FROST: CENTENNIAL ESSAYS II

FROST
CENTENNIAL ESSAYS II

EDITED BY

JAC THARPE

UNIVERSITY PRESS OF MISSISSIPPI
JACKSON
1976

THIS VOLUME IS AUTHORIZED

AND SPONSORED BY

THE UNIVERSITY OF SOUTHERN MISSISSIPPI

Library of Congress Cataloging in Publication Data
Main entry under title:

Frost—centennial essays II.

    Bibliography: p.
    Includes index.
    1. Frost, Robert, 1874–1963—Addresses, essays,
lectures. I. Tharpe, Jac.
PS3511.R94Z6544   811'.5'2   76–26665
ISBN 0–87805–026–4

*For Meyer Chanin
and his family*

Contents

BACKGROUND AND BIOGRAPHY   279

Acknowledgments

Grateful acknowledgment is made to the following:

Holt, Rinehart and Winston, Inc. for permission to quote:

From *The Poetry of Robert Frost* edited by Edward Connery Lathem. Copyright 1916, 1923, 1928, 1930, 1934, 1939, 1947, 1949, (c) 1967, 1969 by Holt, Rinehart and Winston. Copyright 1934, 1936, 1942, 1944, 1945, 1951, 1953, (c) 1956, 1958, 1961, 1962 by Robert Frost. Copyright 1964, 1967, 1970, 1973, 1975 by Lesley Frost Ballantine. Reprinted by permission of Holt, Rinehart and Winston, Publishers.

From *Robert Frost: Poetry and Prose* edited by Edward Connery Lathem and Lawrance Thompson. Copyright (c) 1972 by Holt, Rinehart and Winston. Reprinted by permission of Holt, Rinehart and Winston, Publishers.

From *The Letters of Robert Frost to Louis Untermeyer.* Copyright (c) 1963 by Louis Untermeyer and Holt, Rinehart and Winston. Reprinted by permission of Holt, Rinehart and Winston Publishers.

From *Selected Letters of Robert Frost* edited by Lawrance Thompson. Copyright (c) 1964 by Lawrance Thompson and Holt, Rinehart and Winston. Reprinted by Permission of Holt, Rinehart and Winston, Publishers and The Estate of Robert Frost.

From *Selected Prose of Robert Frost* edited by Hyde Cox and Edward Connery Lathem. Copyright 1939, 1954, (c) 1966, 1967 by Holt, Rinehart and Winston. Copyright 1946, (c) 1959 by Robert Frost. Copyright (c) 1956 by The Estate of Robert Frost. Reprinted by permission of Holt, Rinehart and Winston, Publishers.

From *Robert Frost: The Early Years 1874–1915* by Lawrance Thompson. Copyright (c) 1966 by Lawrance Thompson. Copyright (c) 1966 by The Estate of Robert Frost. Reprinted by permission of Holt, Rinehart and Winston, Publishers.

From *Robert Frost: The Years of Triumph 1915–1938* by Lawrance Thompson. Copyright (c) 1970 by Lawrance Thompson. Copyright (c) 1970 by The Estate of Robert Frost. Reprinted by permission of Holt, Rinehart and Winston, Publishers.

Alfred A. Knopf Inc. for permission to quote from "To The One Of Fictive Music" by Wallace Stevens, from *The Collected Poems of Wallace Stevens*, copyright © 1954.

Macmillan Publishing Co., Inc. for permission to quote from the *Collected Poems of William Butler Yeats*: "All Things Can Temp Me," copyright 1912 by Macmillan Publishing Co., Inc., renewed 1940 by Bertha Georgie Yeats; "The People" and "The Phases of the Moon," copyright 1919 by Macmillan Publishing Co., Inc., renewed 1947 by Bertha Georgie Yeats; "Nineteen Hundred and Nineteen" and

"Among School Children," copyright 1928 by Macmillan Publishing Co., Inc., renewed 1956 by Georgie Yeats.

A. P. Watt & Son, London, England for permission to quote from *The Collected Poems of W. B. Yeats*, "All Things Can Tempt Me," "The People," "The Phases of the Moon," "Nineteen Hundred and Nineteen," and "Among School Children," by permission of M. B. Yeats, Miss Anne Yeats and the Macmillan Company of London and Basingstoke.

Atheneum Publishers for permission to quote from "Keeping Things Whole" from *Reasons for Moving*, reprinted by permission of Atheneum Publishers, copyright (c) 1968 by Mark Strand.

Preface

ECEPTION of *Frost: Centennial Essays* (1974) encouraged the University of Southern Mississippi to sponsor further studies in Robert Frost's accomplishment. Credit is once again given first to the various contributors whose time and energy helped to make up the volume. The administration of the University of Southern Mississippi and both the director and the board of the University Press of Mississippi have been exceptionally generous and cooperative. The director and the staff of the Honors College have been equally helpful and understanding.

Encouragement also came from those several reviewers who, whatever their reservations, found something of value in the *Centennial Essays* and from the many persons who, incidentally or intentionally, sent their compliments. One hopes the failure to mention names—many of them—leaves no one feeling the editor's ingratitude. Despite the tedium of hours spent in proofreading, editing these volumes on Frost has been a fascinating and unusually pleasant experience. Though hardly sentimental, one feels warmly about those who did the slightest kindness.

Among the essays in this volume are those read at Merrimack College, North Andover, Massachusetts, on Robert Frost Day, October 19, 1974, by Professors Warren French, Marie Borroff, and George Nitchie.

The volume also shows the influence of the MLA (1974) seminar on Robert Frost, conducted by Professor Marjorie Cook, Miami University, Oxford, Ohio. These essays are grouped separately under PLAY, the topic of the seminar, and the section unfortunately does not contain some very good essays elicited by that meeting but unavailable for inclusion herein. Coincidentally, some essays not prepared for that occasion deal with some aspect of a very broad definition of the concept of play—those by Professors Borroff, French and Marion Montgomery, for example.

A third group of essays presents several comments on Frost's skepticism regarding philosophy and religion. These were neither commissioned nor planned, and not all appear in the section on Religion. Though these essays show a point of view so consistent as to make them seem repetitive, each writer has simply had the chance to set up his own context and say what he thinks. While the editor generally approves of the defense of Frost, he would have had no objections to publishing essays taking other points of view. No editing or selection of opinion has been done anywhere throughout the collection.

While this volume uniformly cites *The Poetry of Robert Frost*, edited by Edward Connery Lathem (New York: Holt, Rinehart and Winston, 1969) and attempts to document thoroughly, its scholarly paraphernalia is, one hopes, unobtrusive. The easy informality of some essays was temptation often to publish with citation only of the primary materials, but those quoted deserve the credit of being named and located for readers less familiar with the secondary material than the contributors and their colleagues. Yet, to reduce production costs, as well as to make reference easy, primary documents are cited by abbreviation in the text. A short table at the head of the bibliography identifies the abbreviations. The bibliography itself is merely a brief list of works cited without full data in the text or the notes. Those concerned for more bibliographical information may consult *Robert Frost: A Bibliography, 1913–1974*, compiled by Frank Lentricchia and Melissa Christensen Lentricchia (Metuchen, New Jersey: The Scarecrow Press, 1976), scheduled for issue during the latter part of the year.

The two volumes of Lawrance Thompson's biography have, for practical reasons of saving space, been designated as Thompson, I and II throughout the volume. Generally, quotations from the dialogue in Frost's poems are set without double quotation marks, to reduce clutter and avoid mistakes in proofreading and typesetting. Frost's sometimes erratic prose is reproduced as accurately as possible, without editorial comment.

J. T.   Honors College
1976   University of Southern Mississippi

FROST: CENTENNIAL ESSAYS II

FROST COUNTRY

This section borrows its title from Warren French's essay. Frost country is a concept—amenable to broad definition, yet meaningful. Professor French discusses rural New England and local color. He talks also of the association of vice and corruption with the city and of virtue and innocence with the country. An ironic comparison of Frost and the early filmmaker, D. W. Griffith, contributes to a wide-ranging discussion of intellectual background that gradually implies a connection between Frost's poetic landscape and the nation. Frost country is actually a somewhat realistic term for the poet's domain.

Marie Borroff's concept of "To Earthward" is so broad, yet so clear and convincing, as to refer aptly to an essential aspect of Frost country—Man Performing. Professor Borroff finds labor and love closely associated in some of Frost's best work. The discussion incidentally anticipates themes in several other essays—the concept of play and Frost's view of man's relationship to nature. The essay urges on the editor reiteration of the point made in the afterword to *Frost: Centennial Essays*—that Frost's famous line from "Mowing" may be accurately paraphrased to say the artifact—the work of art—whether poem or ax-helve—is the sweetest dream that labor knows.

George Nitchie considers whether the nation itself is Frost country and to what extent Frost is the nation. He still wonders if the United States was stated and if New England was, while he also ponders the relationship between the smaller and the larger areas and studies the man who spoke of both—or spoke from one about the other.

Unless design govern in a thing so small as the editor's organization of essays, coincidence alone accounts for the grouping here of the three essays presented at the Merrimack Conference. But some vague intuition of fitness accounts for inclusion of Peter Stanlis' detailed observations about Frost's view on politics—man en masse

3

in the United States where Frost lived, whether the land possessed us or we it. Frost had reservations not only about the Communism that appealed to the idealists of his time but also about the American tendency to reform human nature through legislation, of which legislating morality is but one endeavor. Professor Stanlis rather more objectively treats the subject than the editor does.

J. T.

Frost Country

WARREN FRENCH

In memory of Cornelius Weygandt,
who came from Philadelphia every year.

Even a stamp has appeared to commemorate the centenary of Frost's birth—an appropriately gray and gnarly stamp to recall the figure seemingly carved from the eternal granite of New Hampshire and Vermont that the poet became during his last days on the lecture circuit. Still this celebration proved no match for that observing—even without a commemorative stamp—the centennial of Longfellow's birth, when on February 28, 1907, the governor of Massachusetts and other political, social, and educational notables assembled in Harvard's Sanders Theatre. William Roscoe Thayer reported to *The Nation* Harvard President Charles Eliot Norton's still timely comment about the value of Longfellow's honesty and vision at a time "when public and private minds are corrupt, and wealth is believed to be able to purchase everything—even immunity from punishment." Tributes to Longfellow glowed on the pages of forty-odd magazines considered suitable for indexing in the still relatively experimental *Reader's Guide to Periodical Literature*. Although the John Greenleaf Whittier celebration at the end of that same year was less lavishly observed, there was a special new edition of his works along with tributes and reprintings of his beloved poems in genteel journals.

Fifty years later there was an exhibition of Longfellow memorabilia at the Harvard Library, but no public celebrations noted by the national press, except in—of all places—Russia and Hungary, the latter boycotted by American representatives because of the chilly relations between the two countries following Hungary's suppression the preceding year of a civil uprising. The sesquicentennial of Quaker Whittier's birth was observed at Swarthmore College, but no magazines indexed in the now venerable *Reader's Guide* recalled the event or printed even a token verse. Clearly among the many things that had happened during the half century between these occasions, something especially drastic had happened to the reputation of those that the still loyal Boston Public Library in its permanent exhibition area names "The Fireside Poets." Although many writers once gone are forgotten, few have fallen so far in such a short time. And the blame cannot simply be put on their *pastness* because the centennial celebration in 1930 of Emily Dickinson's birth proved quite another matter, with the publication in four prestigious national magazines of selections from her work offered to the public *for the first time*. We are also close enough to 1980 to predict confidently that if literary people then have occasion to celebrate anything, they will be celebrating Emily Dickinson's still growing reputation on the 150th anniversary of her birth.

I propose, however, not to examine, except tangentially, the reasons for the decline of the reputation of the "fireside poets" or the rise of Miss Dickinson's, but rather to speculate which pattern Robert Frost's may follow during the next fifty years, since he shares with these New England predecessors the distinction of being widely honored during his centennial year. But a few more facts about the others may prove useful in such crystal-gazing.

The reputations of the "fireside poets" were still secure enough in 1940 for Franklin D. Roosevelt's strategists to choose as part of the efforts promoting the President's pursuit of an unprecedented third term the inclusion of Longfellow, Whittier, and James Russell Lowell (along with Walt Whitman and James Whitcomb Riley) as the poets among only thirty-five "Famous Americans" from all fields of endeavor to be honored by a special series of postage stamps. Despite this pious tribute, Longfellow, Whittier and Lowell had already lost their preeminence as national bards in the high schools of even conservative Philadelphia that I attended during the 1930s. My generation was encouraged to memorize instead of their works the more cheering among the productions of Sara Teasdale, Adelaide Crapsey, Edna St. Vincent Millay, Edwin Arlington Robinson, and Robert Frost. No reputation seemed more secure then than that of Miss Millay, whose "Renascence" was the most frequent choice of the elocutionists who performed at the University of Pennsylvania's grotesquely named "Cultural Olympics." One sees the benignly fatherly hand of Louis Untermeyer already at work in the teacher-training institutions. If we can believe the evidence provided by audiovisual aids catalogs—and the merchandisers' knowledge of what sells must be respected—most of this group has not remained in favor. The only American poets being promoted in this prosy age are Whitman and Frost.

Although I joined my peers in admiring Miss Millay's art of burning her candle at both ends, I would even then have put my money on Frost as the survivor of the group. Our exposure to him was pretty much limited to "Stopping by Woods on a Snowy Evening" (not as later interpreted by John Ciardi), "Mending Wall," "The Road Not Taken," and "Birches"; perhaps simply the fact that this quartette survived and grew in my mind through many stumbling recitals is all the honor that needs be paid them. I would like, however, to probe further into the reasons why Frost is the only poet whose work managed to transcend the timorous classroom and to link later with the writings of T. S. Eliot, Archibald MacLeish, and Wallace Stevens, which were too deep or disillusioning to be welcome in the high school.

My own preference for Frost was early confirmed when I had the good fortune to begin my study of literature at the University of Pennsylvania with the poet's friend, Cornelius Weygandt, who is saluted in "New Hampshire" as

> . . . one I don't know what to call him,
> Who comes from Philadelphia every year
> With a great flock of chickens of rare breeds
> He wants to give the educational
> Advantages of growing almost wild
> Under the watchful eye of hawk and eagle—
> Dorkings because they're spoken of by Chaucer,
> Sussex because they're spoken of by Herrick. (p. 162)

I have recently, however, found the most useful start toward explaining Frost's appeal in one of the most casual and underdeveloped critical statements about him; and since Theodore Morrison has developed his argument in "Frost: Country Poet and Cosmopolitan

Poet" (*Yale Review*, Winter 1970) only sketchily, I feel at liberty to elaborate upon it.

Morrison starts from Frost's own observation that he had never written a "nature poem" and argues that "Frost was not so much a nature poet, if there is such a thing, as a country poet." The difference, he says, is "considerable," but he never fully explains it, though he goes on to say: "A poet can dredge landscape and seascape for images, can offer a philosophy of nature and man's relation to it, without in any profound sense being a countryman. Frost, on one side, was profoundly a countryman. . . . He was deeply and truly penetrated by the mores, the institutions, the economy, the people, the mental horizon of the rural New England he memorialized in his work" (pp. 179–80).

But this description fits Rose Terry Cooke or Alice Brown and makes Frost sound like a local colorist, in the frequent, condescending sense of the term. We need to remember, of course, that Frost, like Mark Twain and William Faulkner, *is* a local colorist; but he is also—even in his country poems—something more than one of those who preserve the folkways of a quaint and usually vanishing culture. Most local colorists are writers and painters of great sensitivity —in the primary *physical* sense of the word. Their eyes and ears and other sensors have a special receptiveness to sights and sounds, odors, tastes, and the very feel of plants and animals, wind and weather. The most gifted give us with extraordinary fidelity a record of the surface look of a particular place at a particular time; but they rarely violate the barriers that are erected against the penetration of their senses. Frost and Faulkner do more. They remove the very walls from New England and Mississippi farmhouses to let us see the dramas that are being enacted behind drawn blinds and closed shutters. They open doors beyond which the public is not invited to pass. They report not the gossip or folk wisdom gathered at the country store or on a field trip ("Blueberries" is a good example of Frost's "local color" as the *Saturday Evening Post* version of "Spotted Horses" is of Faulkner's). Rather they violate the most secret recesses of the house to report the whispered conversations of those who would never speak to the world—Faulkner's Mrs. Compson, the wife in "Home Burial."

As Morrison soundly argues, Lionel Trilling's notorious effort to categorize Frost as a "terrifying" poet ignores another aspect of his work, because "some of the poems that would most justify Trilling's words are country poems, and in a sense much profounder than mere scene and setting." "Terror aside," Morrison continues, "to attempt to subtract from Frost's work" his country idylls "would be to rob him of far more than trappings and locale. It would be to deprive him of the defining, tangible, physical conditions that give body and being and distinctiveness to a large share of his work" (p. 181).

But even to make such an explanation, we cannot put "terror aside." Trilling is right that Frost is a terrifying poet, and what must be done to flesh out Morrison's definition of the "country poet" is to assimilate Trilling's comment into it. The true "country poet" must be a terrifying poet, because life in the country is terrifying, as life anywhere is terrifying. Even the local colorists like Rose Terry Cooke and Alice Brown have grasped elements of this terror at times, but to be a true "country poet" one must be able to face both the heartwarming and the bloodchilling aspects of rural life with equal equanimity. One may prefer one to the other, but must not limit his poetry to his preference. He must offer us scenes not just for the sensations they afford, but so that we can begin to fathom through them what it means to live in *that* country.

In this sense of the term, we have had remarkably few "country poets." I cannot bring to mind others besides Frost and Whittier. Robinson Jeffers is too one-sided and apocalyptic, too exclusively "terrifying." If the Point Sur country is as he pictures it, who would choose to live there? The work of a "country poet" must mix some measure of invitation with warning, must say to us like Frost in his most mellow mood, "You come too."

We have had country fictionists aplenty—Willa Cather, Faulkner, the early John Steinbeck, Elizabeth Madox Roberts, even filmmaker D. W. Griffith—who have been called "poets" at times; but only Whittier and Frost have sought from their New England prospects to capture the bright and dark lyricism of the country in disciplined lines that intensify the preciseness of the perception.

Morrison's essay does not fully explain the nature of the "country poet" because he shares the tendency of others to attribute any current interest in "country poetry" to nostalgia. "From time to time I have found myself wondering," he observes, "whether the rural strain in Frost's poems will prove a help or an obstacle to his reception in the future. . . . A realm of experience once common to the majority is directly and intimately known only to a shrinking minority" (p. 181). He resolves his doubts, however, by universalizing Frost's works—moving from the earthly to what John Steinbeck in *Cannery Row* calls "the cosmic Monterey": "I am far from convinced that the country element in Frost will prove a fatal detriment to his continued reception. . . . Frost's country poems may be trusted to create their own world for readers many years hence, perhaps the more so as the world of these poems grows even more remote than it has become already, and as temptations to view it with nostalgia are removed once for all by time and change" (p. 182).

I go further than Morrison. While I believe that Frost's poetry has been given and is still getting the nostalgia treatment (one of the most personally repulsive projects I have encountered is a series of silver medals for those who like to do their hoarding stylishly bearing Norman Rockwell illustrations for Frost poems—but for some these are devotional objects that spare them from actual reading), I do not believe that his poetry has simply this passive recall value today. I believe that the best of it still possesses an energizing force that helps us to cope with our world, even choose our world. While I would not wish to prophesy complacently that any particular poet's work will become immortal, I am willing to predict that as long as certain shifting trends in our society continue to shift—as one half century's watching makes me think they will for at least another half century —Frost's reputation will continue to flourish and expand as he is recognized as something that I have not heard him often called even by his most perceptive admirers—an artist ahead of his time. Since survivors so minded will have to wait those fifty years to verify these predictions, I must throw scholarly caution to the winds and exercise your patience still longer while I root them in my own schematization of an important aspect of American mythology.

Despite the incessant proddings of our colleagues in the social sciences to "quantify! quantify!" humanists have always insisted upon exploring experience in terms of intuited myths that defy anything so vulgar as empirical verification. That these myths need incessant revision in no way invalidates them, but serves only to confirm the Emersonian pronouncement that revelation requires constant refurbishment. If we no longer often live in the fashion of our fathers, neither do we share their illusions; there are fashions in dreams as in dress. And specifically within the restless American culture, attitudes toward the country and the city have oscillated over rather regular fifty-year periods during the nearly two-century history of the Republic.

From the first stirrings of revolution in the 1770s to precisely 1820, humanistic myth cherished Jefferson's independent yeoman, democratic in manners and politics, yet aristocratic in his aloofness and self-reliance. The date 1820 stands unusually firm because in that remarkable year when James Monroe was reelected President with but one dissenting vote, and that to honor Washington, the country approached consensus as nearly as it would in its history. The Virginia gentleman, scrupulously legalistic and home-and-hound-loving, seemed the figure that America put before the world as representative in contrast to the arrogant and tyrannical aristocrats of such great capitals as Paris and Vienna that Europe had recently reenthroned after the Napoleonic embarrassments.

But hardly had Monroe been reinstalled in the Brazilia of the nineteenth century, the swampy village named for George Washington with its grandiose street plan and scattered hovels, when the Jacksonian spectre reared its head and the acrimonious disputes over the election of 1824 ended consensus and saw the figure of the independent yeoman gargoylized into the illiterate spoilsman from the frontier. The age of the glorification of the city was about to begin.

Although the most respected humanistic voices of the time—Thoreau and Melville—warned against the city, *who*, in those euphorious years of improved street lighting, improved urban transportation, new water works, culminating in the crystal splendor of the New York World's Fair of 1851, was listening to Thoreau and Melville? The popular writers of the period were the "New York literati" that Poe despised. Big city story and sporting papers like the *New York Ledger* began to cater to mass tastes for the mythical figure of the swashbuckling success-artist. An emblem for the age is the Cary Sisters, who abandoned the "Clovernook" of their rural childhood near Cincinnati to establish what was honored as America's first genuine literary salon by such dignitaries as Horace Greeley. The poetic key to the spirit of the age was Walt Whitman's "Give Me the Splendid Silent Sun" (1865), which celebrates the switching of the country-born poet's loyalties from "solitude" and "Nature's primal sanities" to the thronged streets of Manhattan, "the life of the theatre, bar-room, huge hotel."

Actually Whitman was writing as the end of an era approached, just as Monroe's triumph had come as another era—celebrated in Washington Irving's tales—neared its end. During the years between 1870 and 1920, the corruption of the cities during the Gilded Age, relentlessly documented by the turn-of-the-century muckrakers, caused them to lose their hold on the idealistic imagination, so that even as rural districts in many places were decreasing in population (in New England, for example, as many critics of Frost point out), nostalgic images of the innocent life in the country fired the public imagination. It was not Hamlin Garland, E. W. Howe and a few others who chronicled the miseries of backwaters life who won hearings, but Mark Twain, whose Huck Finn gave up "sivilization" to light out for the territory; William Dean Howells, whose Silas Lapham went back to his rugged New England farm to regain his virtue; and, most especially, the popular writers like the Ozarks' Harold Bell Wright and the Indiana Limberlost's Gene Stratton Porter (not to forget James Witcomb Riley, the Hoosier bard whose inclusion in the 1940 postal tribute to poets many have found inexplicable).

We must recall that it was during this fifty-year period that the myth of rural virtue, culminating in the "Great Experiment" of Prohibition, flourished in the very face of the decay of our rural areas. This was the period during which distrust of city corruption allowed rural voters to win such disproportionate influence in our state and national legislatures that it took another fifty years to restore a balance. Frost may be seen as the Irving or the Whitman of this half century, bringing to perfection his myth, just about the time that it is to lose its hold; but I would argue that Frost gives us no image of unmixed rural virtue and that the true mythmaker of the period arose in a newly risen art just as Irving had in the short story and Whitman had in free verse. This was the age of the silent film, and David Wark Griffith, who began to champion the country over the city in his still unequalled spectacle *Intolerance* (1916) and stepped up his mythmaking for the millions in *True Heart Susie* (1919) and *Way Down East* (1920), was its Homer. Frost and Griffith have not been compared; but they were born only a year apart, and there are many similarities between their careers that would provide a fruitful basis for a comparison of the roles of the traditional poet and the new moviemaker in the early twentieth century that cannot be digressed into here, except to suggest that their creative paths crossed most conspicuously when Frost's key poem, "The Need of Being Versed in Country Things," was published only a few months after the release of Griffith's fabulously successful melodrama *Way Down East*. These two works highlight the differences between their creators: Frost's tough vision of the decline of the country and the indifference of nature to man's concerns; Griffith's sentimental defense of rustic virtues against the debaucheries of the city. But even as traditionalists flocked to see *Way Down East*, the cynical sophisticates disillusioned with simplistic myth by World War I were beginning to sing, "How You Gonna Keep 'Em Down on the Farm After They've Seen Berlin?"

Although discontent with what Sinclair Lewis would become a celebrity by isolating as "the village virus" had been stirring for some time, it broke with unexpected and unprecedented force with the publications in quick succession of *Winesburg, Ohio, Main Street*, Cabell's wicked *Jurgen*. The reception of these works was spurred by justified suspicions that it was principally rural areas that had foisted the unpopular Eighteenth Amendment upon the cities under the patriotic cover of the war. The beginning of an agricultural depression in the 1920s, coupled with the development of automobiles, paved highways, motion pictures, suburban bungalows, and clothes and behavior that shocked the hicks, unseated the country myth and turned the attention of the popular mythmakers to the glamorous cities of the East and even Europe. During the Depression a back-to-the-soil movement flourished briefly, more in theory than practice; but when the pressure of World War II accelerated the movement of country people—especially southern blacks and share-croppers—to defense work in the cities and hastened the development of the large scale farming deplored by John Steinbeck in *The Grapes of Wrath*, the myth of the independent yeoman suffered seeming death blows, and later treasured works like James Agee's *Let Us Now Praise Famous Men* attracted only cultist attention. The "country" became the province of Currier and Ives prints and restored semisuburban inns in fashionable retreats like New Hope, Pennsylvania.

And so things went until the late 1960s with *Peyton Place* providing the stock image of village degeneracy and *The Godfather* sentimentalizing violence as the triumph of family solidity in the face of urban temptations. When riots broke out in our big city streets late in the decade, however, those who had been growing uneasy about megapolitan spread and the greedy upward reaching of skyscrapers found their worst nightmares about the city confirmed. Whatever else one may say about Chicago's Mayor Daley, his handling of the protesters during the 1968 Democratic convention resulted in his city's becoming a symbol of oppression rather than of the boisterous optimism Carl Sandburg's poetry had made it. But by then Sandburg had long since retired to a hill farm in North Carolina, and country and city were once again reversing their roles in American mythology.

This latest turnabout in the American vision has, however, found the country itself, especially Frost's New England, changed. While I think a friend too cynical when he says that ten years ago one could have bought a central Vermont village for $5,000, there is a measure of truth in his remark; and the same place would surely cost half a million today if it were possible to pry loose the present proprietors. The houses that Frost saw abandoned are being restored and reoccupied, with even blackened ruins being reclaimed from the phoebes as the basis for rebuilding. The long neglected cellar holes are being searched by collectors for treasured bottles.

This latest reversal may be no longer-lived than the others; but if it is to have any vitality, people must return to the country with an awareness of its terrors as well as its joys. *Way Down East* is no longer an adequate guide to one's expectations. If crowds of young people rush back to the country with the same fatuous enthusiasm they rushed to the cities with early in the nineteenth century and again early in the twentieth century but without an awareness of the potential nightmare side of their dreams, they will become even more embittered than their predecessors did by nineteenth century working conditions and twentieth century urban blight.

With so few country poets part of our legacy, there are few places to turn for the kind of awareness that blends a lyric response to the country with a dark insight into its terrors. Whittier no longer helps; it is his poems that should inspire medals designed by Norman Rockwell. A brief consideration of one of his most often anthologized works indicates why the "fireside" poets are not likely to share in the revival of the very firesides they once helped brighten.

"Among the Hills" is a complex story-within-a-story-within-a-story poem, giving voice to Whittier's sentiments about just about everything. I will not linger over the summary; but since it may not be generally familiar today, I will briefly mention those parts I wish to comment upon. A summer visitor to the New Hampshire hills is out driving with his hostess, who tells him the story of a "city's fair, pale daughter," who came "from school and ball and rout" to regain her health by drinking "the wine of mountain air" and who remained to marry a rude but ambitious farmer with "his own free, bookless lore,/The lessons nature taught him," who goes on to become a successful politician whose "civic service shows/A purer-toned ambition" through her influence. Whittier's narrator ends with the musing that " 'T were well . . ./If more and more we found the troth/Of fact and fancy plighted,/And Culture's charm and labor's strength/In rural homes united."

Three things give this piece the kind of quaint charm of a faded painting of a nineteenth century farm that provokes only nostalgia today. First, we hear the basic story of the farmer's courtship of the city girl at three removes—through the local busybody, the summer visitor, and the remote poet controlling the obtrusive meter and polite vocabulary. The second problem is this language. After an introduction of some twenty-four quatrains just to set the scene, the narrator gets around to his story at last, presumably quoting his hostess, but commenting, "Her rustic patois of the hills/Lost in my free translation." What puzzles us today is why the translation? I fear that George Santayana provides the explanation in his essay, "The Genteel Poets," arguing that the failure of these worthies was that "their poetry was indeed without sensuous beauty, splendor, passion, or volume. Their culture was half a pious survival, half an intentional acquirement; it was not the inevitable flowing of a fresh experience." Finally, T. S. Eliot has somewhere remarked that the poet must be able "to see beneath both beauty and ugliness; to see the boredom, and the horror, and the glory." The "fireside poets" were too exclusively preoccupied with the glory; they only rarely acknowledged the horror and never the boredom, which their long poems may be seen as a busy effort to dispel. The result is a narrative vitiated of the energy that acknowledged tensions might have given it in order to arrive at a moral that today strikes us as exactly backwards because the monotonous routine of industrial life has become the characteristic of most of our charmless cities, while the strong and imaginative qualities of our culture are found in the revival of country handicrafts. Frost may have sounded simply whimsically cynical in the 1920s when he wrote in "New Hampshire": "I choose to be a plain New Hampshire farmer/With an income in cash of, say, a thousand/ (From, say, a publisher in New York City)" (p. 172), but he prescribes here precisely the pattern of life that has been chosen by many concerned with reinvigorating our decaying culture or at least shaping a new myth for lives become aimless since the "go-getter" legends of the first half of the century have been exploded. Inflation lends quaintness to Frost's "thousand" but one can live much more cheaply and healthfully—physically and mentally—in the country today than in the smoggy city. Frost's choice to live modestly in the country and try to channel some fruits of the better life there back into our polluted cities—however flippant his words may have sounded at a time when they had to be uttered defiantly—has today more application to the conservation and replenishment of our physical, intellectual, and moral lives than it had when he made it fifty years ago.

The difference between Frost's dramatic narratives and Whittier's is, furthermore, that Frost does not give us situations at four removes from actuality with the language prettied up a bit by each middleman. Contrast Whittier's pastoral idyll, for example, with Frost's picture of a household among the hills in "The Housekeeper"—Frost introduces no explanations, no judgments. We are simply plunged directly into the episode in the kitchen to hear the situation illuminated in the language of those helplessly involved. The reader is thrown upon his own resources, not even to arrive at some judgment, but simply to contemplate in the light of these naked revelations how he could respond, what he would do if he were there and involved himself. This demand that the poem makes suggests the quality in Frost's work that would make me wish, were I writing a book like George W. Nitchie's *Human Values in the Poetry of Robert Frost*, to title it *The Humanly Valuable in the Poetry of Robert Frost*. Through this contrast I try to stress that in Frost's work, we are not led—as I think we customarily were in the work of the "fireside poets"—to apply with Olympian detachment preconceived theories to people's situations; we are thrown, rather, on our own resources to develop an adequate response. The ability to make this demand upon our sensibility is, I think, the result of "the new consciousness" that Lionel Trilling senses forming underneath the "old consciousness" of postRenaissance European humanism, though he could not yet identify it. (His difficulty, I think, was the result of his being too completely steeped in an urban culture that led him to seek "the glory, the horror, and the boredom" through artistic experiences rather than direct confrontations with human situations. Certainly his fiction like *The Middle of the Journey* shows that he can conceive of the country only in terms of the pastoral tradition and of people only projecting images to each other rather than exposing their naked selves.) Frost is reputed to have said—most appropriately in Jerusalem—"I am American civilization." He could have said, "If there ever is an American civilization, I'll instigate it."

One of the invariable characteristics of Frost's best dramatic poems is that they deal—as "The Housekeeper" does—with situations in which recourse to theories or institutions—the church, state, or school—would be of no help whatsoever. We are confronted with people who have created their own situations and who must resolve them for themselves or simply put up with them. There is no comfort in describing them as private hells or the products of economic exploitation. There is no place for the characters to turn, and observing them offers the reader nowhere to turn but to his own internal resources.

A further advantage of Frost's giving us only the "bare scene" is that his poetry—as I have already suggested briefly about the lines from "New Hampshire"—can change with changing times. The "fireside poets" are burned-out cases today, for one reason, because of the inflexibility—formally and morally—of their postures. Whittier's very language and distancing in "Among the Hills" makes it a local color poem that is limited to a particular culture at a particular time; but in a period during which the myths that give us our values are changing—as I have argued I believe they are now as they have been over the past two centuries—Frost's work transcends nostalgia by lending itself to new interpretations.

"A Brook in the City," for example, with its picture of a country stream thrown deep in a city's "sewer dungeon," is obviously closely related to the theories about America's oscillating city-country myths that I have been advancing. Although there has always been a thin stream of protest against urbanization, the poem was surely generally read when it appeared fifty years ago plaintively and nostalgically, as though the brook were forever buried beneath the asphalt of the city, even though it might continue to haunt us; but today when cities are crumbling, and we see many of their centers returning to grass, the poem can be read in a vengeful and triumphant tone as the brook flows on after its oppressor is gone.

Other Frost poems have experienced "restorations" comparable to the restorations of the weathered graying houses that they often describe to fresh greens and yellows. "The Census-Taker" can be less melancholy today; life has gone on living. A poem hitherto usually neglected as perhaps too nostalgic and mournful, "In the Home Stretch," assumes major importance sixty years after its appearance. Today in reading this poem about the revelation of the moment of truth for those returning from the city to the farm, we might like to change the "fifteen miles" to "one hundred and fifty," but the wife's answer to the moving man's question, "But I ask,/ What are you seeing out the window, lady?" might remain the same:

"What I'll be seeing more of in the years
To come as here I stand and go the round
Of many plates with towels many times." (p. 111)

Sixty years ago, however, I suspect that most people read these lines
in the resigned and fretful tone of one driven to an unattractive
course by the lack of an alternative; today they can be read in the
triumphant tone of one freed from the city. The "voices" in "The
Generations of Men" are heard more strongly now than when Frost
wrote the poem.

I predict that we'll be seeing more of Frost in the years just ahead.
Something is lost—Frost himself, the backbone of the public poetry
reading program, "speaking" his poems to many who had never
really *heard* a poem before. Even with the legacy of recordings that
he left, we cannot again feel the electric surge of his contrary pro-
jection of lyric genius and cutting pettiness. Yet something is gained,
because Frost may no longer be the right one to speak his own poems.
He spoke them for his time, but he made them so that others could
speak them in their own way for their own time.

Frost's "country" exists not just in his poems. It is the real land
that we have alternately embraced and spurned as we have sought to
impose upon it visions that have successively faded in the face of its
stubbornly insistent realities, and it is a land that finds new spokesmen
who may give different voice to the same words. And while the following question is one that the social scientists' computers can never
quantify, we can indeed ask how much Frost did to create not just
the "country" in his poems, but this real country as well. What could
better satisfy a poet than to have made a poetic landscape—not just
as Emily Dickinson did in the wonderful world of her imagination,
though such a shaping must be the grandest dream of any poet—but
of the enduring soil of the mountains and valleys of New Hampshire
and Vermont? Not a treasured and lost country of legend like the
"fireside poets" fashioned, but a country to which those conscious
of the burning out of old myths can turn with fresh hopes of creating
—at least for a while—a new reality that may foster a new myth. To
create such a country that might give us new energy to fashion a
dream to replace our dying dreams—that would be indeed to be a

country poet. And while someone else may come along to create this country, as Frost did to replace Whittier's with his own, we haven't seen anything of him yet. Until such a one appears—if he does—the country that may inspire a new myth remains the "Frost Country."

Robert Frost: "To Earthward"

MARIE BORROFF

My starting point is two of Frost's early poems: "To Earth-ward" and "Bond and Free." The first is a nostalgic reminiscence of the emotions of youth, when "love at the lips was touch" almost too sweet to bear, the second a disquisition on Love and Thought in which Love is described as sheltering herself in "hills and circling arms" while Thought soars off on "dauntless wings." These poems share a dramatic motif that seems to me of considerable importance to the designs, in both strategic and structural senses, of most of Frost's best poems. I have in mind the "scarring" or "printed trace," left by the pressure of earth against body in "To Earthward," of body against earth in "Bond and Free." But the motif works differ-ently in the two poems, and the poems themselves differ radically in theme and dramatic unfoldment, in such a way that one—"To Earth-ward"—represents Frost's major and most characteristic achieve-ment, and expresses the experiential vision at its heart, while the other—"Bond and Free"—is tangential, charming and witty though we may find it, and agree though we may (and as I do) with the doctrine it preaches. It is minor Frost; not a mere "quantulum," per-haps, yet falling short of the mark in profundity and substance.

Both poems say they are about love, and *love* is the first word in both. We note in them, first, a tacit analogy between love for another human being—the "love at the lips" of "To Earthward," the cir-cling arms" of "Bond and Free"—and love for the earth. This latter, impersonally directed feeling also involves a physical attraction, of the human body for the world's body. It may well remind us of medieval celebrations of love on a cosmic scale, as manifested in the force of gravity. In "To Earthward," the speaker's recollections are associated not only with "lips" but with the scent of "grapevine springs" and the handling of dewy "sprays of honeysuckle"; he longs to recapture their intensity:

> When stiff and sore and scarred
> I take away my hand
> From leaning on it hard
> In grass and sand,
>
> The hurt is not enough:
> I long for weight and strength
> To feel the earth as rough
> To all my length. (p. 227)

In "Bond and Free," love is said to cling to "earth" as well as to hills and circling arms, and to have "left a printed trace," visible on "snow and sand and turf," with "straining in the world's embrace." The wording of this last image makes one think of footprints (the more so since Thought's contrasting behavior consists of shaking his ankles free), and suggests that taking a walk in the snow, on grass, or on sand is a manifestation of love for the earth, as indeed Frost would say it is.

In any case, love in both poems is portrayed in terms of the pressure of the human body against the physical world it emanates from and lives in. The impact point of this encounter—what I like to call Frost's "kinesthetic crunch"—figures in poem after poem, treated now seriously, now comically, now with latent, now with explicit symbolic force. Pushing against resistance, lifting or climbing against the downward force of gravity, bumping into things, being battered by wind and weather—such actions and experiences provide narrative details and episodes and even whole plots of poems in Frost from first to last. "Birches" is about climbing trees as far up as they can be climbed before they bend over; "Two Look at Two" opens with two persons walking up a mountainside as far as they can before being forced to turn back; in "Lodged," the speaker describes flowers in a storm pushed by wind and pelted by rain, and adds, "I know how the flowers felt"; in "Bereft," leaves lifted from a porch floor by wind strike at his knee; in "The Armful," he is overwhelmed by the weight of the many parcels he is carrying and finally has to "sit down in the middle of them all"; in "The Door in the Dark," he walks into a door left ajar; in "Willful Homing," "the storm gets down his neck in an icy souse" and "the snow blows on him and off him, exerting force Downward to make him sit astride a drift."

The marshalling of physical force against natural counterforce is made into a vivid and moving symbol of survival itself in "A Leaf-Treader," which begins,

> I have been treading on leaves all day until I am autumn-
> tired.
> God knows all the color and form of leaves I have trodden
> on and mired.
> Perhaps I have put forth too much strength and been too
> fierce from fear.
> I have safely trodden underfoot the leaves of another year.

Here the leaves are portrayed as "threatening," falling from the trees as if "with a will to carry [him] with them to death," but the threat is vigorously defied:

> . . . it was no reason I had to go because they had to go.
> Now up, my knee, to keep on top of another year of snow.
> (pp. 297–98)

(Limitations of space and topic forbid me to make more than fleeting mention of other poets, but it is clear that the central character of Wallace Stevens' poems, as compared with Frost's, is almost spookily detached from the palpable world, rarely touching or handling anything; in Yeats, though we learn more from him than from Stevens what it is like to inhabit a body, physical consciousness is introspective, as when the sweetness of memory makes the lover "shake from head to foot," or cry and tremble and rock to and fro.)

More than once, the kinesthetic motif in Frost is figured forth specifically in terms of hands. In "To Earthward" the speaker remembers "dew on the knuckle," shaken by honeysuckle sprays as he once gathered them. In "A Brook in the City," he knows the strength of a brook that has now been forced to run underground, "having dipped a finger length/And made it leap my knuckle"; the two neighbors of "Mending Wall" are said to "wear their fingers rough" handling the fallen stones they pick up and replace in the wall. Most movingly, in "The Death of the Hired Man," the wife, Mary, during a pause as she and her husband sit on the porch talking about Silas's return, makes a small and seemingly inconsequential gesture:

> She put out her hand
> Among the harplike morning-glory strings,
> Taut with the dew from garden bed to eaves,
> As if she played unheard some tenderness
> That wrought on him beside her in the night. (p. 38)

In terms of what I take to be the meaning of the kinesthetic image in Frost, she thereby expresses a continued emotional involvement in reality—the ties that bind us to life.

In still another of Frost's dramatic poems, "Wild Grapes," the central character recalls an incident in which, as a little girl, she had unexpectedly been lifted off the ground by a birch tree her brother had bent down so that she could gather grapes from it. She remembers sinking lower and lower, while still frighteningly far from the ground, her "small wrists stretching till they showed the banjo strings." Once she has been set back on earth again, she says,

> I know I looked long at my curled-up fingers,
> Before I straightened them and brushed the bark off.

The conclusion of the poem shows that, for the speaker as for Frost himself, hanging on to tangible reality is an expression of love.

> I had not learned to let go with the hands,
> As still I have not learned to with the heart,
> And have no wish to with the heart—nor need,
> That I can see. The mind—is not the heart.
> I may yet live, as I know others live,
> To wish in vain to let go with the mind—
> Of cares, at night, to sleep; but nothing tells me
> That I need learn to let go with the heart. (pp. 198–99)

The most painful of these encounters, of course, takes place in "Out, Out—," where a boy helping some adults work with a power saw loses his right hand to the saw and then, as a result, life itself. The implicit epigraph to this poem is contained in the passage in *Macbeth* that follows the words of the title:

> Out, out, brief candle!
> Life is . . . a tale
> Told by an idiot, full of sound and fury,
> Signifying nothing.

These lines, as I have pointed out in another connection,[1] express not Frost's cynical view of life, but his tacit condemnation of a world in which people make things go wrong, starting with the refusal of the unnamed "they" to allow the boy an extra half-hour at the end of the day to watch the sunset.

The engagement of the self in material actuality—the meshing of gears between body and world—is an essential part of Frost's experiential vision. It is dramatized as contending forces, of muscular effort on the one hand, and the obdurate solidity and heaviness of things on the other. The collision between these two, insofar as it is a manifestation of love, brings joy, but it inevitably is attended by pain and weariness as well. What the speaker longs for in "To Earthward" is an intensity of contact, a roughness such as would leave his whole body "stiff and sore and scarred." Fulfilment comes not from an easy transcendence, but from the shock of meeting reality head-on; the pain of this encounter is not masochistically pleasurable, it is simply an inescapable qualification of human happiness as Frost conceives of it.

To talk about the pitting of muscular effort against the resistance of matter is to formulate a parodic definition, in quantum mechanical terms, of "work"—the "potential energy" and "foot-pounds" of my schooldays. It follows that work, in that it is a form of willed encounter between body and world, is also, for Frost, a form of love. The thematic identification of the two kinds of physical action, hinted at more or less broadly in a number of poems, is most clearly implied in "Putting in the Seed," where the man planting beans and peas describes himself as "Slave to a springtime passion for the earth." In "Mowing," the wielder of the scythe speaks of "the earnest love that laid the swale in rows"; in "Two Tramps in Mud Time," the householder chopping his own wood says, of the interruption that has just occurred, "The time when most I loved my task/These two must make me love it more/By coming with what they came to ask." But the identification cannot be taken for granted. It would be more accurate to say that the performance of the task with love is an ideal, not always realized—an ideal that separates man from the rest of the creaturely world with both desirable and undesirable consequences.

Labor in Frost, when all goes well, is shown as yielding an esthetic perception or contemplative insight, something above and beyond the defined goal of the task itself. What is yielded can appropriately be termed a "reward"—even if in Frost's world there is no guarantee of a supernal rewarding agency—in that it is conditional on accomplishment, on the deed done. In "Mowing," the esthetic perception is embodied in "pale orchises" and a "bright green snake," but neither of these would have appeared had the grass not been mown. So also, to give one additional example, in "The Pasture," the speaker is "going out to clean the pasture spring." He will "rake the leaves away," but he will then "wait to watch the water clear." (He says he *may* wait, but this has to be understood as plain old New England caution.) The culmination of work in seeing is linked to human love in this poem by the invitation that follows—"You come too." The necessary and unending labor that is a part of human destiny—in Biblical terms, of the state of fallen man—is, one might say, "redeemed" in Frost's ideal, invested with a saving grace.[2]

A famous and problematic poem of the task, "After Apple-Picking," lends itself well to a reading in these terms. We are now alerted to the kinesthetic motif, and it duly makes an appearance halfway through the speaker's soliloquy:

> My instep arch not only keeps the ache,
> It keeps the pressure of a ladder-round.
> I feel the ladder sway as the boughs bend.

The incantatory cadences and riddlesome ending of this poem—according to Frost, it was "the one thing in *North of Boston* that could be intoned"—have misled some, at least, of its readers into thinking it is about knowledge. But Frost is usually at least as much morally as epistemologically preoccupied, and so it is here.

You will recall the dramatic situation set forth in the opening. The picking of the apples is done. The scent of the fruit is on the air—alluding playfully to the nomenclature of perfumes, Frost calls it "essence of winter sleep." The drinking-trough is frozen over, so that the speaker is able to pick "a pane of glass" from it. He holds this to his eyes, looking through it at the hoarfrost that dims the grass.

> It melted, and I let it fall and break.
> But I was well
> Upon my way to sleep before it fell,
> And I could tell
> What form my dreaming was about to take.
> Magnified apples appear and disappear,
> Stem end and blossom end,
> And every fleck of russet showing clear.

Despite the preternatural vividness of the imagined apples, this is not a contemplative vision of essence in the Platonic sense, but something more mundane. The dream the speaker uneasily looks forward to having is the kind of dream we all experience after working at any-thing too hard and too long, in which we continue vainly to try to cope with the minutiae of the preceding day's task. It is, in other words, an anxiety dream of the occupational sort; and, to the degree that anxiety is a peculiarly human state, it is a peculiarly human kind of dream. The source of the speaker's anxiety, and hence of his dream, is made plain in the lines that follow:

> For I have had too much
> Of apple-picking: I am overtired
> Of the great harvest I myself desired.
> There were ten thousand thousand fruit to touch,
> Cherish in hand, lift down, and not let fall.
> For all
> That struck the earth,
> No matter if not bruised or spiked with stubble,
> Went surely to the cider-apple heap
> As of no worth.

What has made the speaker "overtired" is not simply the gathering of an enormously large crop of apples but the necessity of "cherish-ing" each one, of lifting it down and not letting it fall, lest it be judged worthless and so lost from the harvest. (We might note that the exact wording is "cherish *in hand*.") The symbolic purport of these lines needs scarcely be made explicit. For apples, substitute any series of things—or persons—with which one is responsibly con-cerned, each of which must be not merely handled but handled with love. This is the source of the kind of tiredness that is peculiarly human, the kind of tiredness that leads to a troubled, not a dreamless, sleep. We find it also in "Stopping by Woods on a Snowy Evening" in the significant contrast between the driver and his horse. The beast, oriented simply toward the end of the journey in food and rest, "think[s] it queer" that they are stopping along the way with neither food nor rest at hand. The man is torn between a weariness that makes darkness deeply welcome and his knowledge of "promises to keep," hence "miles to go" before sleeping. Both here and in "After Apple-Picking," is a tacit analogy between the end of one day, or of one harvest-time, and the end of all the tasks of a man's life.

If we interpret the dream in "After Apple-Picking" and the description of the task that follows it along the lines I have suggested, the ending of the poem ceases to be obscure:

> One can see what will trouble
> This sleep of mine, whatever sleep it is.
> Were he not gone,
> The woodchuck could say whether it's like his
> Long sleep, as I describe its coming on,
> Or just some human sleep. (pp. 68–69)

The woodchuck's "long sleep" is of course the dreamless oblivion referred to in Anglo-Saxon diction early in the poem as "winter sleep," i.e., hibernation. If he were there to be asked, the woodchuck would have to say that the night's sleep to which the speaker looks forward is not at all like hibernation, or even the daily sleep of animals. It *is* "just some human sleep," a restless sleep of poor quality. What vitiates it is an anxiety bound up with the responsibilities to which only human beings are subject, the ideals of behavior making them at once less fortunate than animals and—I think Frost would agree—more interesting and important. But I have already indicated that the end of the poem leads us to look beyond the time-scope of one harvest season, and even beyond the scope of human life itself, when the endless carrying out of the task under the pressure of altruistic responsibility will be over for good. This wider dimension, transcending mortality, is, I think, alluded to by the pane of ice lifted from the drinking-trough, through which the speaker sees the world as through a glass darkly; it has left a "strangeness on his sight" that cannot be rubbed off. Yet the New Testament promise of a life beyond this, in which we will see face to face, has no part in the meaning of the poem or in Frost's sceptical vision generally. The pane of ice is there, rather, to remind us that the nature of human life, the inescapable imposition of the ideal upon fleshly being, is a mystery, and that here on earth it will remain so.

In Frost's poetry, as in life itself, happiness in the performance of the task depends on a balance between effort and resistance, a "poise" neatly symbolized, in "Two Tramps in Mud Time," in the speaker's description of what it feels like to be chopping wood:

> The time when most I loved my task
> These two must make me love it more
> By coming with what they came to ask.
> You'd think I never had felt before
> The weight of an ax-head poised aloft,
> The grip on earth of outspread feet,
> The life of muscles rocking soft
> And smooth and moist in vernal heat. (p. 276)

The lifting of the ax aloft and the gripping of the earth below, combined in the physical act of chopping, seem to correspond to the union of abstract and concrete, "love and need," play and work, in the task, a union threatened here by the encroachment on the scene of the two tramps whose joblessness is a symptom of social malaise. In "Out, Out—," the union of love and need is thwarted by a rigid insistence on work for work's sake. In "After Apple-Picking," satisfaction in the completion of the task is marred by a weariness that comes from having worked too long under the pressure of the responsibility of cherishing each object. The fault in this last poem is neither in society nor in Puritanical narrowness, but in the conditions of human nature and life itself. In "Mowing," "Putting in the Seed," "The Pasture," and elsewhere, labor is shown achieving its dream of fact under ideal conditions, involving an ideal balance between effort and resistance.

The kinesthetically rendered engagement of body and world, the additional, specifically human, burden of responsibility—both these key-components of Frost's experiential vision are found in "The Grindstone." Reading this poem, we cannot fail to be struck by what may well be Frost's greatest gift: his ability to develop symbolic meaning with cumulative force, seemingly without art or effort, in naturalistically portrayed scene and action. On the literal level, the poem is a reminiscence of a boyhood incident. The speaker recalls how once, on a summer afternoon, he had cranked a grindstone for an old man sharpening a scythe. The man was a difficult taskmaster; once the boy got the stone spinning, he bore down on the scythe blade, forcing the boy to increase his efforts.

> I gave it the preliminary spin,
> And poured on water (tears it might have been);
> And when it almost gaily jumped and flowed,
> A Father-Time-like man got on and rode,
> Armed with a scythe and spectacles that glowed.
> He turned on willpower to increase the load
> And slow me down—and I abruptly slowed,
> Like coming to a sudden railroad station.

As the contest between man and boy continues, the boy turns to "bitter thoughts":

> I wondered who it was the man thought ground—
> The one who held the wheel back or the one
> Who gave his life to keep it going round?

It is the man who has the authority to say when the blade is done, and his standard of keenness is so high that the work of whetting seems destined never to conclude. The boy, though he does not relax his efforts, becomes not only resentful but anxious:

> The thing that made me more and more afraid
> Was that we'd ground it sharp and hadn't known,
> And now were only wasting precious blade.
> And when he raised it dripping once and tried
> The creepy edge of it with wary touch,
> And viewed it over his glasses funny-eyed,
> Only disinterestedly to decide
> It needed a turn more, I could have cried
> Wasn't there danger of a turn too much?
> Mightn't we make it worse instead of better?
> I was for leaving something to the whetter.
> What if it wasn't all it should be? I'd
> Be satisfied if he'd be satisfied. (pp. 189–91)

And so the poem ends. Just as the neighbor in "Mending Wall" metamorphoses with complete plausibility into a cave man standing armed in primeval gloom, so the man in "The Grindstone" is at once a real old New England farmer and Father Time, armed with a simultaneously real and emblematic scythe. So too the grindstone is both a real contraption and the popular emblem of work itself; and the "work" being carried on in the poem perfectly embodies the paradigm of effort and resistance, the push against the crank versus the weight of both stone and blade, the friction of blade against stone. Needless to say, kinesthetic imagery is not lacking; we know from reading the poem exactly what it must be like to work a grindstone by hand. As an allegory, "The Grindstone" raises the question whether too strict a standard imposed on the task may not only take away the joy that should ideally be a part of labor but also thwart the successful completion of the task itself, the keenness of the "precious blade" wasted by oversharpening. The poem treats humorously, as frustration recollected in tranquillity, what in "Out, Out—" is shown leading to a tragic disaster.

The fruit of labor, in the poems I have been discussing, is won by physical effort from tangible reality, and is itself tangible, a crop of hay, a spring raked clear of leaves, a cellarful of apples, a perfectly sharpened scythe blade. Ideally, it also involves something intangible or abstract, perhaps not named outright but hinted at; I have called it by such names as love, esthetic perception, fulfilment. A similar pattern can be detected in another important group of poems, in which the encounter between man and world is not active but contemplative. The speaker in these poems is not actually at work; he may be out for a walk, or perhaps simply thinking. What corresponds to the physical effort of labor is the exercise of externally directed powers of observation. The object is seen clearly; no idealizing vision is imposed upon it. In "Hyla Brook," the brook on the farm that by June has disappeared is meticulously portrayed in all its drabness as it looks in summer:

> By June our brook's run out of song and speed.
> Sought for much after that, it will be found
> Either to have gone groping underground
>
> . . . .

> Or flourished and come up in jewelweed. . . .
>
> .   .   .   .
>
> Its bed is left a faded paper sheet
> Of dead leaves stuck together by the heat—
> A brook to none but who remember long. (p. 119)

The conclusion of the poem shows that the mental engagement of self and world, like the physical, has its "yield," something above and beyond the accurately rendered record itself which can be seen both as a reward for work done and as an enlargement of consciousness. Retrospectively acknowledging the truth, that this brook of his doesn't amount to much in comparison with other brooks, the speaker simultaneously attains and expresses the insight of the final line: "We love the things we love for what they are." Faithful observation of the world around us is then, or should be, a labor of love, as is shown in other poems such as "The Tuft of Flowers," "The Wood-Pile," "Two Look at Two," and "The Most of It" in ways that limitations of space forbid exploration of here. All are thematically concerned with the winning of significance from unfalsified reality. This is what they are about, but they are as dramatically powerful as they are because this is also how they work; they show first the undistorted perception of facts and then the emergence of meaning.

The meditative enterprise as portrayed in "Hyla Brook" has another dimension that must be fully recognized if we are to understand the full import of the labor-love analogy in Frost. The speaker's rueful disclaimer concerns his brook, to be sure, but it also, and quite explicitly, concerns his poem. "This," he says, "as it will be seen is other far/Than with brooks taken otherwise *in song*" (emphasis added). The scope of reference of the demonstrative pronoun widens out as we consider it. What is "other far" than with other brooks is not only the brook itself but the description of the brook, and not only the content of the description but the way that content is presented. The importance of our making the comparison between this poem and other poems is guaranteed by the fact that a second term, a brook that is indeed "taken otherwise in song," springs instantly to mind.[3] "The Brook," by Alfred Lord Tennyson, is a registered poetic classic, inhabitant of dozens of anthologies, and it contrasts with Frost's "Hyla Brook" as neatly as one could wish in all relevant respects. Far from having run out of either song or speed, Tennyson's brook is able, nay eager, to speak for itself. It says,

> I come from haunts of coot and hern,
>   I make a sudden sally,
> And sparkle out among the fern,
>   To bicker down a valley. . . .
>
> I chatter, chatter, as I flow
>   To join the brimming river,
> For men may come and men may go,
>   But I go on for ever.

Confronted by these breathless intimations of immortality, we strongly suspect that Frost, in making his demurely self-deprecatory comparison, was at the same time having a bit of fun.

"Hyla Brook" tells us that for Frost, to love things as they are leads one to write poetry in which things are portrayed as they are. The fruit of the mental engagement between self and world is not insight alone, but a work of art in which that insight finds definitive expression. Thinking of "Hyla Brook" in this way, as a poem that asks to be compared with other poems, we are led to think also of "The Oven Bird." The point of this poem has been generally recognized to lie in its insistence on the bird's "saying" rather than "singing." The question the speaker sees as implicit in this paradoxically prosaic song, "what to make of a diminished thing," irresistibly takes on general significance for the reader as bearing on the problem of making poetry in a prosaic world. "The Oven Bird" is Frost's modern version of that august symbol of poetic tradition, the nightingale, and the answer to the question raised by the poem is the poem itself, "made" out of the sympathetic acceptance of diminishment as truth.

Making poetry is obviously akin to physical labor in that it is literally productive, yielding a visible fruit or harvest. But the analogy applies to the two actions as well as to their results, and we can see more clearly what this means by considering a poem that ostensibly has nothing to do with the writing of poems, "The Ax-Helve." The central emblem named in the title unites the themes of labor and love: an ax-helve is made by the French-Canadian, Baptiste, as a gift for his neighbor, who is the narrator of the poem. In the account of the making of the helve, Frost pays characteristic attention to kinesthetic detail. Baptiste is said to have "plowed the grain" of the speaker's old ax-handle "with a thick thumb-nail," and later, to have "chafed the long white body" of the unfinished new one "from end to end with his rough hand shut round it." The making of a fine helve, as expected, involves an element of perception above and beyond mere manual strength and skill. "He showed me," the narrator says,

> that the lines of a good helve
> Were native to the grain before the knife
> Expressed them, and its curves were no false curves
> Put on it from without. And there its strength lay
> For the hard work. (p. 187)

A little later, he exclaims, as if in surprise, "Do you know, what we talked about was knowledge?" and this is indeed a clue that what he has learned applies to things other than ax-handles, but the real theme of the poem is not knowledge; as usual with Frost, it remains implicit. In a note on "The Ax-Helve" in a book of his poems belonging to Elizabeth Shepley Sergeant, Frost wrote, "This is as near as I like to come to talking about art, in a work of art."

The skilled craftsman's ability to capture the lines native to the grain of the wood in the imposed shape of the helve corresponds nicely to what Frost thought was the poet's single most important gift, his ability to create "sentence sounds," the intonation patterns of living speech, in lines having metrical form.[4] This process was often described by him in physical terms. Everyone remembers his scoffing remark, that writing free verse is like playing tennis with the net down. And he once said in a newspaper interview that he liked "to drag and break the intonation across the meter as waves first comb and then break stumbling on the shingle."[5] To make the lines of a poem *say* themselves dramatically, the way people actually speak, is to write a kind of verse quite different from the insistently metrical lines of Tennyson's "The Brook," or the grandiloquent accents of Keats's "Ode to a Nightingale," and it is something much like whittling a supple, springy ax-handle out of a length of tough second-growth hickory. The writing of poems is, then, yet another form of what Frost in "Two Tramps in Mud Time" called the deed truly done, in which the pitting of human effort against resistance is motivated by love and yields a value belonging to the domain of the imagination. To put it in terms of an etymological link, labor for Frost, whether on the concrete or the abstract plane, is, ideally, expressive; and "expression" requires the existence of a reality against which "pressure" can be brought to bear.

For a final example of this experiential vision, in which a number of the themes we have been discussing are brought together, we may turn, briefly, to "Birches." In this poem, as in "Two Tramps in Mud Time," work and play are united, but now it is play that takes on the aspect of work rather than the other way around. Climbing birches is a game that is also an art, created in solitude by a boy "too far from town to learn baseball." It is difficult, involving a complicated technique that must be perfected by laborious repetition.

> He learned all there was
> To learn about not launching out too soon
> And so not carrying the tree away
> Clear to the ground. He always kept his poise
> To the top branches, climbing carefully. . . .
> . . . .
> Then he flung outward, feet first, with a swish,
> Kicking his way down through the air to the ground.

Painstaking application is rewarded by a sense of mastery in the final moment of release and fulfilment. Such fulfilment is contrasted with the frustration and thwarting of impulse that occurs when

> . . . life is too much like a pathless wood
> Where your face burns and tickles with the cobwebs
> Broken across it, and one eye is weeping
> From a twig's having lashed across it open

—kinesthetic imagery with a vengeance! The speaker, under such circumstances, longs for what Dorothy Parker once called "temporary suicide," but prays that no fate may wilfully misunderstand him

> And half grant what I wish and snatch me away
> Not to return. Earth's the right place for love:
> I don't know where it's likely to go better. (p. 122)

Pain, weariness, frustration and, on a broader time-scale, decline, aging, and death—all have their source in the human predicament as Frost conceived it: the rootedness of spirit in body and of body in world. But this same predicament is the indispensable precondition of all the love, all the accomplishment, all the satisfaction that we can know or imagine. Frost's poetry tells us this; it also, as I have said, enacts it and thus makes it a part of our own imaginative experience. The simile in "Birches" that describes the art of birch-swinging applies with uncanny aptness to the gradual building up of symbolic meaning that is of the essence of Frost's poetic artistry. The boy is said to have learned to climb "carefully/With the same pains you use to fill a cup/Up to the brim, and even above the brim."

We hear a great deal of the "dark side" of Frost,[6] and it is true that the world we are presented with in his poetry is largely, in the words of the hymn, "a world of toil and a world of pain/And a world of sorrow and care." But given the nature of Frost's vision, the true source of fear for him is not suffering, not the harsh impingement on mortal flesh of the branches and brambles of the pathless wood, but nothingness, the subtraction of reality. This is the blankness or white nightmare unforgettably portrayed in "Desert Places," where the speaker, passing by a field on which snow is falling heavily, sees a few last weeds and bits of stubble disappearing into a whiteness that threatens to obliterate him as well. In this loneliness he sees the portent of a more all-encompassing emptiness and silence—looking, perhaps, toward the end of the world:

> And lonely as it is, that loneliness
> Will be more lonely ere it will be less—
> A blanker whiteness of benighted snow. . . . (p. 296)

Most dreadful of all, in such a landscape there will be "no expression, nothing to express."

It is against the terrifying emptiness of "Desert Places" that the hills and circling arms of "Bond and Free" form a reassuring bulwark:

> Love has earth to which she clings
> With hills and circling arms about—
> Wall within wall to shut fear out. (p. 120)

And this brings me back to the two poems which were my starting point, and my reasons for thinking that "Bond and Free," in contrast with "To Earthward," is both peripheral to Frost's real concerns as a poet and of minor importance in the canon of his works.

"To Earthward," for all its seeming lucidity, never really explains itself. The two physical actions, real and hypothetical, which it describes in its two final stanzas—the pressing down of hand on earth, and the longing to press the whole self against earth with equal weight—are themselves fraught with a weight of meaning that resists paraphrase. We can recognize the speaker's feelings, disturbingly, as our own, yet we cannot fully understand them; the attraction of spirit toward earth remains a mystery. And there is an additional dimension to the mystery, whether or not we spell it out in paraphrase. The act of straining against earth with the *entire* body is intrinsically impossible; we cannot press against it without also pushing away. We can be possessed wholly by the force that draws us to earthward only at the end of our existence as separate beings.

"Bond and Free" portrays Love and Thought as personified abstract entities, and exalts the former at the expense of the latter. Concerning the treatment of Love, with its imagery of clinging and straining in the world's embrace, I need say nothing further; the pervasiveness and key significance of such imagery in Frost has been a major theme of my essay. Thought, on the other hand, is personified as a spirit who, having effortlessly "shaken his ankles free" of the terrestrial world, "cleaves the interstellar gloom"

> And sits in Sirius' disc all night,
> Till day makes him retrace his flight,
> With smell of burning on every plume,
> Back past the sun to an earthly room.

I take it that in the "smell of burning on every plume" we are to see an allusion to the fall of Icarus, whose wings melted when he flew too close to the sun and let him fall; in that case, Thought is to be considered similarly presumptuous, and engaged in an enterprise similarly dangerous if not doomed. The poem continues,

> His gains in heaven are what they are.
> Yet some say Love by being thrall

And simply staying possesses all
In several beauty that Thought fares far
To find fused in another star. (pp. 120–21)

The message is superficially both clear and plausible: concrete multiplicity has at least as much to offer as abstract unity; the enslavement of Love brings at least as much fulfilment as the free-wheeling liberty of Thought. We may find mildly objectionable the pretense of coy understatement in "some say," since the poem gives every indication otherwise that this is the view of the speaker as of all right-minded men. But there is a far deeper objection to the poem than this, namely, that for Frost at his most serious (and at his most serious he is usually also at his best), not only love but thought, creativity, all human achievement whether material or spiritual, arises from an engagement with actuality in which the latter is a powerfully resistant force. The "Thought" of "Bond and Free" does not take part in such an engagement; when we first hear of him, he has already soared off into space. What he is described in the poem as doing is almost totally lacking in interest and suggestiveness; it is difficult to imagine what might be meant by sitting in Sirius' disc all night, or how what Love finds on snow and sand and turf could also be found "fused" in "another star" than earth. "Bond and Free" presents, not a concept of abstractive thought that we can seriously respect, but a parodic "Superthought" figure, a comic-strip Icarus. If we agree with the poem before we read it, we may assent to its final statement while taking pleasure in the grace and wit bestowed on it by Frost's verbal Midas touch. But "To Earthward" leaves us both moved and troubled. In it, as in all of Frost's most authentic poems, we not only find a parable that lingers in the memory, but are also made more vividly aware of what it is like to be alive.

Notes to *Robert Frost: "To Earthward"* by MARIE BORROFF

1. "Robert Frost's New Testament: Language and the Poem," *Modern Philology*, 69 (1971), 47–48.

2. Frost's ideal of labor may also be considered to represent a humane enlargement of the so-called "work ethic" associated in America with traditional Puritan or Calvinistic views concerning man's nature and duty. For a recent discussion of this tradition, see Kenneth Keniston, " 'Good Children' (Our Own), 'Bad Children'

(Other People's), and the Horrible Work Ethic," *Yale Alumni Magazine*, 37, no. 7 (1974), 6–10.

3. See, e.g., Reuben Brower, *The Poetry of Robert Frost: Constellations of Intention* (New York: Oxford University Press, 1963), pp. 82–83.

4. See "Robert Frost's New Testament," p. 44 and n. 12.

5. Quoted by Elaine Barry, *Robert Frost on Writing* (New Brunswick, New Jersey: Rutgers University Press, 1973), p. 20.

6. See, e.g., Eben Bass, "Frost's Poetry of Fear," *American Literature*, 43 (1971–72), 603–15. According to Bass, nature is an object of fear for Frost in its threat to "reclaim everything" if man neglects the work necessary to hold it at bay (p. 608). I see as primary in this threat the prospect of obliteration rather than of hardship or suffering; white is a major fear symbol in Frost because it symbolizes emptiness, the absence of an "other" that can guarantee by opposition the existence of the self.

Robert Frost: Some Reflections
on Poetry and Power

GEORGE W. NITCHIE

I want to start with recollection of an occasion, one that is for me chiefly images, oral, visual, and emotional. The occasion is that of John Kennedy's inauguration, as it exists in my memory: dazzling cold sunlight, so bright that Frost could not read his manuscript; Lyndon Johnson (was it Johnson?) attempting to shade the podium with his hat; an obstreperous breeze that kept riffling Frost's papers and hair; everybody smiling vividly—Kennedy, Johnson—as the almost botched performance went on, Frost mumbling his lines, then giving it up and simply speaking "The Gift Outright" from memory. I remember it as a moving, awkward, almost embarrassing occasion, probably all the more moving and movingly awkward for the resonance it acquired when, three years later, with Robert Frost dead, John Kennedy spoke in Frost's praise at the dedication of the Robert Frost Library at Amherst; and then a month after that when the still unstoried, artless, unenhanced land did something about one more of those deeds of gift that were many deeds of war, and John Kennedy was dead, and Robert Frost was dead, and Lee Oswald was dead. And the next effort to bring poetry and power into focus was Lyndon Johnson's White House Festival of the Arts, with Robert Lowell's movingly awkward refusal to participate because of his repudiation of Johnson's Vietnam policy. But that is another chapter.

In the last couplet of his unread inaugural poem, Frost had donned Virgilian robes and prophesied

> A golden age of poetry and power
> Of which this noonday's the beginning hour. (p. 424)

But in a televised interview quoted by the editors of a collection of poems prompted chiefly by the assassination, John Kennedy cited "a story that some years ago an interested mother wrote to a principal of a school: 'Don't teach my boy poetry; he's going to run for Congress.' "[1] And I suspect we can recognize in that anecdote an authentic American principle. Kennedy, of course, rejected that principle.

What about Frost? Really?

I think the answer is complicated, as most answers probably are. I believe two things among others about Frost. One is that he was the kind of poet he was able to be, perhaps the kind it was given him to be; I believe, that is, that he could not have been other than he was. And I believe that when he was doing the kind of thing it was given him to do, he was a great and fine poet. But I also believe that the kind of poet it was given Frost to be was in some way at odds with the kind of poet he wanted to be, and I think that that is partly because Frost was in some way at odds with the kind of country it was given him to be a citizen of. He was a citizen of a very large country that has always had trouble in taking its poets seriously, even in knowing what to do with them at all. No matter how far back one goes, European America has no tradition of *using* its artists, including its poets. Chaucer was a public servant; Donne became Dean of St. Paul's at a time when that meant you were recognized by authority; Milton was a kind of sub-cabinet minister in a revolutionary government; Swift served Queen Anne; Tennyson held that peculiar position the Laureateship. Yeats took part in revolutionary or near-revolutionary political activity; he set out to organize Ireland; he became a senator, and a working senator, of the Irish Free State.

Now, as a young man Frost had admired Yeats. In the spring of 1910, while he was teaching at Pinkerton Academy in Derry, New Hampshire, Frost put on five plays; only two of them were modern, and both were by Yeats, *The Land of Heart's Desire* and *Cathleen ni Houlihan.* In 1913 he met Yeats in London and was disappointed that no real friendship developed. In 1928, during a visit to Ireland, he met Yeats again through Padraic Colum and A.E., and he wrote in a letter to a friend: "If I have forgotten anything or anyone it is not invidiously. Oh yes there was Yates [sic]. He was the best I ever saw him and quite seemed to see me in the room. I had been scared by stories I had heard about his senatorial greatness" (Thompson,

II, 639). One does not have to be too deeply versed in country things to detect something very like envy, like resentment, in the 54-year-old Frost toward the 63-year-old Yeats.

"How Hard It Is to Keep from Being King When It's in You and in the Situation" Frost titled one of his more wistfully jocular late poems. Nobody asked him to be king. That sounds so silly. They gave him Pulitzer prizes and visiting professorships and congressional citations, but they never made him a senator or a cabinet minister, not even in John Kennedy's Camelot. Yeats could talk about "The seeming needs of my fool-driven land." He could write:

> 'What have I earned for all that work,' I said,
> 'For all that I have done at my own charge?
> The daily spite of this unmannerly town,
> Where who has served the most is most defamed,
> The reputation of his lifetime lost
> Between the night and morning.'

He could write:

> We, who seven years ago
> Talked of honour and of truth,
> Shriek with pleasure if we show
> The weasel's twist, the weasel's tooth.

He could write as, and present himself as, "A sixty-year-old smiling public man,"[2] because in fact that is what he was. Edwin Muir remarks, "A public man is a man who is entitled to be listened to by the public; a great public man is one who can tell his public, on occasion, what he thinks of them, knowing that they will listen." Robert Frost was never really that; no American poet has been.

Muir, in fact, adds, "It is easier to be the voice of a small nation than of a great one."[3] Can't one say, it is easier to be the voice of New England than of the United States? And wasn't Frost that? But that won't do. For one thing, nobody was ever inaugurated President of New England. New England has been identified as a temperament, a history, a state of mind, a chronic disease. But not a nation. Ireland had the Easter Rising; New England had the Dickie-Raymond power project. The scale is different; you have to pretend more. Frost even pretended to be a New England native; Lawrance

Thompson has told us how Frost taught himself to speak New Hampshire Yankee (I, 371). And this has something in common with Yeats, perhaps quite a bit; both men invented themselves, out of much the same unpromising materials. To drop one more name, John Wain usefully compares Yeats and Milton: "They write in a similar way because they have a temperamental affinity. Both were shy, proud men who forced themselves, not without a self-consuming inner delight, to play a part on the public stage. Both were in love with pride—Milton half-consciously, Yeats openly—and both write superbly in praise of the proud character." And you can easily substitute the name of Frost for that of either Yeats or Milton without ever losing your stride. You can carry the point further. Wain notes Yeats's use of the word *arrogant* as a term of praise, and adds: "Since arrogance is in fact an unpleasant characteristic, one is driven to ask how Yeats manages to enlist our sympathy, even momentarily, for people who suffer from it. And the answer comes quickly. These people are on the losing side. The impoverished Irish gentry, who helped Yeats to do his life's work, were going down before the advance of modern bureaucracy and commerce; the politician and the 'huckster,' both egalitarian and rationalistic though in conflicting ways, were inexorably treading the 'renowned generations' into the mire. This, of course, is the major theme of Yeats's poems, and it is what reconciles one to the endlessly asserted *hauteur* of the characters he writes about. Pride such as theirs would be intolerable in a governing class that was actually dominant."[4] As with Yeats and the Irish gentry, so with Milton and the Roundhead saints. And so with Frost and the galaxy of moving or amusing or exasperating losers with whom his poetic world is peopled.

What might have happened if Frost had set out, like Yeats in Ireland, to remold New England; or like Milton, into that real exercise of poetry and power, when men risked their heads in the political hustings, and sometimes lost them? What, even, might the Watergate tapes sound like if Frost had been part of the Nixon team? The thought seems inconceivable; but does its inconceivability say more about Frost's integrity or about the relationship (I want to say, the nonrelationship) between poetry and power, art and politics in our time and place? Does it, in fact, say something about not teaching one's boy poetry if he's going to run for Congress?

In the inaugural poem for John Kennedy, once more, Frost had called for

> Less criticism of the field and court
> And more preoccupation with the sport. (p. 424)

But there had been no way for him into that necessary preoccupation, no way for him to become a sixty-year-old smiling public man, no way for him into that country beyond politics from which Milton could write with earned authority, whole again beyond confusion, "One's country is wherever it is well with one." In a way, Frost had *chosen* that there should be no way there; nothing could tempt him from this craft of verse. Not farming, really; not public life, certainly; only sporadically teaching, "barding around," doing the things poets do in America, as distinct from the things, one is sometimes tempted to say, that *real* people do, people who don't want their boy taught poetry because he's going to run for Congress. Milton postponed poetry for twenty years and spent himself in public life; Yeats spent himself in organizing Irish literary societies, in the Abbey Theater—spent himself and very greatly found himself in the process, made himself whole again—I will not say beyond confusion, because that is one of the things one dare not say of our time. These were great, public gestures, like Byron and Greece, Wordsworth and France. Frost, it is tempting to say, gave us only the great private gesture: storming off on a solitary hike through the Dismal Swamp when Elinor White first refused to marry him; selling his farm and going to live in England with no prospects except poetry. Except poetry. Like Keats, Frost wanted to be a poet or nothing—and by the time Keats was twenty-two or twenty-three, he was already turning against that decision, as is clear from the alterations he was making in his long poem about Hyperion.

Lawrance Thompson tells us (I, 472) of a long talk Frost had with Robert Graves in 1914 about whether he, Frost, should enlist in the British army. There would have been public gesture. Frost evidently rejected it. I suspect that he was right in doing so, right as a poet, as the kind of poet it was given him to be. Milton could not have written *Paradise Lost* or *Samson Agonistes* or *Paradise Regained* without the experience of commitment and disillusionment that public life had given him. Wordsworth could hardly have been a poet at all without the experience of France and the redemptive experiences that followed, and would not have happened without France. Frost was different. In *North of Boston* he knew all about violence and terror, pity and fear, everything he could have learned in the trenches. Though perhaps he learned something more when Elinor Frost died in 1938 and did not ask for him; or in his daughter's weeping, hysterical refusal to have him make his home with her, after Mrs. Frost's death, lest he damage her children the way he had his own (Thompson, II, 494–96). And none of it had anything to do with public gestures, with the reflections of a sixty-year-old smiling public man. They had nothing to do with America, or New England, or with that participation in the august affairs of state that he publicly thanked John Kennedy for making possible. It was not given him to be that sort of poet, whatever he may have believed, or wished to believe. Or wished others to believe.

As American poet, it seems to me, Frost was an authentic stateless alien, as much so as Wallace Stevens, or Ezra Pound, or T. S. Eliot. Some time ago I devoted some time and energy to some speculations on what Frost really drew on among his contemporaries and immediate predecessors. Did the local green and universal blue of "The Middleness of the Road" and "Fragmentary Blue" owe something to Mallarmé's images of blueness, of l'azur? Does man's (or woman's) role in naming in "The Aim Was Song" or "Never Again Would Birds' Song Be the Same" owe anything to Rilke's aesthetic metaphysics in the *Duino Elegies?*

Well, one says, obviously not. From Mallarmé and Rilke to Frost: from the neurotic, deracinated, rootless, alienated, European decadent to the American cousin of, at his most European, Thomas Hardy and Edward Thomas? Clearly, the distance is too great. After all, who wrote to a friend, "You will understand that it was only by jumping the rails in the most rebellious and aggressive way that I could take possession of my own temperament and blood"? Who wrote, "What I write as an artist will probably to the last somewhere show traces of the rebellion by means of which I entered into my own..."?[5] "Into my own": the last phrase clearly gives the game away; we know who that is. And we are wrong: not the author of *A Boy's Will*, but that alienated, rootless, neurotic and utterly European wanderer, Rainer Maria Rilke, a man without a country if there ever was one.

Frost, I suppose, was such another. That he ever seemed to be otherwise—so American, so Ours, so much the one to get the United States stated, our 60-, and 70-, and 80-year-old not-quite-smiling public man—that he ever seemed to be is a triumph, and a very substantial triumph, over the system that didn't want its boy to be taught poetry because he was going to run for Congress. In the end, Congress came to him, with citations and medals, and Presidents took him at his own evaluation. He may not have corrupted Hadleyburg, but he did become Poetry Consultant to the Library of Congress—and what a position of political power that is! And as he had said about his wife when she finally agreed to become his wife, "I bent her to my will." Or as he wrote to Louis Untermeyer in 1916, "The poet in me died nearly ten years ago. . . . The calf I was in the nineties I merely take to market. I am become my own salesman" (Thompson, I, 606).

He was wrong, of course; there was plenty of poetry left after 1916, though I think none better. But it is suggestive that, as early as 1916, he was already prepared for the role of self-salesman, for the effort at proving that he at least (perhaps no one else, but he at least) could make it as a poet, could compel New England and America to make him their own, the "great public man" identified by Edwin Muir as one who can "tell his public, on occasion, what he thinks of them, knowing that they will listen." And of course prove it he did, choosing like Yeats's man of the third quarter "whatever whim's most difficult/Among whims not impossible" (p. 161), telling us of his own desert places and convincing us or making us convince ourselves that they were cozy; looking into a great emptiness and letting us suppose it was full of meaning; embodying emotional chaos, suspicion, resentment, alienation, insecurity, and showing us, or pretending to show us, stability, wisdom, rootedness and love.

What a performance! What an enterprise!

I do not know, finally, what I think of Robert Frost; but I want to end, as I began, with an image. When Professor Murphy first wrote me about the Merrimack conference, his letter was stamped, appropriately, with the ten-cent Robert Frost commemorative stamp. This is clearly design. But the stamp was cancelled by a device commemorating twenty years of service by the Small Business Administration. This, it seems to me, is Providence. How hard it really is to keep from being king when it's in you and in the situation.

Notes to *Robert Frost: Some Reflections on Poetry and Power*
by GEORGE W. NITCHIE

1. Erwin A. Glikes and Paul Schwaber, eds., *Of Poetry and Power: Poems Occasioned by the Presidency and by the Death of John F. Kennedy* (New York: Basic Books, Inc., 1964), p. 4.
2. *The Collected Poems of W. B. Yeats* (New York: The Macmillan Company, 1951), pp. 95, 148, 207, 213.
3. *The Estate of Poetry* (Cambridge, Mass.: Harvard University Press, 1962), p. 52.
4. "Strength and Isolation: Pessimistic Notes of a Miltonolater," in Frank Kermode, ed., *The Living Milton* (London: Routledge & Kegan Paul, 1960), p. 5.
5. Quoted in Eudo C. Mason, *Rilke* (London: Oliver and Boyd, Ltd., 1963), pp. 3–4.

Robert Frost:
Politics in Theory and Practice

PETER J. STANLIS

How small, of all that human hearts endure,
That part which laws or kings can cause or cure!
(Goldsmith, *The Traveller*, ll. 429–30)

Me and mine are below the threshold of legislative
cognizance. Beyond participation of politicians
and beyond relief of senates lie our sorrows.
(Frost, Letter to Louis Untermeyer, Feb. 23, 1932)

THE personal life of Robert Frost was filled with great and frequent tragedies. His father died of tuberculosis at age thirty-four; his mother of cancer at fifty-six; he lost his infant son Elliott in 1900, and his infant daughter Elinor-Bettina soon after; his sister Jean became insane shortly after World War I; his beloved daughter Marjorie died young of septicemia fever in 1934; his wife died of an unexpected heart attack in March 1938; his son Carol committed suicide in the fall of 1940; and his daughter Irma lost her mind and was institutionalized in 1947. In addition to these strong billows of calamity which rolled over Frost's family for decades, the poet himself suffered much illness, and for many years the family endured poverty. These personal afflictions, together with Frost's reading, observations of life, and reflections on the general human condition throughout history, provided the basis for the poet's tragic vision of man's life on earth.

In a letter to his Marxist friend, Louis Untermeyer, on the occasion of his daughter Irma's confinement, Frost clearly made the reality of his tragic vision of man's life paramount to the subordinated realities of politics in theory and practice: "Cast your eye back over my family's luck and perhaps you will wonder if I haven't had pretty near enough. That is for the angels to say. The valkyries and eumenides. My own objection to your communism (socialism for safety) is that realized to perfection it can't come within three strata of the stratosphere of touching the reality of our personal life."[1] Frost always believed that the terrible, natural, unavoidable afflictions suffered by men in their daily lives were beyond the help of politics.

Such cosmic sorrows implied a great injustice built into the very frame and order of man's trial by existence in his temporal life: "The chiefest of our sorrows is that the world should go as it does—that thus all moves and that this is the justice that on earth we find. What justice? . . . Why injustice, which we either have to turn on the other fellow with a laugh when it is called comedy or we have to take like a spear-point in both hands to our breast when it is called tragedy. . . . But let what will be be. I am so deeply smitten through my helm that I am almost sad to see infants young any more" (pp. 219–20). The phrase "let what will be be" underscores the stoicism bearing upon fatalism that were elements compounded into Frost's tragic view of man's life, elements that were beautifully captured in a passage in his poem "The Wind and the Rain":

> I sang of death—but had I known
> The many deaths one must have died
> Before he came to meet his own!
> Oh, should a child be left unwarned
> That any song in which he mourned
> Would be as if he prophesied?
> It were unworthy of the tongue
> To let the half of life alone
> And play the good without the ill.
> And yet 'twould seem that what is sung
> In happy sadness by the young
> Fate has no choice but to fulfill. (p. 336)

In a quatrain, "A Question," Frost raised the question of the tragedy in man's life on earth from the viewpoint of God:

> A voice said, Look me in the stars
> And tell me truly, men of earth,
> If all the soul-and-body scars
> Were not too much to pay for birth. (p. 362)

To Frost there was no universal or final answer to the question whether the terrible price of tragedy was sufficiently compensated by birth and the joys of life. Each man had to answer that question out of his own experience and philosophy.

There was never anything maudlin or sentimentally romantic about Frost's tragic view of man's life. He always accepted the personal tragedies of poverty, disease, failure, public unrecognition and death with quiet dignity and stoical courage. When Untermeyer was divorced, Frost wrote to him that this sorrow "must be kept away down under the surface where the great griefs belong" (p. 191). To Frost the great "griefs" of mankind were subjects for religion and philosophy, and were in a realm of reality beyond the mere "grievances" of politics. His tragic vision of life derived from his religion and philosophy and involved the most profound metaphysical and spiritual problems of human life and death. In contrast, politics dealt with man's merely physical and social temporal problems. Like Samuel Johnson, Frost believed that political solutions of public grievances, however perfectly realized, were merely palliatives of recurring problems and that they could not cure men's irremedial tragic griefs.

Frost's tragic vision of life made him highly skeptical that revolutionary changes in the form of government, or in the structure of an economic system, could vitally affect the most important concerns of men. Indeed, such changes could do nothing even in the more limited area of human character and ability. On this point he wrote to Untermeyer in 1934: "I consider politics settled by the conclusion I reached last night amid the many movements of my mind that no change of system could possibly make me a bit better or abler, the only two things of any importance to me personally" (p. 243). A well-based and balanced tragic vision of life was of great practical value in politics, Frost believed, because it prevented men from having delusions about reality; it dissipated their unrealistic faith in miracles through social systems, political programs and politicians.

Political ideologies such as Marxism were to Frost among the great intellectual illusions of human nature, promising a heaven on earth beyond man's capability. Early in his friendship with Untermeyer, the poet invited his friend to join him in his tragic view of life, on a plane of reality above the struggles of mere political good and evil: "Leave the evils that can be remedied or even palliated. You are of an age now to face essential Hell. Cease from the optimism as much that makes good as that sees good. Come with me into the place of tombs and outer darkness" (p. 136). This melodramatic appeal was not successful, and Untermeyer remained an ideological Marxist throughout their decades of friendship until Frost's death in 1963.

Since politics fell far short of redeeming men from the "essential Hell" of human tragedy, Frost knew that as a writer he would never place his ultimate faith in any political optimism: "There's one thing I shan't write in the past, present, or future," he wrote in 1917, "and that is glad mad stuff or mad glad stuff. The conviction closes in on me that I was cast for gloom as the sparks fly upward. . . . I am of deep shadow all compact like onion within onion and the savor of me is oil of tears" (p. 59).[2] Frost's prophesy about himself as a writer proved true: he never abandoned his tragic view of man's life and never adopted any "mad glad" political ideology that promised temporal salvation for mankind. Yet Frost's tragic sense did not plunge him into gloom; within the limitations of temporal life he often experienced an exhilarating joy. Throughout much of his life Frost was a profoundly pessimistic man with an enormous zest for living, who thoroughly enjoyed talking about politics in theory and practice.

Faith in the power of politics to redress men's temporal injustices rested upon the common belief of modern men that human knowledge acquired through empirical study and scientific methods, and human reason, will and moral character, were competent to solve the great problems of poverty, ignorance, disease, crime, and war on a regional, national and even international basis. Frost's tragic vision of life was reinforced by his conviction that even within the temporal order the power of politics was severely restricted by limitations within human nature.

To Frost one of the most important of human limitations was that human nature, and especially human intelligence, does not improve much, if at all: "It all comes down to this: We have ways of knowing that human nature doesn't change much. Maybe it gets worse— maybe not. Only the denouement tells the story, the end. Human intelligence, for all our worship of evolution, stays pretty much the same. We'd be hard put to it to show an intellect in our day the equal of Aristotle's or Immanuel Kant's. These, I take it, appear to be capstones, at least of their periods, maybe of all time."[3] If "the denouement tells the story," then the scientific idea of progress, as applied to the nature of man, is an illusion: "A scientist like Vannevar Bush must be full of a feeling of progress . . . but a man who feels deeply about humanity must feel we are back in ancient Egypt."[4]

An important consequence of man's limited intelligence, as he wrote to Untermeyer in 1925, was that general human knowledge was limited: "I might sustain the theme indefinitely that you nor I nor nobody knows as much as he doesn't know. And that isn't all: there is nothing anybody knows, however absolutely, that isn't more or less vitiated as a fact by what he doesn't know" (p. 175). Frost applied to himself his intellectual skepticism against the power of human reason to know anything absolutely, and therefore he refused to translate logic into practical life through speculative argument: "Not for me to argue anything where I don't know" (p. 178). Frost believed that speculative logical reasoning through induction and deduction was never the basis of reality in life, because in the abstract high singular there isn't any universal reason. Indeed, strict logic tended to put a man outside of any subject he considered. To Louis Untermeyer he wrote: "The logic of everything lands you outside of it: the logic of poetry outside of poetry . . . ; the logic of religion by nice gradations outside of Catholicism in Protestantism, outside of Protestantism in agnosticism, and finally outside of agnosticism in Watsonian behaviorism . . ." (p. 188). In this vital sentence, Frost summarized the historical course of rational secularism in the Western world since the sixteenth century.

Like David Hume, Frost always doubted that human knowledge could ever become absolute and thorough, regardless of how systematically men applied the scientific method in establishing factual and empirical truths and general principles of physical nature and supposed laws of history. Also, there were truths of a mystical kind that science could not reach, such as were the great concerns of the humanities, psychology, the arts, and especially religion. In practical affairs also, Frost believed, the discipline modern man often needed to learn most was his submission to unreason.

Finally, beyond the limitations of intelligence and knowledge and the illusions of rational ideology were the finiteness and fallibility of the human will, and the moral weaknesses of men's characters. Even when men had knowledge adequate to their political and social purposes, they often failed for lack of prudence, temperance, or moral courage, or through expediences of ambition, or a lust for power. Because of all these intellectual and moral limitations in human nature, Frost was skeptical of the claims of modern social scientists that they could ever bring man's social environment under scientific or rational control and, thus, through politics, determine the course and end of human history. A scientifically controlled social order might result in more evil than good for man. Frost's contempt for sociological and psychological behavioralists, whom he called "the guild of social planners,"[5] remained constant throughout his life, and increased as their claims for dominance over society increased.

Although men simply did not know enough and were not Godlike enough to control the course of social history, Frost was convinced that men had to act in society on self belief, out of their inadequate knowledge and limited character. Frost distinguished sharply between social knowledge and self-belief. Despite their uncertain general knowledge, men had to have self-belief, and Frost admired decisiveness in a man's self-belief: "Belief is better than anything, and it is best when rapt, above paying its respects to anybody's doubt whatsoever" (p. 16). Even at the risk of being dead wrong, Frost believed, a man should firmly assert his philosophical position about life: "What I love best in a man is definiteness of position. I don't care what the position is so long as it is definite enough. I mean I don't half care. Take a position and try it out no matter who sets up to call you an unhanged traitor. My God how I adore some people who stand right out in history with distinct meaning" (p. 58). Undoubtedly, Frost's preference of decisive personal belief over faith in human intelligence, knowledge, and character parallels the superior position in his total philosophy of his tragic view of life over politics. It was the commitment of a man of leadership as the tragic hero in public affairs, in the political drama of life. Frost was aware that when a leader imposed his beliefs on others the consequences could be disastrous.

Frost's view of human nature led him to doubt that drastic changes in social machinery, based upon ideological revolution, would solve men's basic economic and social problems. He mocked lightly at Untermeyer's Marxist faith in revolutionary ideology: "Pity me for not knowing what would set everything right" (p. 86). Frost recognized the irony that it took superior intellectual power and moral wisdom to reject theories that the revolutionary ideologue accepted because of his excessive faith in his own reason and self-esteem. In practical politics the revolutionary ideologue was a doctrinaire fanatic, anything but liberal and tolerant, even when the substance of his politics was called "liberal," because he was prepared to impose his ideological theories upon society as official "truth." A fervent revolutionary was prepared to use force to bring about immediate and drastic changes in society, without regard to the human suffering caused by his changes. Frost particularly disliked the Marxist theory that the violent destruction of existing capitalist society was a necessary and constructive act that would lead to greater good in the future. In his satiric portrait of an American ideological Marxist, "A Case for Jefferson," Frost expressed his dislike of violent total revolution:

> Harrison loves my country too,
> But wants it all made over new.
> He's Freudian Viennese by night.
> By day he's Marxian Muscovite.
> It isn't because he's Russian Jew.
> He's Puritan Yankee through and through.
> He dotes on Saturday pork and beans.
> But his mind is hardly out of his teens:
> With him the love of country means
> Blowing it all to smithereens
> And having it all made over new. (p. 393)

With bland irony the poet indicated the kind of social revolution he favored: "I don't mind a revolution if I start it. The kind of revolution I don't like are those someone else starts" (*Interviews*,

p. 170). Frost favored a revolution within the individual that would enrich and improve his intellectual, moral, aesthetic and social nature, without changing the structural forms of institutions in the use of political power. Frost called this inner change in men "a one-man revolution" ("Build Soil," p. 324). It was a revolution which took into account all the individual differences of men and did not seek to level out distinctions into a homogenized mass society.

Frost believed that perhaps the most constantly recurring modern problem in society was that of distributive justice in economics, and that most social changes and revolutionary movements were concerned with securing greater equity between rich and poor. Too great extremes between rich and poor was very bad for any society. Periodically some equalization between the economic extremes of rich and poor had to take place. Frost expressed this social need in "An Equalizer":

> And when we get too far apart in wealth,
> 'Twas his idea that for the public health,
> So that the poor won't have to steal by stealth,
> We now and then should take an equalizer. (p. 363)

Frost's deep concern for securing greater equity in distributive justice in general prompted him to write Untermeyer: "Count on me as in favor of reforming a whole lot of things downward" (p. 127). Frost even entitled one of his poems "On Taking from the Top to Broaden the Base." But a policy of equity in economic justice, aimed at establishing greater equality of condition between classes in society, if carried to an extreme could mean the destruction of individual freedom and individual differences in more than wealth and poverty. To Frost, solving the problem of distributive justice in economics did not mean that equality should replace freedom, or that parliamentary forms of government should be weakened in a free society. He felt that, within the framework of a free society, parliamentary government remained the constant and immediate necessary means and that distributive justice was an imperfect and occasionally realized remote end. This meant that in making economic changes in society, political moderation was central in Frost's philosophy.

Frost's criticism of most social and political reformers was only slightly less severe than his criticism of ideological revolutionaries. In an interview in 1957 the poet confessed that he "didn't like reformers" (*Interviews*, p. 169). Too many social reformers were mindless and untalented activists: "I am not for the reformer, who is always active but usually has nothing to give" (*Interviews*, p. 78). To Frost, reformers were too interested in "bending the flame," whereas his interest was more basic—"to keep the candle from going over" (p. 98). He summarized his general prejudice against reformers in a couplet in "To a Thinker":

> I own I never really warmed
> To the reformer or reformed. (p. 326)

Even in times of crisis, when drastic social changes seemed necessary, Frost favored withholding the full force of such change. He expressed this conviction in "A Semi-Revolution":

> I advocate a semi-revolution.
> The trouble with a total revolution
> (Ask any reputable Rosicrucian)
> Is that it brings the same class up on top.
> Executives of skillful execution
> Will therefore plan to go halfway and stop.
> Yes, revolutions are the only salves,
> But they're one thing that should be done by halves. (p. 363)

Frost favored gradualism in making necessary changes in society, and therefore he was highly critical of the impatience of those who wished immediate drastic changes. In his *Masque of Reason* the poet has Job voice his criticism of impatient reformers:

> God needs time just as much as you or I
> To get things done. Reformers fail to see that.—(p. 478)

Just as it required time for God to create the universe, and to recreate it in its ongoing process, it had also required eons and eons of evolutionary time for mankind to improve itself, until it produced modern man. In a mock-serious thrust at Untermeyer, Frost wrote: "Think of all the human pains that went to uplifting Pithecanthropus Erectus into the Piltdown man and the Piltdown man into the Neanderthal and the Neanderthal into the Heidelberg and him into the likes of me and Woodrow Wilson" (p. 86). Extending this idea logically, Frost pretended to believe that modern revolutionaries, by virtue of their claim to have the golden key to establish a perfect society, must hold their superior political wisdom through holding a higher place in the evolutionary scale of human beings than that of retrograde skeptics such as he. In a witty reductio ad absurdum application of this point to several of Untermeyer's revolutionary friends, Frost suggested to Untermeyer: "Why by osteopathic manipulation . . . couldn't you . . . effect the next great change of me into Max Eastman or Jack Reed?" (p. 87). Indeed, Frost suggested, if modern man were intelligent enough to perceive the truth and value of the evolutionary metaphor in understanding past human development, then for that very reason he should be wise enough to reject unwanted changes in society, as part of that very process. This included the power and right to choose to hold fast to a position: "Since we all agree that we're now smart enough to go on with what we are in an evolutionary way, we ought to be smart enough to stop where we are. And I am in favor of stopping where we are" (*Interviews*, p. 213).

Where is contemporary man in his evolutionary development? According to Frost, he is in a state of "uncertainty . . . between being members and being individuals" (*Interviews*, p. 213). Frost preferred to maintain the ambiguous state of modern man, between the claims of individual freedom and the desire of revolutionaries and radical reformers to force him into fixed social memberships. He believed that society would be improved more easily if the individual remained free; revolutionaries believed that individual freedom had to be sacrificed in favor of a collectivism that improved society. When Marxian revolutionaries argued through historical necessity that they would eventually triumph, and therefore invited people to help bring about their supposed inevitable changes more quickly, Frost turned the tables on them by noting that if the social changes they favored were indeed "inevitable," why hurry them along? It made more sense to postpone inevitable changes. Frost agreed with John Dryden's couplet about the best way to make changes in society:

> 'Twas not the hasty product of a day,
> But the well-ripened fruit of wise delay.
> (*Astraea Redux*, ll. 169–70)

Frost did not believe in preordained or inevitable changes, as ideological revolutionaries claimed. Social changes often involved reason and choice on the part of many individuals in determining the course of their personal lives, and also of history. Individual reason and free will remained constant elements to Frost, in determining the best relationship between man and his society. Frost rejected the metaphor of evolution, which assumed that social changes were determined without reference to man's reason and will, and that they were necessarily improvements.

Robert Frost never wrote a sustained discourse on politics, and he never constructed a systematic political philosophy. But he was unusually consistent in his statements about his political convictions, and from his many impromptu remarks over many years a set of basic political principles about man as a social animal is clearly discernible.

Frost was highly skeptical about politics in theory when the speculative thought was separated from practical affairs: "Politics is a joke because it is as speculative as philosophy. I lump them together, politics and philosophy, as things a young fellow might toy with in his salad days" (p. 70). His severe skepticism about doctrinaire rational ideologies of any kind made him dismiss them as inconsequential: "I'm against all the isms as being merely ideas in and out of favor. The latest ideologies are formidable equations that resolve themselves into nothing more startling than that nothing equals nothing" (p. 212). The delusive plausibilities of speculative theory had no place in Frost's own political philosophy. To Frost, as to Aristotle and Burke, politics was a branch of ethics, not of science; it was concerned with the good, not with the true. Therefore, a political philosophy had to be tested by its practical consequences to men in society. Speculative ideology which assumed it had the "truth" reversed this process by being indifferent to the practical consequences of its supposed truth to men in society. On this vital point, in July 1940, at Bread Loaf, Vermont, Frost put the question to me: "How else can anyone explain Stalin's willingness to 'liquidate' (dread word) millions of Russian farmers in order to establish their collective farms?" Frost's view of the relationship between politics in theory and in practice can perhaps be best understood in terms of the usual political terminology used to describe the spectrum of categorical positions: "radical," "liberal," "conservative," "revolutionary," "rebel," and "reformer."

Although Frost always refused to pin any of these labels on himself, and always objected when anyone attempted to label him, he had some significant things to say about all these political terms. In an interview he once said: "Two lines from one of my earlier verses sum up my whole viewpoint . . .

> I never dared be radical when young
> For fear it would make me conservative when old" (*Interviews*, p. 85).

This statement itself reveals Frost's characteristic political moderation between extremes, which enabled him to avoid disillusionments by avoiding illusions. His early political convictions remained with him throughout his life. His famous couplet from "Into My Own,"

> They would not find me changed from him they knew—
> Only more sure of all I thought was true (p. 5)

applies especially to his politics.

From very early in life Frost rejected any form of radical socialism. In July 1940 at Bread Loaf, he said to me: "In my boyhood I read the radical works of Edward Bellamy and Henry George, but I have never been a radical." He remarked that upon reading George's socialism he rejected it immediately, "because like all socialism it is bad arithmetic, in which two comes before one." Frost never believed that politics based upon compulsory social benevolence was superior to politics based upon freedom to pursue legitimate self-interest.

Another objection that Frost had to political radicalism was that it claimed to be original but was not: "More than once I should have lost my soul to radicalism if it had been the originality it was mistaken for by its young converts."[6] Frost had great reservations about the common variety of young radical, and he even wrote a satirical poem on this type of dogmatic ignorance or illusion of youth, called

"Young, Sure and Twenty." He wrote to Louis Untermeyer about this poem: "It was in mockery of conventional young radicals. I never stand young radicals till I see how long they are going to stay radicals. I hate to see people get over either their radicalism or their conservatism. You are still about as radical by the litmus test as you were that Sunday you met me at the Grand Central and took me down for my first and last visit with Floyd Dell and Max Eastman at the Masses office" (p. 366).

Frost contrasted "conservative" and "radical" as follows: "The most conservative thing in the world is that like produces like." . . . "The most radical thing is a certain dissatisfaction that that is so" (*Interviews*, p. 283). The aphorism captures perfectly the essence of the radical temperament.

As early as 1920, in a letter to Untermeyer, Frost inverted the conventional viewpoints of conservatives and radicals toward social change, in an effort to see if there was a meeting point between them. He raised the fascinating and original question: which social changes would conservatives favor, and which social changes would radicals be sorry to see occur? Frost's answer to this question, in which he imagined himself both a conservative and a radical, is extremely significant for an understanding of his politics: "In the general rush of change with almost everything going, I should think there would be danger that some things would be carried away that even the wildest revolutionary would be sorry to see carried away. Well then that's where I come in. Delegate me to hold on to those. 'Here hold these,' you could say. You would find me so serviceable that never again would you hurt my feelings by calling me a conservative. I should count my life not spent in vain if I were permitted to sit and hold in my lap just one thing that conservatives and radicals were alike agreed must be saved from being changed by mistake in the general change of other things. I am interested in what is to stay as it is; you are interested in what is not to stay as it is. We can't split on that difference. We operate in mutually exclusive spheres from which we can only bow across to each other in mutual appreciation. If I am a conservative it is the kind of conservative you want in your pay to take care of what you don't want to take with you. And just so if I am radical it is the kind you can have no kick against because

I let you take with you all you care to load up with. The fact is I am neither a conservative nor a radical and I refuse henceforth to be called either. I am a strainer. I keep back the tea leaves and let the tea flow through" (pp. 97–8). Some of the specific substantive things which both conservatives and radicals "would be sorry to see carried away" are to be found in Frost's poem, "The Black Cottage." But this passage reveals that Frost regarded what exists in society as the norm which contains the irreducible minimum of enduring necessary and desirable things, and that the burden of proof in making social changes rests more with the proposers than with the opposers of change.

Frost also distinguished sharply between a political radical and a rebel; he had considerable sympathy with rebels: "Being rebels doesn't mean being radical; it means being reckless like Eva Tanguay. It means busting something just when everybody begins to think it so sacred it's safe" (p. 32). To Frost, a radical was bound to an ideology and a doctrinaire political program, whereas a rebel was a free critical spirit, free to be critical of all ideologies and political programs, policies, propaganda and slogans. In this sense, Frost was himself a freewheeling rebel. His criticism of the established social order in his country was out of love of America; his quarrels were like lover's quarrels. But in another sense, that of rejecting social institutions as the necessary instrumentalities for men in society, his position as critic was not that of a rebel. Two lines from "Not Quite Social" summarize his position:

> The way of understanding is partly mirth.
> I would not be taken as ever having rebelled. (p. 306)

The freedom to rebel from ideology and strong governmental controls was the basis of Frost's rebellious individuality. His originality in politics was best expressed in his skepticism about all forms of social conformity and togetherness, whether radical, conservative, liberal or revolutionary. As a "rebel" he remained free to choose or reject whatever political "truths" he found in any of these general positions, but he remained uncommitted to any of them.

Although Frost refused to be categorized as either political radical or conservative, he clearly and explicitly rejected twentieth century "liberalism" as a political ideology. He was quoted by an interviewer: "He said his definition of a liberal was 'someone who is unhappy because he is not as unhappy as other people' " (*Interviews*, p. 170). The bland neutrality of the uncommitted academic liberal was well summarized by the speaker in Frost's Horatian poem, "The Lesson for Today," in distinguishing himself from his debating aristocratic opponent:

> I'm liberal. You, you aristocrat,
> Won't know exactly what I mean by that.
> I mean so altruistically moral
> I never take my own side in a quarrel. (p. 354)

To Frost, the modern political liberal was too often a sophisticated, sentimental, unprincipled humanitarian, with no definite or strong convictions about anything, who held to a position more by default than by depth of conviction.

In a letter to Untermeyer in 1950, Frost described how he responded to a group of academic pacifist liberals, who indulged themselves in the liberal cliché that no one ever wins a war: "The great thing is to win in war and peace. I have no patience with the casuistry that will persuade undergraduates that neither side wins a war—both sides lose it. Among a lot of liberal Northerners who were talking that way I once asked the only Southerner present who won the Civil War between the states. It was a cruel thing to do—crueler to the liberals than to the unreconstructed Southerner, though it hurt him, too. No sir, never from sophistication or anything try to make yourself think meanly of victory" (p. 363). Such decisive criticism did not endear Frost to political liberals. The poet was aware that he ruffled the feathers of many modern liberals, and noted that their defense against him, more often than not, was simply to dismiss him as of no political account: "Some liberals don't think I am anything to worry about. But you know how liberals are. You know how they were about the Russian Revolution and the German Revolution. You can pack the Supreme Court for all of them. Nothing is crucial" (p. 292).

Frost believed that one of the practical consequences of the indecisiveness of political liberalism was that it encouraged convinced revolutionaries of a totalitarian ideology that nations dominated by liberalism would not resist their aggressions. This had been a large factor in the success of Hitler, who had perceived that the liberal governments of France and Britain would not resist him. Frost noted that the same conviction existed among the leaders of the Soviet Union toward the United States. In September 1962, after Frost's interview with Premier Khrushchev, the poet reported: "Khrushchev said he feared for us modern liberals. . . . He said we were too liberal to fight. I suppose that he thought we'd stand there for the next hundred years saying, 'on the one hand—but on the other hand' " (*Interviews*, p. 291). Frost admired decisiveness and courage in politics and preferred a man take a wrong position than remain paralyzed in indecision. Adlai Stevenson was to Frost too indecisive to be a strong leader. Frost once said that, between them, Stevenson and his wife together would make a good president. Such liberalism was helpless to resist the revolutionary ideologies of the twentieth century, Frost believed, and the decline of the Liberal Party in Britain was in part the result of the public's recognition of this fact. On a trip to England in May 1957, Frost looked up his old friend Lord Beveridge, who had once been a radical and had fathered the welfare state in Britain, and the poet asked Beveridge where the Liberals had all gone to: "When I was here last they were a big party. Now they're just a handful" (*Interviews*, p. 170). Such was the fate of those who equivocated in politics during an age of revolutions.

Frost's political philosophy can be understood in part through his comments on democracy as a form of government. In general, he held it to be superior to other forms of government. In 1960 Frost had occasion to compare the Soviet Russian type of so-called "democracy" with American "democracy," and in making his comparison the poet traced out his understanding of the historical origins of American democracy: "The world . . . is being offered a choice between two kinds of democracy. Ours is a very ancient political growth, beginning at one end of the Mediterranean Sea and coming westward—tried in Athens, tried in Italy, tried in England, tried in

France, coming westward all the way to us. A very long growth, a growth through trial and error, but always with the idea that there is some sort of wisdom in the mob.

"Put a marker where the growth begins, at the eastern end of the Mediterranean, and there's never been a glimmer of democracy south of there. Over east, in Asia, there have been interesting ideas, but none bothered by the wisdom of the mob" (*Interviews*, pp. 240–41). In extending his comparison between the Soviet Russian type of "democracy" and American "democracy," Frost put the differences between them in an analogy centered in food and medicine: "Our democracy is like our bill of fare. That came westward, too, with wheat and so on, adding foods by trial and error and luck. I think, when corn comes in good and fresh, what would I have done if Columbus hadn't discovered America? . . .

"What is this Russian democracy? . . . Ours, I say, is like our bill of fare—kills a few people every year probably, but most of us live with it. The Russian democracy is like a doctor's prescription or a food fad. That's all there is to that. That finished them off. . . .

"I have pretty strong confidence that our kind of democracy is better than a trumped-up kind. . . . I'm pretty sure we're going to win. I'm on our side, anyway" (*Interviews*, p. 241).[7] In comparing the Russian Soviet system and the American, Frost noted wryly that "By courtesy, we call them both democracies" (*Interviews*, p. 289). Both the Russian totalitarian form of government and the American parliamentary form, as "democracies," meant "a more earnest desire than the world has ever had to take care of everybody. To bestow . . . bread and butter, yes; but that's not the top thing. The top thing to bestow is character" (*Interviews*, p. 289). As a form of government that went beyond a concern for distributive justice, and also bestowed character, and thus justified faith in the political wisdom of ordinary people, Frost favored the extension of democracy through the world: "I am out to see a world full of small-fry democracies even if we have to fill them two deep or even three deep in some places" (p. 77).

One of the most significant of Frost's statements about political democracy was made in August 1917, concerning the newly established Kerensky government in Russia. Just two months before the

Bolshevik revolution of October 1917, Frost engaged in some speculation and guesses about the Kerensky government. He noted that it spoke for the Russian middle class as distinct from both the old Russian aristocracy and the new proletariat, and he expressed the hope that free and constitutional parliamentary government had at long last been established in Russia: "Middle class government, which is to say liberal democratic government, has won a seat in Russia and it is going to keep its seat for the duration of the war and share with us in the end in a solid out-and-out middle class triumph such as the Germans enjoyed when they marched into Paris. The lower class seeing nothing in all this for itself may do its worst to create divisions, but it will fail. This may be the last war between bounded nations in the old fashioned patriotism. The next war may be between class and class. But this one will be to the end what it was in the beginning, a struggle for commercial supremacy between nations. I will not guess further ahead than that. The lower class will kick a little on street corners and where it can find a chance in journalistic corners. But it will be suppressed—more and more brutally suppressed as the middle class gains in confidence and sees its title clearer. We are still surer of nationality than we are of anything else in the world—ninety nine millions of us are in this country. I don't say this to discourage you—merely to define my position to myself. Live in hope or fear of your revolution. You will see no revolution this time even in Germany until Germany goes down with a perceptible crash, and I'm not so sure you'll see one there even then. Everybody is entitled to three guesses, and this is one of mine" (pp. 57–8). Like many other men, Frost overestimated the courage, foresight and will to power of the Kerensky government and greatly underestimated these traits in Lenin and the Bolsheviks, whom he disliked for their appeal to mob rule based upon class. Frost erred in his guess about which party would triumph in Russia, because he hoped for the triumph of democracy, which was to him essentially a middle class parliamentary government—not a proletarian-based dictatorship masquerading as a democracy. But his prophecy that the First World War was the last war to be based on "old fashioned patriotism," and that future wars may be "between class and class," was a remarkable insight to make in 1917.

To Frost the essence of American parliamentary democracy was the many constitutional provisions which gave freedom to the individual, against the political and legal power of the state, and not an egalitarianism that leveled out all individual and class differences. Frost rejected the egalitarian theory of popular sovereignty, with its modern slogan of "one man, one vote." When Carl Sandburg published what Frost called his "New Deal-Fair Deal" propaganda poem, "The People, Yes," Frost responded (to me in August 1941) by saying that his view of American Democracy was, "The people, yes; and the people, no." Frost's faith in the people under democratic government included an awareness of their weaknesses as well as their strengths and virtues. In an interview he said: "Someone once asked me if I was for democracy or against it, and I could only say that I am so much of it that I didn't know. I have a touchiness about the subject of democracy, of America. It amounts to a touchiness. I know how much difficulty there is about democracy, and how much fun it is too" (*Interviews*, p. 124). Frost rejected popular sovereignty as the sole basis of American democracy in favor of three other principles: (1) a concept of territorial democracy; (2) the federal-states constitutional system; and (3) a concept of representative republican government based upon both territory and population.

In commenting on his poem, "The Gift Outright," Frost said: "What gives us our freedom is having a territorial basis, belonging to the land" (*Interviews*, p. 158). Frost's belief in territorial democracy included a strong emphasis upon the autonomy of state and local governments, but it was also the result of the poet's strong historical sense concerning the founding of America. Frost believed that the settling of America was a unique experience for Western man and that the character of the American people was in part created by their eventual awareness of how they belonged to the land, and not just how the land belonged to them. Politically, this sense of belonging to the land was most intense on the regional, state, or local level, prior to manifesting itself on the national level. The poet undoubtedly derived this vital element in his view of American democracy from his father, William Prescott Frost, Jr., who was convinced that the geographical extent of the United States was too vast for it to be one nation. He thought that it would split up into six or seven regional independent nations. Frost recalled that when he was a boy his father once spread out a map of North America and drew out the approximate boundaries of his hypothetical future nations. Although Frost's father's vision of the future never materialized, his regional concept of sovereignty manifested itself in the poet's adherence to a belief in states' sovereignty. Frost always believed that for democracy to be effective the political unit of society and the state should not be too large. His view on this vital aspect of democracy and sovereignty was not unlike that of Jean-Jacques Rousseau in *The Social Contract*. As a states' rights, free-trade Democrat, Frost called himself a "sep-a-ra-tist." The poet accepted fully the federalism of the United States, but he interpreted federalism to include a strong emphasis upon territorial democracy, retained on the state and local levels.

Frost's belief in the federal constitutional system was voiced in response to a question put to him on why he believed in American democracy: "Somebody once asked me why I believed in this wasteful democratic system of government we call a republic. I told 'em it was because it was full of checks and balances. Maybe we've got too many checks in it sometimes—we can't have too many balances. Its a system of power divided against itself, so that nobody can get more than is good of power—I mean more than's good for the rest of us" (Mertins, p. 310). The federal constitution provided form and legal structure in American society on a national scale and prevented the anarchy of "unchartered freedom" on anything but an individual or small group level. Frost had great confidence in the enduring power of the American constitution: "the Constitution," he said, "will keep America American after other countries have all broken down and run together from mutual imitation" (Mertins, p. 207).

To Frost one of the most important parts of the Constitutional form of the American republic was the electoral system used in putting men in public office; therefore, he resisted any attempt to change it: "The electoral system we have worked under politically for so long's got to be preserved, basically unchanged, only modified somewhat" (Mertins, p. 402). Since the electoral system included representation on the state level, by units of electoral votes for the presidency, by population districts for the representatives, and by equal representation of each state in the Senate, Frost's endorsement of the established electoral system was another indication that he rejected popular sovereignty as the basis of American democracy. To Frost, the United States was a representative democratic republic, and not a pure democracy based on direct popular will through numbers. In holding fast to the electoral system, Frost was consistent with his conviction that the protection of individual and minority rights, and not the triumph of simple majority will, or unchecked popular power, was at the core of the American system of government. To Frost the great objective of the American republic was to maintain individual freedom, and not to establish equality of economic or social condition.

Throughout his long life Frost frequently stated that he was born a Democrat, that he always remained a Democrat, and that he would probably die a Democrat. What kind of a Democrat was Robert Frost? In "Build Soil—A Political Pastoral," the chief character in the poem says:

> I was brought up
> A state-rights free-trade Democrat. What's that?
> An inconsistency. (p. 324)

When Frost himself was accused of being politically inconsistent, or "mixed-up," he replied: "No, I'm not mixed up, I'm well mixed." As the poet himself has noted, the political mixture of his partisan politics began at birth: "You know, I inherited my status as a States'-rights Democrat from my father—maybe my grandfather. I've never outgrown it" (Mertins, p. 402).

Whether mixed-up or well-mixed, Frost was certainly one of the most original and unstereotyped Democrats that the Democratic Party ever had. The wideranging class and nationality groups which comprised the Democratic Party certainly suited his individualism. As a party man, Frost was very much like Will Rogers, another famous nonpolitical Democrat, who once quipped: "I'm a Democrat. I don't belong to any organized party." Similarly, Frost once said: "Being a Democrat is like being a woman; you can always change your mind." And then added: "There are more different ways of being a Democrat than of being a Republican." Frost made this remark in Cambridge, Massachusetts, to a middle-aged couple, conservative, Republican, Harvard friends of his, and the wife listened intently to the poet's statement and then responded vehemently: "You're right, Mr. Frost, there's only one kind of Republican," pointing to her husband, "and there he sits!" Frost told this story to a group of the faculty at the Bread Loaf School, during the summer of 1961, in the presence of Donald Davidson, a southern Jeffersonian Democrat. Davidson then asked Frost: "What kind of Democrat are you? Democrat with a capital 'D,' or with a lower case 'd'?" Frost answered: "I'm a G-D Democrat." The "G-D," Frost went on to say, stood for "Godawful Disgruntled," and that he had been a "G-D" Democrat since 1896, when Grover Cleveland's second term of office ended.

Frost identified his party politics by calling himself, at various times, "a Madisonian-Washingtonian-Jeffersonian Democrat," or a "Grover Cleveland Democrat," or a states' rights Democrat. Certainly he took his party stand in the light of the public philosophy of the Founding Fathers of the American republic, whom he greatly admired. His party politics also functioned within the agrarian virtues that stressed individual freedom on the state level and self-reliance on the individual level. In a conversation with President Eisenhower, Frost is recorded to have said: "I was talking with Eisenhower in the White House awhile ago. He got confidential—no secret, I take it—and told me he supposed he was a Jeffersonian Democrat—not a Jacksonian. I told him I was a Democrat (upper case) by training, a democrat (lower case) by birth" (Mertins, p. 377).

Robert Frost's first political experience was as a boy of ten, in San Francisco, where his father was a Democratic precinct worker and campaign manager, and later a candidate for city office. To Untermeyer the poet wrote in July 1918: "I mewed my infancy among political bosses and in party bigotry"(p. 73). Later, Frost told an interviewer: "My first experience was working with my father for the election of Grover Cleveland. The Mugwumps made the difference. Now we call them independent voters" (*Interviews*, p. 118). And again: "As a child I did what I could by marching and shouting and burning oil to throw the country to Grover Cleveland in '84. And I lived to vote for Debs!" (p. 45). Looking back over six decades, Frost noted his reasons for admiring Cleveland, and it is worth noting that personal character rather than partisan loyalty took prior claim: "I keep reading about old Grover, and after sixty years I have to admit there were one or two things that could be said against him; but I concede it reluctantly. As Mencken said, Cleveland got on in politics, not by knuckling to politicians but scorning and defying them. He didn't go around spouting McGuffy Reader slogans or wanting to be liked" (*Interviews*, p. 178). Although Frost's loyalty was with the Democratic Party, he was a bit diffident about party politics when it clashed with his scale of higher values, such as human character. He put his diffidence as follows: "I can stand a great deal of change in politics. But what I care about isn't settled by elections. I was brought up a Cleveland Democrat and in an off-hand playful way I've remained that" (*Interviews*, p. [94]). But since "Yankees are what they always were," he thought of himself as a "politician at odd seasons" (*Interviews*, p. 87). But as an American he valued what he believed was best for his country far above party politics and was often highly critical of the leaders and program of his own party.

As a loyal Democrat, Frost wrote to Untermeyer on November 14, 1916, immediately after the presidential election: "Surely you won't mind my taking a little common ordinary satisfaction in the election of Wilson" (p. 45). But it was not very long after Wilson's re-election that Frost began to have second thoughts about the Democratic president. The poet had no respect for Colonel House, Wilson's chief advisor and friend, and he even wrote a parody of House's work, "Philip Dru, Administrator: A Story of Tomorrow." Some of Frost's contempt for House spilled over to Wilson.[8] The president's main political interest, his international pacifism and proposal for a League of Nations, called forth Frost's harshest criticism. In a letter to his Amherst College friend George Whicher, in 1919, Frost commented savagely on Wilson's message to Congress regarding the League of Nations: "Does Wilson at last stand revealed to you in his last message to Congress? . . . It seems he came not to bring peace but a League of Nations. Anyone who could use the word afraid as he does there! He is afraid we won't have to be afraid of European nations for some time yet. Does he mean he's afraid we can't look for them to give us a fight worthy of our steel industry or rather chemical industry? Is it like Richard the Lion-Hearted he talks. No, I'm afraid he talks like a fraud. Afraid am I?"[9] Frost came to have more and more reservations about Woodrow Wilson, both as a Democrat and as a man. Many years later, when the poet was interviewed in the Woodrow Wilson Room of the Library of Congress, surrounded by Wilson's personal library, Frost noted that the library had no works of imaginative literature, that it consisted mainly of legal and political works: "Look around at the books, and you'll see the limitations. Someone said he was so busy he had no time for frills—that's one way of looking at poetry. A noble, conscientious man, but he strained himself. We need somebody who is unstrained, who has time to read poetry and wear flowers" (*Interviews*, p. 282).

From the time of Woodrow Wilson on through the rest of the twentieth century, Frost continued to despair for the Democratic Party, much as a father might despair about a wayward child. On July 23, 1920, right after James Cox was nominated by the Democrats for the fall election, Frost wrote to his friend Untermeyer: "Catch on to the New Radicalism and vote for Harding" (p. 116). Two months later in another letter Frost clearly stated his opposition to Cox, for following Wilson's international politics, yet he was not quite sure about Harding: "I should like to see [Harding] elected if only I was surer he was anti-international" (p. 117).

Soon after the election of Franklin D. Roosevelt in 1932, like many other "old-line" Democrats such as Alfred E. Smith, Frost realized that the "States' Rights" Democratic Party he had lived with had been captured by the Democratic socialists, whose doctrine of political sovereignty, and whole political philosophy, was directly contrary to his own. As the poet's friend Louis Mertins has observed: "As a States' Right Democrat, his soul was burdened by the centralization of power in Washington and all the alphabetical agencies which sprang up almost overnight" (Mertins, p. 208). Frost perceived the terrible irony of history, that during the great Depression the defeated Republican Party in reacting against the absolute control of Congress and the presidency by the Democratic Party— on partisan grounds was forced to assume a policy that reversed its political origins and historical position on federal sovereignty: "Funny thing, isn't it, the Republicans getting into a lather over states' rights—the thing they fought the Civil War over. Now they're on the other side" (Mertins, p. 333).

Since the political parties had apparently reversed their positions on centralized authority and other important matters after 1932, why didn't Frost become a Republican? In part, because he simply refused to be driven out of the Democratic Party by its socialist wing, just because they were then in command. In an interview in February 1936, Frost said: "I'm going to stay a Democrat if I have to push everyone else out of the party but Carter Glass." He then added, significantly: "I'm a pursuitist, not an escapist. And I'd rather cast an idea by implication than cast a ballot" (*Interviews*, p. 83). Frost was probably convinced that he could be more effective as a critic of the socialist heresy within the Democratic Party than he could be if he were driven out of the party and himself declared politically unorthodox by the New Deal Democrats. After all, had he not always believed there were more different ways of being a Democrat than of being a Republican?

Frost considered the concentration of executive and legislative power, and Roosevelt's desire to centralize all authority (through packing the Supreme Court), as aberrations from the true principles of the old Democratic Party. The poet's position was one which even a good New Deal Democrat like James Farley finally came to adopt. For Frost the New Deal was much too big a step in the direction of the twentieth century ideological totalitarianism. The emasculation of American parliamentary government in favor of government by executive decree could not be justified in Frost's mind by an appeal to solving the problems of the great Depression and of distributive justice. But the American republic survived the great Depression, the New Deal, and the Nazi and Japanese challenge, with its parliamentary form of government intact. Shortly after Roosevelt's death, when someone suggested to Frost that the twentieth century needed a political Messiah to solve its economic and social problems, the poet wrote: "How can any one fail to see we have one and of the Messianic race, namely Karl Marx. And I'm not joking. F. D. R. came as near being one as I suspect a Democracy can feel the illusion of. Thrice mayor of London Town. No four times" (p. 345). Frost believed that the greatest danger to the United States during the 1930s was not its failure to solve the problems of the Depression, nor even the Nazi threat from abroad, but rather F. D. R.'s New Deal program, in its movement towards left wing collectivism.

Frost's satirical poem on Franklin D. Roosevelt, "To a Thinker," begins:

> The last step taken found you heft
> Decidedly upon the left.

A few lines later, after describing the unstable movements of the early New Deal, Frost wrote:

> Just now you're off democracy
> (With a polite regret to be)
> And leaning on dictatorship;
> But if you will accept the tip
> In less than no time, tongue and pen,
> You'll be a democrat again. (pp. 325–26)

Frost claimed that his satire was not really aimed at Roosevelt personally, but only as the recognized leader of those "easy despairers of the republic." The poem had first been printed in *The Saturday Review of Literature* on January 11, 1936, under the title, "To a Thinker in Office." In a letter to Henry Leach, editor of *The Forum*, Frost wrote an explanation of "To a Thinker": "You will see that it was only by restriction of meaning that it was narrowed down to fit the President. Changing the title from 'To a Thinker' to 'To a Thinker in Office' helped do the business. As a matter of fact it was written three years ago and was aimed at the heads of our easy despairers of the republic and of parliamentary forms of government. I encounter too many such and my indignation mounts till it overflows in rhyme. I doubt if my native delicacy would have permitted me to use the figure of walking and rocking in connection with a person of the President's personal infirmities. But I am willing to let it go as aimed at him. He must deserve it or people wouldn't be so quick to see him in it" (*Interviews*, pp. 87–8). The political satire in this poem is actually playful and light, not savagely indignant.

There were several other important points of criticism that Frost levelled against the Roosevelt New Deal administration. The immediate occasion for his writing "To a Thinker," according to an interview in the *Baltimore Sun* (February 26, 1936), was his intense anger against the New Deal farm policy, which he believed was posited upon a view of American farmers as possessors of what he labeled "submarginal minds." This was the result of the supposed intellectually "holier-than-thou" assumptions of Roosevelt's so-called "Brain Trust." Frost always distrusted any separation of the intellectual virtues from the moral virtues, and he believed the academicians in Roosevelt's "Brain Trust" stressed intellect above ethics to a stupid degree. In place of traditional ethics they had a social consciousness and sentiment. To Frost the New Deal brain trust advisors of Roosevelt were like clever, corrupted shyster lawyers, morally decadent, sententious, self-pitying, like such sentimental English poets of the 1890s as Ernest Dowson. In a letter to Untermeyer (July 6, 1936), Frost wrote: "Dowson is often in my mind these days of Tugwell and the New Deil (I told you Tugwell reads him to Mrs. Roosevelt . . .)" (p. 280). In this criticism of the New Deal Frost was attacking the whole philosophical and moral basis of the Roosevelt administration, as manifested in his anger over its farm policy.

One of Frost's major criticisms of the New Deal was based upon his case for personal freedom in the economic sector against a planned economy. During January 1935 while Frost was living in Key West, Florida, he wrote an account to Untermeyer of how debilitating the New Deal public works economic program was on the people and leaders of Key West: "The only thing at all socially disturbing is the presence in force of Franklin D. Roosevelt F E R A (Federal Emergency Relief Administration). This has been one of the administration's pet rehabilitation projects. No taxes had been paid on anything. Everybody was riding round in cars without silencers and without licenses. There was talk of transporting seventy five percent of the crowd. But Nobody could think of anybody who would want them. So the author of a book called *Compulsory Spending* is here with a staff to put everybody at work on public improvements, some building, some tearing down, and some general cleaning up of filthy vacant lots. We had to get our rent thru them. They are mildly and beneficently dictatorial. Both the Mayor of the town and the Governor of the state have abdicated in their favor. Their great object they say is to restore the people to their civic virtue. When in history has any power ever achieved that?" (p. 251). About a month later Frost again commented upon his view of Key West: "If I seem irritable it is probably due to the horribleness of having to look on at the redemption of a city that has lost its self respect to the New Deil" (p. 258). Most of the economic pump-priming attempts of the New Deal met with Frost's caustic criticism.[10]

Another major criticism that Frost had against the New Deal was its use of economic appeals in elections, its setting the poor against the rich, and its exploitation of envy and discontent for political purposes. This type of neoMarxism called forth Frost's sharpest attacks. The very idea of judging a person by his economic condition or status was repellent to Frost. In July 1939, during a reading of his poems to an audience at Bread Loaf, he asked: "Don't you think that the poor are disgusting, and the rich are disgusting—as such?" He then asked, if men are to judge people by their class, why concede anything to the Marxists by using "class" only in its economic sense? Why not judge people by their psychological class? "To which class do you belong," the poet asked, "the neurotic class?"

Frost never wrote poetry for "the welfare minded," although some New Deal political friends approached him hoping that he would. As Frost noted, their hope was based upon a misunderstanding of what he had written early in his life: "I don't consider myself to blame for their mistake. Ferner Huhn (Henry Wallace's ghost writer) is still at me for having led him on with *North of Boston* to expect better of me than *A Further Range*. Its his damned party politics. I tried to tell him and his like in 'The Need of Being Versed in Country Things' that my subject was not the sadness of the poor. He puts his finger on 'The Lockless Door' with uncanny shrewdness, but not enough to quite bring him through. He says the rich in their top hats knocked at my cottage door and through having provided no way to keep them out I retired through a back window and left the place to them, it was only to join them mischievously by circling round behind and taking their view of the house I had built. Funny but except for one person . . . all the rich who ever came to my door were the condescending welfare minded and they came under the mistaken impression that what I had built was a house of the poor. I was flattered by their attention and I decided to let them have the house any way they would. I wanted to be honest with them in all gentleness: and I satisfied my conscience with hints at the truth, as in the last part of the poem 'New Hampshire' and in 'The Need of Being Versed in Country Things.' But lately I have been getting cross with their fatuosity. My house may be only a one-room shack but it is not the Poor House: it is the Palace of Art. *North of Boston* is merely a book of people, not of poor people. They happen to be people of simplicity or simple truth miscalled simplicity. Before I get through I'm going to drive these social servitors back to the social settlements or to concentration camps where I can starve their sympathies to death. For myself I never sought anyone I wasn't thrown with and I never thought of anyone I was with as a possible subject for literature or charity or the literature of charity" (pp. 304–05). This vital letter reveals not only how true to his self-reliant politics Frost was, but also how true he was to his own integrity in his poetry, in refusing to make it the vehicle for social or economic propaganda. Poetry was for truth about human nature, not a propaganda vehicle for political solutions of social problems such as poverty. As Frost noted on another occasion: "It's neither the rich nor the poor that I was writing about. Just about people like us" (*Interviews*, p. 108). Clearly, Frost was consciously and strongly opposed to economic class consciousness as a legitimate basis for judging his art, or for judging people through politics.

Frost perceived both advantages and disadvantages in being rich and being poor. In listing seven disadvantages that Franklin D. Roosevelt had to overcome, in order to rise to the presidency, Frost included Roosevelt's wealth. He then pictured Roosevelt at the pinnacle of his career, beyond wealth, beyond even his presidency, engaged in world politics toward the end of World War Two: "then he sits on top of the world along with Stalin and Churchill! That row is forever in my mind" (*Interviews*, p. 157). Frost admitted that "sometimes wealth has its bad things and poverty has its bad things and limits to our freedom," yet, contrary to Mrs. Roosevelt's expressed desire to get rid of poverty, Frost noted something to be said for poverty in terms of men's achievements: "Poverty has done so much good in this way in the world that I should hesitate to abolish it" (*Interviews*, p. 156). Besides being a spur to ambition, Frost observed, poverty made people realistic about life: "Things belong to the poor by their having to come to grips with things daily. And that's a good one on the poor. They are the only realists" (p. 80). But Frost was also aware that the poor, in wishing to raise themselves above their poverty, were as vulnerable to the delusions of ideology as anyone else: "If the poor promised themselves no more than vengeance in the oncoming revolution I'd be with them. It's all their nonsense about making a better or even a different world that I can't stand" (p. 80).

But the middle classes always remained for Frost the backbone of a free and democratic nation. He feared for the world if the middle ranks of people should ever be destroyed through a Marxist or other kind of ideological revolution. He doubted that such a revolution could succeed: "Sometime the world will try cutting the middle class out of our middle. But my mind misgives me that the experiment will fail just as the eighteenth century experiment of getting rid of the lowest class by cutting it out and dumping it on distant islands failed. You know how the lowest class renewed itself from somewhere as fast as it was cut out" (p. 58). On attempts to raise people economically through political power, Frost agreed with Balfour that the result would be a levelling downward, that no government can "make people equally rich; you can only make them equally poor" (p. 347).

Frost was acutely aware that the very political virtue he esteemed most—individual freedom—could be indicted as perhaps one of the causes of the most acute problem of distributive justice, the extremes of wealth and poverty. Under the open conditions of a free society, competent, ambitious and energetic people could take full advantage of their freedom to amass great personal wealth and power. In contrast, as a nation's population increased, large masses of people who lacked the traits of character that would enable them to compete successfully in a free society remained very poor. Freedom meant little to the masses, as compared to economic security. This problem of inequitable distribution of the productivity of society was especially acute during the great Depression. In light of this conviction Frost moderated his criticism of the efforts of the New Deal to secure greater equity between rich and poor. An extended passage in Frost's *A Masque of Mercy* (1947) contains the essential position the poet held about egalitarian distributive justice accomplished by political means. The character Paul notes that in a free society success, "by its own logic" comes to concentrate "all wealth and power in too few hands," and then he says:

> The rich in seeing nothing but injustice
> In their impoverishment by revolution
> Are right. But 'twas intentional injustice.
> It was their justice being mercy-crossed.
> The revolution Keeper's bringing on
> Is nothing but an outbreak of mass mercy,
> Too long pent up in rigorous convention—
> A holy impulse towards redistribution.
> To set out to homogenize mankind
> So that the cream could never rise again
> Required someone who laughingly could play
> With the idea of justice in the courts,
> Could mock at riches in the right it claims
> To count on justice to be merely just.
>
> . . . .
>
> The thing that really counts, though, is the form
> Of outrage—violence—that breaks across it . . .
>
> . . . .
>
> And if you've got to see your justice crossed
> (And you've got to) which will you prefer
> To see it, evil-crossed or mercy-crossed? (pp. 509–10)

Frost has left no doubt that the character "Keeper" (short for "My Brother's Keeper") was epitomized by Franklin D. Roosevelt, whose New Deal administration sought to "homogenize mankind." In a comment on egalitarianism in education, Frost remarked: "The matter of giving a pupil an A or a B whether he deserves it—has earned it—or not, made me say awhile ago to some of my New Deal friends that they are trying to homogenize things so that the cream will never rise to the top again" (Mertins, p. 369). Justice for the rich had to be qualified by mercy for the poor, and in certain of its social legislation the New Deal achieved this goal, and thus prevented a complete "evil-crossed" or violent revolution.

Frost believed that the duty of all good government was to foster the general welfare in a great many ways that the private interests of citizens could not. As Frost noted in a passage in "Build Soil," this meant that in the public sector of society "socialism" was a part of every government:

> Is socialism needed, do you think?
>
> We have it now. For socialism is
> An element in any government.
> There's no such thing as socialism pure—
> Except as an abstraction of the mind.
> There's only democratic socialism,
> Monarchic socialism, oligarchic—
> The last being what they seem to have in Russia.
> You often get it most in monarchy,
> Least in democracy. In practice, pure,
> I don't know what it would be. No one knows. (p. 318)

The conflict between Frost and the New Deal was over the extent to which the government's socialistic welfare programs intruded into the private sector of American life and violated the individual's freedom of action. But just as there was "no such thing as socialism pure," there was also no such thing as pure laissez-faire individualism in society. Frost's conception of human nature in society was corporate; man is by his nature a political and social animal. Therefore, Frost rejected both the anarchy of pure laissez-faire and the tyranny of pure socialism. Frost's comment on the criticism of the New Deal by "a hard-boiled inhumanitarian" Republican named Nock indicates that pure laissez-faire was not his alternative to excessive socialism: "What did he think? That the Republican party would repudiate in its toryism everything from old-age pensions and unemployment insurance to rural free delivery, free public schools and the graduated income tax! Nock is a wonderful idealist of the old school. No least taint of socialism and paternalism for him.

Absolutely all enterprise private" (p. 282). Obviously, Frost was not nearly as severe in his well-considered criticism of Roosevelt and the New Deal as were some of its other detractors, such as Henry Mencken.[11]

Partly as a Democrat, and partly on the basis of close friendships among New Deal leaders, and partly out of his conception of man and society, Frost's criticism of the New Deal became more qualified than severe. In 1944 an interviewer recorded Frost's view of the last years of the New Deal: "Despite the present Administration's attempts to do everything for the individual, Frost still supports portions of it, because of a personal friendship with many of the leaders, including Vice-President Wallace.

"Maintaining that the present Administration is more interested in promoting the arts than any previous one has been, the poet declared that most of the programs have been successful. He believes that most of these state-sponsored programs are mere dilettantism and do not tend to produce great artists" (*Interviews*, p. 112). When Wallace broke with the Democratic Party and became leader of the "progressive" socialists, their friendship ended. In a letter to Untermeyer (August 9, 1947), Frost referred to "my former friend Henry Wallace."

It would be inaccurate to conclude that Frost began as a severe critic of the New Deal and gradually mellowed into greater tolerance toward it. He was always acutely sensitive to the suffering of the poor and shared the general compassion of the American people toward the victims of the great Depression. On November 25, 1936, Frost commented to Untermeyer on the recent reelection of Roosevelt: "I don't mean it is humanity not to feel the suffering of others. The last election would confute me if I did. I judged that half the people that voted for his Rosiness were glad to be on the receiving end of his benevolence and half were those overglad to be on the giving end. The national mood is humanitarian. Nobly so—I wouldn't take it away from them" (pp. 284–85). Clearly, Frost's criticism of the New Deal transcended his and the government's common humanitarian sympathies for the poor, and their desire to solve the complex problems of the great Depression.

Frost's lifelong faith in the parliamentary system of the American republic, as the whole basis of individual freedom in a society under law, made him reject the New Deal's radical modifications of that system in favor of greater socialism. He believed that every loss in personal freedom was a loss in individual self-sufficiency and a corresponding gain for collectivist paternalism and totalitarian government. A free society, making maximum use of individual initiative and motivation, was a far more economically productive society than a controlled or slave society. The problem in America was not inadequate productivity but the inequitable distribution of its overabundance. In any conflict between the constitutional freedom of the individual and the unconstitutional uses of power by the state, Frost was invariably on the side of individual freedom. Also, Frost clearly distrusted political ideology as a speculative science aimed at establishing theoretical perfection in society, because he regarded politics as a part of practical reason, as the art of the possible. Therefore, he doubted that men's greatest social problems—distributive justice versus freedom and order, and poverty, crime, war and ignorance, ever have final or absolute solutions. At best, through government and other institutions, men applied palliatives and secured partial and temporary solutions to these constant problems. Frost rejected historical determinism, because he believed that conscious and deliberate human decisions, and not a supposed law of historical necessity, determined the course of human events. His conception of freedom and individualism was not nihilistic or anarchical; he opposed "unchartered freedom," but his defense of the private person in a society under constitutional law was probably his most essential political principle. Throughout his long life he remained true to his own vision of the ideals of democratic government, as contained in the American republic, and in both theory and practice he held fast to a politics that provided the maximum of personal liberty against all the claims of the modern totalitarian state. For the ultimate basis of Frost's view of man as a political animal was that, consistent with the need of maintaining order and justice in civil society, each man should be as true to himself as possible, a free and self-reliant individual within his society.

Notes to *Robert Frost: Politics in Theory and Practice* by PETER J. STANLIS

1. *The Letters of Robert Frost to Louis Untermeyer*, ed. Louis Untermeyer (New York: Holt, Rinehart and Winston, 1963), p. 346 (hereafter in text with page numbers only).

2. There was a Gothic strain in Frost's tragic sense of life that made his laughter sardonic. He adds, "No man can tell you the sound or the way of my laughter. I have neighed at night in the woods behind the house like vampires. But there are no vampires, there are no ghouls, there are no demons, there is nothing but me."

3. Louis Mertins, *Robert Frost: Life and Talks-Walking* (Norman: University of Oklahoma Press, 1965), p. 62 (hereafter in text as Mertins).

4. *Interviews with Robert Frost*, ed. Edward Connery Lathem (New York: Holt, Rinehart and Winston, 1966), p. 128 (hereafter in text as *Interviews*).

5. See "The Planners" in *Steeple Bush*.

6. "The Figure a Poem Makes," in *Selected Prose of Robert Frost*, ed. Hyde Cox and Edward Connery Lathem (New York: Holt, Rinehart and Winston, 1949), p. 20.

7. Both in his explanation of the historical origins of American democracy out of ancient Greece and in his firm faith that it is a superior form of government and will prevail against its competitors, Frost again reveals some important points in common with Orestes Brownson's *The American Republic*.

8. See *Untermeyer*, pp. 67–9, for Frost's lampoon and burlesque of House's political romance and his dig at Wilson.

9. Frost to George Whicher, May 23, 1919, Amherst College Library.

10. See, for example, Frost's comments about a scheme proposed by Edward Bruce, a New Deal official, to encourage poets through granting them pensions rather than by putting them on relief (*Untermeyer*, p. 258).

11. See *Interviews*, p. 84. Frost summarized his objections to the New Deal in a pithy phrase: "I can't stand coercion."

RELIGION

Studying the poetry rather than the man, for the most part, Laurence Perrine discusses Frost's concept of immortality, actually a discussion of Frost's metaphysics. And the statement implying that Frost believed in reincarnation, which comes at the end of Professor Perrine's introduction, is explained and elaborated at the end of the essay—with a pleasant originality. The greater, remaining portion of the essay is so clear an exposition that summary would be travesty. While Professor Perrine, he says, prefers explication to more general interpretation, his explication is remarkably suggestive.

Like Thomas McClanahan, Professor Perrine is in effect dealing with the influence of William James on Frost, specifically in the suggestion of (conflicting) varieties of religious experience (in the same man). Professor McClanahan not only extends the study of the influence of William James on Frost but also specifically uses James to account for Frost's direct yet skeptical and pragmatic approach to metaphysical problems, especially of course concerning religion. While both Frost and James were probably very much aware of Emerson, neither was willing to accept Emerson's blithe pronouncements about the unity of the trinity of man, nature and deity. Some of Professor McClanahan's observations coincide with those of Marjorie Cook (in PLAY) and Joseph Kau.

Joseph Kau discusses what he calls the "incarnation" poems—from the early "Trial by Existence," which Frost retained in his collections, to "Kitty Hawk," in examining the ambiguous statements or statements of ambiguity from a man reflecting upon the question of faith in a concept his heritage categorizes as the deus absconditus—the hidden God. This is too the stuff of poetry. And so long as Frost is himself absconditus, the question continues to arise to what extent his poetry expressed his beliefs—even ambiguously, or in ambiguity.

A line from *A Masque of Reason,* which must come directly from William James's "Pragmatism and Religion," possibly offers another insight into Frost's approach, both poetic and personal. Job says, "God needs time just as much as you or I/To get things done" (p. 478). And whatever the influence of Emerson on either James or Frost, an Emerson who hated reformers could have appreciated the remark immediately following: "Reformers fail to see that.—"

J. T.

Robert Frost
and the Idea of Immortality

LAURENCE PERRINE

I n *A Masque of Reason* Job, pondering "the wisdom of having children" (p. 483) in a world where "there is still injustice" (p. 477), says to God:

> You could end this by simply coming out
> And saying plainly and unequivocally
> Whether there's any part of man immortal. (p. 483)

He does not receive an answer. That he does not points up the first important fact regarding Frost's beliefs concerning life after death. At its foundation Frost's position on this question is agnostic. Unlike such nineteenth-century predecessors as Browning ("But God has a few of us whom he whispers in the ear;/The rest may reason and welcome; 'tis we musicians know") and Tennyson ("Peace, let it be! for I loved him, and love him forever; the dead are not dead but alive"), Frost was willing and able to rest in a state of uncertainty about the matter. He accepted the inability of man to answer the ultimate questions. "We dance around in a ring and suppose,/But the Secret sits in the middle and knows" (p. 362) he wrote in a couplet-poem. Man's strength and courage, indeed, are tested by his ability to rest in doubt about what happens to him beyond death: "There may be little or much beyond the grave,/But the strong are saying nothing until they see" (p. 300).

I do not, however, wish to force a nonexistent consistency on Frost's thinking. As every student of his poetry knows, Frost's ideas on religious matters are often contradictory. He did not write out of or into any fixed system of belief. He characteristically reached differing answers to the questions he persistently put to the universe. His poems are explorations of truth, conceivable ways of looking at things, not assertions of unquestioning dogma. They express temporary insights, "momentary stays against confusion," not rigidly fixed intellectual positions.

Frost knew how deeply embedded in the human psyche is the hope of future existence for one's friends or for oneself, and he expresses this knowledge in a late untitled quatrain:

> We vainly wrestle with the blind belief
> That aught we cherish
> Can ever quite pass out of utter grief
> And wholly perish. (p. 469)

Though belief that our friends cannot wholly perish is a "blind" one, we unsuccessfully try to give it up, even when cessation of existence might be a respite for the cherished one—a passing out of "utter grief." Frost himself could not consistently wrestle down that "blind belief." In "A Soldier," occasioned by the death in battle of his most cherished friend, Edward Thomas, Frost abandoned any uncertainty about future existence. His friend, he says, is "that fallen lance" that has intersected the curve of earth and "lies un-lifted now."

> But this we know, the obstacle that checked
> And tripped the body, shot the spirit on
> Further than target ever showed or shone. (pp. 261–2)

With the words "this we know," Frost sounds a note of certainty about the future life unequalled in the rest of his poetry.

What I wish to contend in this essay, however, is that there is a general drift or tendency, despite inconsistencies, in Frost's thinking about immortality and that this thinking is grounded in agnosticism but does not end there. His acceptance of our inability to know did not cut off speculation on the subject. I shall attempt to show that he found value both in uncertainty about a future life and in faith in it; that his own poetry is nevertheless thoroughly earth-centered, not heaven-centered; and that he increasingly leaned toward a conviction that the soul would continue to exist after death, not disembodied in some other world, but reembodied upon earth. This belief, foreshadowed in his first volume, becomes explicit in his last.

In *A Masque of Reason* Job does not receive an answer to his question about immortality. What he does receive is a defense from God for keeping man in uncertainty (ll. 347–358). If man were certain, God argues, that virtuous behavior would be rewarded in another life, then its essential disinterestedness would not exist, "And if it did, it wouldn't be a virtue" (p. 485). The very definition of virtue, that is, involves the willingness to suffer without expectation of reward. Otherwise the so-called "virtuous" man would only be serving God "for pay," as the Devil's followers serve him for pay. Though presumably the Lord's followers would be "stronger"—better able to postpone present satisfactions for the sake of even greater future satisfactions—their motivation would be equally mercenary. Uncertainty about a future reward is therefore necessary for the existence of virtue.[1]

But if, in *A Masque of Reason*, Frost finds it important that we not be certain of a future life, he elsewhere finds it important that we not be certain there is no future life. Indeed he finds a value in the belief, regardless of its truth. It makes, or helps to make, our lives significant to us. Something like this I take to be the point of "A Steeple on the House" (a poem wrongly interpreted by some readers as an expression of orthodox belief)[2]:

> What if it should turn out eternity
> Was but the steeple in our house of life
> That made our house of life a house of worship?
> We do not go up there to sleep at night.
> We do not go up there to live by day.
> Nor need we ever go up there to live.
> A spire and belfry coming on the roof
> Means that a soul is coming on the flesh. (p. 386)

"What if it should turn out" (here is the agnostic attitude, we can't be sure how it will turn out) that eternity "Was but the steeple on our house of life . . . ?" That is, what if it should turn out after death that there is no eternal life—that eternity "Was" (the past tense is important) only a belief we had erected on top of our house of life to make it into a holy place, a place of worship? Though the steeple has no functional value (we cannot go up there to live), still it is not useless. Its value is symbolical and psychological. It gives spiritual meaning to our lives, saves them from being purely materialistic—

"nasty, brutish, and short." It makes us something more than mere flesh—makes us capable of disinterested behavior, of goodness and of love.

A recurrent theme in Frost's thought is that belief shapes reality by shaping behavior. Some things have to be "believed into existence." His fullest expression of this idea is found in the prose piece "Education by Poetry." There he speaks of four beliefs: the self-belief (a young man has to believe into existence his foreknowledge of his worth); the love-belief ("a relationship of two that is going to be believed into fulfilment"); the art-belief (poems cannot be written by cunning and device; they must "begin in something more felt than known"); and the God-belief ("that the belief in God is a relationship you enter into with Him to bring about the future") (*SP*, 44–5). Most important for Frost, however, though he does not mention it here, was the life-belief, the belief that life is worth living. Flowing through his poetry like an ocean current is the idea that life can have value only if you believe it has. Conversely, if you believe it hasn't, it hasn't. This is the burden of Frost's poem "The Times Table," where he remarks on a farmer's saying ("A sigh for every so many a breath,/And for every so many sigh a death"):

> The saying may be ever so true;
> But it's just the kind of a thing that you
> Nor I nor nobody else may say,
> Unless our purpose is doing harm,
> And then I know of no better way
> To close a road, abandon a farm,
> Reduce the births of the human race,
> And bring back nature in people's place. (p. 263)

For a similar reason Frost, in *A Masque of Mercy*, makes Keeper jokingly refer to Robinson Jeffers and Eugene O'Neill as "stokers" in his imaginary hell (p. 516). Frost felt that their pessimism about human life helped destroy the real value of human life by undermining the life-belief. In "A Steeple on the House" the importance of the belief in eternity is that it enhances the life-belief. Even should the belief turn out false, it has given worth, for those who have believed it, to their lives.

Our beliefs, hopes, and fears, then, profoundly affect the quality of our living. Base hopes and fears diminish human life, noble ones enhance it. The hope of eternity in "A Steeple on the House" makes a soul grow on the flesh. The noblest fear, for Frost, was "the Fear of God" expressed by Paul at the end of *A Masque of Mercy*:

> We have to stay afraid deep in our souls
> Our sacrifice—the best we have to offer,
> And not our worst nor second best, our best,
> Our very best, our lives laid down like Jonah's,
> Our lives laid down in war and peace—may not
> Be found acceptable in Heaven's sight.
> And that they may be is the only prayer
> Worth praying. May my sacrifice
> Be found acceptable in Heaven's sight. (p. 520)

The obverse of fear is hope, and Paul's "Fear of God" is obversely a prayer which may be interpreted as a hope for salvation. But salvation is an ambiguous concept in Frost. It may mean the attainment of everlasting life, or it may mean the preservation of one's integrity in this life. Without abandoning the first possibility, Frost holds the second meaning, I think, as the essential one. In his "Letter to *The Amherst Student*" he writes, "Whatever progress may be taken to mean, it can't mean making the world any easier a place in which to save your soul—" and then immediately adds, "or if you dislike hearing your soul mentioned in open meeting, say your decency, your integrity" (*SP*, 106). In "A Steeple on the House" *soul* means decency and integrity, not some portion of the human being that survives the death of the body. In "The Lesson for Today" (for which the "Letter to *The Amherst Student*" was a prose rehearsal) Frost's statement "Earth's a hard place in which to save the soul" (p. 353) means essentially that earth is—and always will be—a hard place in which to preserve one's integrity. The poem ends with Frost's proposed inscription for his tombstone—an inscription that makes no mention of a hope for heaven but states, instead, "I had a lover's quarrel with the world."

For medieval Christianity this life was an insignificant prelude to eternal life: we live in a world of appearances, the substance is in the life to come. For Robert Frost the relationship was almost the reverse; the idea of heaven or an afterlife was important as it gives value to this life. The steeple was an appendage to "the house of life," not vice versa. I say the "idea" of heaven, for I do not believe that Frost, for any length of time, ever seriously considered heaven as an actually existent place or state of existence.[3] It was, rather, a metaphor, a symbol, a concept created by man to give value and significance to his life. In the couplet-poem "An Answer" he wrote:

> But Islands of the Blessèd, bless you, son,
> I never came upon a blessèd one. (p. 363)

This, taken in conjunction with the quatrain shortly preceding it called "A Question," suggests that the answer to the question there asked (whether "all the soul-and-body scars/Were not too much to pay for birth") must be found on earth or nowhere. When we examine Frost's earth-centered poetry for speculation about a future life, we find that the characteristic movement is always a movement from heaven to earth, or from earth to earth, not from earth to heaven. Two lines spoken by God to Job in *A Masque of Reason* ("But it was of the essence of the trial/You shouldn't understand it at the time" p. 475) send us back to a poem in Frost's first volume— "The Trial by Existence."

The scene in "The Trial by Existence" is heaven—charmingly pictured in conventional religious terms; but the poem begins with a twist:

> Even the bravest that are slain
>   Shall not dissemble their surprise
> On waking to find valor reign,
>   Even as on earth, in paradise;
> And where they sought without the sword
>   Wide fields of asphodel fore'er
> To find that the utmost reward
>   Of daring should be still to dare. (p. 19)

In short, the souls of the dead are given a choice—whether to remain in paradise and enjoy eternal bliss, or to return to earth and undergo "The trial by existence named,/The obscuration upon earth." The noblest and bravest are those who accept the challenge, "who for some good discerned/Will gladly give up paradise"— and who do so despite the severe condition laid down by God:

"One thought in agony of strife
The bravest would have by for friend,
The memory that he chose the life;
But the pure fate to which you go
Admits no memory of choice,
Or the woe were not earthly woe
To which you give the assenting voice."

Frost's concluding stanza sums up the meanings of the poem:

'Tis of the essence of life here,
Though we choose greatly, still to lack
The lasting memory at all clear,
That life has for us on the wrack
Nothing but what we somehow chose;
Thus we are wholly stripped of pride
In the pain that has but one close,
Bearing it crushed and mystified.

Clearly, "The Trial by Existence" is a myth, a fanciful story designed to convey certain "truths" or perceptions about human life. It is not to be read literally. The heaven depicted in the poem is part of the myth. What are the "truths"?

(1) The poem asserts, first of all, through overstatement, Frost's belief in free will, in the capacity of man to make meaningful choices in the government of his life. It rejects the mechanistic scientific determinism so prevalent in the early years of the century. (2) The poem asserts the importance of courage as a human virtue—a value Frost emphasized all through his life, notably in *A Masque of Mercy*. (3) The poem asserts that hardship and suffering are inescapable conditions of human life and that much of this suffering—like Job's—simply *happens* to man, is not a punishment for sin or only a consequence of his own foolish actions. (4) The poem asserts our inability to know whether any life to come will compensate for our sufferings in this one. At the end we are "wholly stripped of pride/In the pain that has but one close,/Bearing it crushed and mystified." I single out these thematic concerns of the poem in order to separate them from its mythical framework. But most important for us here is the mythical framework, which shows brave souls turning their backs on the joys of heaven and choosing instead the pains and uncertainties of life on earth.

Heaven is a recurrent word in Frost's poetry. Most often it substitutes for *sky*, with favorable overtones, but frequently it is a metaphor or symbol standing for some *imagined* state of perfect bliss or for some *ideal* goal of human aspiration. In "The Silken Tent," for instance, the "central cedar pole" which is the tent's "pinnacle to heavenward" explicitly "signifies the sureness of the soul"—the integrity and love—of the woman whom the poem celebrates. Perhaps the most famous use of the word is in "Birches." Here, Frost says, when life gets too difficult ("is too much like a pathless wood"),

> I'd like to get away from earth awhile
> And then come back to it and begin over.
> May no fate willfully misunderstand me
> And half grant what I wish and snatch me away
> Not to return. Earth's the right place for love:
> I don't know where it's likely to go better.
> I'd like to go by climbing a birch tree,
> And climb black branches up a snow-white trunk
> *Toward* heaven, till the tree could bear no more,
> But dipped its top and set me down again. (p. 122)

Surely the words "Earth's the right place for love: /I don't know where it's likely to go better" voice a deep skepticism that any actual, attainable heaven exists. A Milton or a George Herbert could not have written these lines. In any case, here, as in "The Trial by Existence," the important movement is a movement from heaven to earth.

The phrase "Toward heaven" recurs in "After Apple-Picking":

> My long two-pointed ladder's sticking through a tree
> Toward heaven still. . . . (p. 68)

"After Apple-Picking"—whatever else it is about—is a poem of fulfilment in earthly labor; it expresses a deep satisfaction derived from working close to the earth. The ladder pointing *toward* heaven symbolizes the enriching and joyful nature of this activity, enabling one to partake on earth in that joy which we imagine to be pure in heaven (where one would not get "overtired"). But the work is here its own reward; it does not look toward heaven for its fulfilment. Even the dream envisioned as troubling the speaker's sleep—"whatever sleep it is"—presents a continuation of earthly activity.

Two other poems—though they do not use the word *heaven* or concern a future life—take a similar direction. "Mowing" is another poem in which labor—the love of the work—is its own reward. It specifically rejects "the gift of idle hours,/Or easy gold at the hand of fay or elf" (p. 17)—a kind of heaven substitute. Like "Birches" it insists that the place for love—in this case, love of work—is here; and it rejects the need for other compensation—in a form that makes the very possibility of other compensation seem illusory. "To Earthward" contrasts youth and maturity. In youth the poet "lived on air," experiencing paradisiac bliss in the fragrance of grapevine springs and honeysuckle sprays; in maturity he finds that "no joy but lacks salt" for him "That is not dashed with pain/And weariness and fault" (p. 227). He has descended "Earthward"—from heavenly to earthly experience—and strongly implies a preference for the latter.

> When stiff and sore and scarred
> I take away my hand
> From leaning on it hard
> In grass and sand,
>
> The hurt is not enough:
> I long for weight and strength
> To feel the earth as rough
> To all my length.

All of these poems point in the direction of Frost's final thinking about immortality, though it does not emerge explicitly until his final volume, *In the Clearing*. Here in three poems he expresses belief in some kind of continued life, or renewal of life, beyond the grave— not, however, in heaven or hell, not in some place of eternal bliss or eternal torture—but on earth.

The central poem of *In the Clearing*, philosophically speaking, is "Kitty Hawk," and especially those lines from it that Frost chose as epigraph for the volume as a whole:

> But God's own descent
> Into flesh was meant
> As a demonstration
> That the supreme merit
> Lay in risking spirit
> In substantiation.

> Spirit enters flesh
> And for all it's worth
> Charges into earth
> In birth after birth
> Ever fresh and fresh.
> We may take the view
> That its derring-do
> Thought of in the large
> Is one mighty charge
> On our human part
> Of the soul's ethereal
> Into the material.[4]

Frost here puts the Christian story of the incarnation to metaphorical use, but gives it a meaning considerably different from the traditional one. For the Christian believer the significance of the incarnation is summed up in the crucifixion. "For God so loved the world, that he gave his only begotten Son, that whosoever believeth in him should not perish, but have everlasting life." Christ suffered and died for man in order to bring eternal life in the Kingdom of Heaven to the truly repentant. Frost stops with the incarnation itself and makes it symbolize the recurrent entry of spirit into flesh "In birth after birth." He reverses the traditional emphasis, suppressing the escape of the immortal spirit *from* the temporal body, putting his entire stress on the entry of eternal spirit *into* the temporal body.

What it comes down to is perhaps something like this. Eighteenth-century science had mathematically validated the ancient doctrine of the indestructibility of matter. Matter is not destroyed; it is only changed into some other state. PostDarwinian poets, robbed of the traditional belief in immortality, made a melancholy creed of this scientific law. "We die and push up the daisies" was its popular expression. Edward FitzGerald put it more poetically in the *Rubaiyat*:

> I sometimes think that never blows so red
> The Rose as where some buried Caesar bled;
>   That every Hyacinth the Garden wears
> Dropped in her Lap from some once lovely Head.

Frost himself touched obliquely upon this idea in his early poem "In Hardwood Groves." The leaves renew themselves year after year, he observes, but only by going "down into the dark decayed" and later mounting "To fill the trees with another shade" (p. 25). In *In the Clearing*, however, Frost emphasizes, not the indestructibility of matter, but the indestructibility of spirit. Yet, at the same time, he emphasizes that the characteristic disposition of spirit is in combination with matter.

"Kitty Hawk" expresses Frost's view in general terms. Two other poems from *In the Clearing* express it in personal terms. In "Away!" the speaker is the poet himself, imagining himself as dead, a ghost "walking," a disembodied spirit:

> Now I out walking
> The world desert,
> And my shoe and my stocking
> Do me no hurt.

He ends, quoting the refrain from the folk song "Shenandoah":

> Unless I'm wrong
> I but obey
> The urge of a song:
> "I'm—bound—away!"
>
> And I may return
> If dissatisfied
> With what I learn
> From having died. (pp. 412–13)

The agnosticism is still there. The poet does not know what he will "learn/From having died." But his thought is focused on a possible return to earth, not on elevation to some realm of heavenly bliss.

More positive in its statement is the final poem in the volume:

> In winter in the woods alone
> Against the trees I go.
> I mark a maple for my own
> And lay the maple low.
>
> At four o'clock I shoulder ax,
> And in the afterglow
> I link a line of shadowy tracks
> Across the tinted snow.
>
> I see for Nature no defeat
> In one tree's overthrow

> Or for myself in my retreat
> For yet another blow. (p. 470)

Some have read this poem at a purely literal level: Frost retreats to his cabin at the end of the day to return on the morrow and renew his task.[5] But the winter and the twilight setting, words like *shadowy* and *afterglow*, and the equation of the tree's overthrow with his own "retreat" clearly mark it as symbolical. Its position as the final poem in Frost's final volume reinforces a symbolical interpretation. This, in short, is Frost's "Crossing the Bar." His "retreat" is his death. Death is "no defeat," however, but only a "retreat," for he means to come back from it and strike another blow for life. But if this is Frost's "Crossing the Bar," how different it is from Tennyson's! Tennyson will sail far "from out our bourne of Time and Place" into "the boundless deep" of eternity where he will see his Pilot "face to face." Frost will retreat from our bourne of Time and Place only temporarily and not very far, and then will come back to it to strike "another blow." Immortality, for Frost, if it exists— and he increasingly inclined to think that it did—will be here on earth, and not in some other place.

In this final paragraph I should like to be almost entirely speculative. That is, I should like to record my own intuitions as to where Frost's thought was headed. What exactly did Frost mean when he spoke of coming back "To strike another blow"? Richard Eberhart, speaking of Frost's poem "Away!", comments: "He says that if he is dissatisfied with what he learns from having died he may return from beyond death to this life, something no man has ever done. . . . I do not believe that man can come back from the dead whether he wishes to or not. Nobody has done so as far I know."[6] Eberhart's remarks strike me as naive. Frost was a poet. He spoke in metaphors. I cannot think that he meant anything as strictly literal as Eberhart envisions. Nor do I think that Frost was thinking of reincarnation in the doctrinal form that had such appeal, for instance, to Yeats. The word *reincarnation* does not occur in his poetry, nor do I recall it from his prose. I do not think he meant that some future clairvoyant could point to a particular man or animal and say that it had been Robert Frost in a previous incarnation. He meant, I think, something more nearly conformable to a scientific world picture.

Frost, after all, had "a lover's quarrel" with science. He quarreled with it whenever it became overdogmatic, whenever it went beyond its evidence in making large generalizations about the world, and especially when these generalizations were reductive in their interpretations of the mysteries of life. But he also took pains (or, rather, joy) in keeping up with science; he understood it remarkably well; and he appropriated many of its conclusions for his thinking and his poetry. In his poetry, for poetic reasons, Frost clung to a vocabulary that dichotomizes spirit and matter. In his mind he may have been closer to the concept that spirit perpetually enters matter because in fact they are never separated. Matter and spirit, in other words, may be seen as simply different aspects of the same reality. The smallest "particles" of the universe (if we choose to call them that) may be particles of matter-spirit. (Scientists in this century, as Frost himself has noted (*SP*, 38), have stressed that the movements of individual atoms are spontaneous and unpredictable: only in large masses may the movements of "matter" be predicted.) The emergence of "spirit" out of "matter" then becomes a function of complexity of organization. Organize these matter-spirit particles simply, and the result is what we call "matter"—inert spirit—as in a stone. Organize the matter-spirit particles more complexly and the result is life—vegetable, animal, or human, depending on the complexity of the organization. The matter-spirit particles never cease to exist; they merely reorganize. At death a pattern disintegrates. The individual matter-spirit particles scatter, to recombine with other matter-spirit particles into new patterns, some of which are human. Thus spirit perpetually reembodies itself or, as Frost puts it, "charges into earth." Something approximating this, I think, is the direction which Frost's thought was taking. At any rate, it is well to keep in mind his culminating remarks on metaphor in "Education by Poetry": "Greatest of all attempts to say one thing in terms of another is the philosophical attempt to say matter in terms of spirit, or spirit in terms of matter, to make the final unity. That is the greatest attempt that ever failed. We stop just short there. But it is the height of poetry, the height of all thinking, the height of all poetic thinking, that attempt to say matter in terms of spirit and spirit in terms of matter" (*SP*, 41).

Notes to *Robert Frost and the Idea of Immortality* by LAURENCE PERRINE

1. Several critics of *A Masque of Reason* have taken God's final answer to Job's question "Why did You hurt me so?" to be His flippant remark "I was just showing off to the Devil, Job" (p. 484) and have been, quite understandably, profoundly dissatisfied with the poem. Randall Jarrell says in "The Other Frost," *Poetry and the Age* (New York: Alfred A. Knopf, 1953), p. 34: "When common sense has God justify His ways to Job" by making this remark, "the performance has the bleak wisdom of Calvin Coolidge telling you what life comes to at 2½%." "The God of *A Masque of Reason*," says Arthur M. Sampley in "The Tensions of Robert Frost," *The South Atlantic Quarterly*, 65 (1966), 432, "is callous, flippant, capricious: he does not seem very far removed from the Setebos of Browning's poem." Yvor Winters, in "Robert Frost: or, the Spiritual Drifter as Poet," *The Function of Criticism: Problems and Exercises* (Denver: Alan Swallow, 1957), p. 175; George W. Nitchie, in *Human Values in the Poetry of Robert Frost* (Durham: Duke University Press, 1960), p. 172; and Lawrance Thompson, in *Robert Frost* (Minneapolis: University of Minnesota Press, 1967), p. 36 have made similar complaints. All of these critics have taken overseriously what is essentially a joke. The moral center of *A Masque of Reason* does not lie in the quoted line 327 but in lines 347–58. Only if "Virtue may fail and wickedness succeed" (p. 475), these lines explain, is virtue truly possible. At this point in the poem Frost goes beyond the Old Testament Book of Job in offering a rationale for the existence of injustice.

2. Sampley, p. 433 calls it "almost orthodoxly religious in expression."

3. At the end of "A Fountain, a Bottle, a Donkey's Ears, and Some Books," Frost pictures the poetess Clara Robinson in heaven responding with a sigh of gratitude when the speaker (Frost) takes home one of her books (p. 217). Each reader will have to decide for himself to what extent this passage is imagined seriously or whimsically on Frost's part, but the fact that the poetess in the supposed place of perfect bliss feels unease in her heart over her unread books inclines this reader to a whimsical interpretation.

If Frost, as I believe, is not inclined to take the possibility of eternal future bliss very seriously, he is not inclined to take the possibility of eternal future torment seriously at all. In *A Masque of Mercy* he has Keeper joke, "We send our wicked enemies to Hell,/Our wicked friends we send to Purgatory" (p. 519). Later, Keeper says, more seriously, "I'm no more governed by the fear of Hell/Than by the fear of the asylum, jail, or poorhouse,/The basic three the state is founded on" (p. 520).

4. I give the passage here as printed in the epigraph of *In the Clearing*. In the poem itself, the sixth line is separated from the seventh by an intervening passage, and the verb *Is* is replaced by *Was* at the beginning of the fifteenth line (pp. 435–6, 577).

5. The poem is apparently so read by Lewis H. Miller, Jr., in "Design and Drama in *A Boy's Will*," *Frost: Centennial Essays* (Jackson: University Press of Mississippi, 1974), p. 367 and by Margaret Edwards in "Pan's Song Revised," *Frost: Centennial Essays*, pp. 116–17. Donald J. Greiner in "Robert Frost's Dark Woods and the Function of Metaphor," *Frost: Centennial Essays*, p. 385 makes a similar reading but curiously sees the retreat as a retreat "to" the woods rather than "from" them. Perhaps an examination of the poem's structure is needed. In stanza one the poet goes "Against the trees" (attacks them). In stanza two, with the sun setting and a maple felled, he retreats. In stanza three he comments on the experience, the first two lines paralleling stanza one, and the last two (which speak of his "retreat") paralleling stanza two. (The word *blow* in the last line should be compared with its use in "Two Tramps in Mud Time": "The blows that a life of self-control/Spares to strike for the common good,/That day, giving a loose to my soul,/I spent on the unimportant wood," p. 275.)

6. "Robert Frost in the Clearing," *The Southern Review*, 11 (1975), 265–6.

"Trust . . . to go by contraries": Incarnation and the Paradox of Belief in the Poetry of Frost

JOSEPH KAU

ROBERT FROST is often viewed as a twentieth century American poet of rugged individualism, yet in his poetry one detects an individualism vitiated by a dilemma which has plagued the humanist since the birth of the modern age, whether to use religion or science as the guide to metaphysics. The dualism of Descartes, the pantheism of Spinoza, and the materialism of Hobbes, all conceived in a century more credulous than ours, offer less assurance to the humanist of the twentieth century than to his brethren of the seventeenth century. Science and religion have divided the loyalties of the modern humanist: on the one hand is the theism of Eliot and on the other the materialism of Stevens; inhabiting the middle region between belief and unbelief, between religious faith and materialism, are poets like Frost. While Eliot assumes a moral stance and Stevens an intellectual one in their attempts to resolve the dichotomy, Frost assumes an ambivalent stance. Though his sensibilities are on the side of religion, his scientific reason argues against acceptance. Caught between contraries, a predicament which fosters much of the tension in his poetry, Frost opts frequently for a resolution that, while seemingly accepting the proof of science and the logic of reason, still indicates a religious bias.

Frost's dilemma is essentially that of an agnostic and is, not surprisingly, the source of the powerful attraction of his poetry of belief. But he is not a rigid agnostic. If by "agnostic" one means a person who holds that both the ultimate cause and the essential nature of things are unknown or unknowable, or that human knowledge is limited to experiences, then Frost is hardly agnostic. If one understands "know" in the materialist experiential sense, all men are of necessity agnostic. But if one accepts belief as knowledge, again the poet is not agnostic. He accepts Divine Cause, just as he accepts the spiritual nature of things, on faith; however, since man is limited to experiences and hears no confirming voices this side of eternity, "faith" as metaphysical knowledge is always called into question. The quandary in Frost's poem pertains not to cause; he is agnostic in the sense that he does not trust God wholeheartedly in the matters of existence and destiny. The tension between the desire to trust completely and the skepticism of the agnostic is apparent in his "incarnation" or "creational" poems which affirm that questions concerning the human condition and human destiny remain unanswered. Frost refuses docile acceptance of their mystery.

In the "creational" poems, Frost deals with spirit becoming flesh. Not only in his last collection, *In the Clearing*, but also in poems early and late, the incarnation theme is developed in various mythic or legendary settings: "Trial by Existence" is neoPlatonic; "Sitting by a Bush" Old Testament and rural; "West-Running Brook" New Testament, evolutionist, and rural American; "Kitty Hawk" modern American; "A Never Naught Song" evolutionist; and "One More Brevity" homely and classical. These poems show that the problem of faith, acceptance and fear has always bothered Frost in his poetry. Metaphysically, he is never "in the clearing." The "incarnation" poems reveal the challenges that mystery presents to faith.

In a sense they form an article of faith, for they postulate that if man derives from spirit, which is immortal, then he should return to spirit. "The Trial by Existence," an early poem (1906), sets forth in detail an argument which Frost found most comforting and satisfying in his early years: from an existence in Paradise, the soul courageously chooses life, his "trial by existence." Spirit is transformed into flesh,

> And God has taken a flower of gold
> And broken it, and used therefrom
> The mystic link to bind and hold
> Spirit to matter till death come.

But with no memory of its choice, the spirit incarnate finds life mystifying with no consolation but the impression of choice:

> 'Tis of the essence of life here,
> Though we choose greatly, still to lack
> The lasting memory at all clear,

> That life has for us on the wrack
> Nothing but what we somehow chose;
> Thus are we wholly stripped of pride
> In the pain that has but one close,
> Bearing it crushed and mystified. (p. 21)

Poetically, however, the mystery is resolved by showing the bold spirits' return, at the opening of the poem, to Paradise, home for the Browningesque journeying spirit. "Trial by Existence" views life as a cosmic game with a precondition of forgetfulness, and the amnesiacs in it cope as best they can through choice. Frost's note for this poem is that it contains a youth's resolution "to know definitely what he thinks about the soul" (p. 530). The resolution here is rather too easy, almost cant, and far from definite. Later poems indicate less certainty and a greater awareness of the challenges to belief.

In "Sitting by a Bush in Broad Sunlight" (in *West-Running Brook*, 1928), incarnation and revelation are linked directly with faith:

> When I spread out my hand here today,
> I catch no more than a ray
> To feel of between thumb and fingers;
> No lasting effect of it lingers.
>
> There was one time and only the one
> When dust really took in the sun;
> And from that one intake of fire
> All creatures still warmly suspire.
>
> And if men have watched a long time
> And never seen sun-smitten slime
> Again come to life and crawl off,
> We must not be too ready to scoff.
>
> God once declared He was true
> And then took the veil and withdrew,
> And remember how final a hush
> Then descended of old on the bush.
>
> God once spoke to people by name.
> The sun once imparted its flame.
> One impulse persists as our breath;
> The other persists as our faith. (p. 266)

The title establishes a matter-of-fact setting which the poet later develops as an analogue both for Creation and the episode of Moses and the Burning Bush. The poem opens with a quite ordinary observation as the persona tests a ray of light, a physical test which is a prelude to metaphysical reflection. In the second stanza, the persona claims that man was created from dust and inspired with life from the sun. He goes on further to say that though the act of creation (or evolution) has ceased, man must not scoff at the idea of creation. As a comparison, he cites God's appearance to Moses by means of the Burning Bush; such appearances have ceased. But as he asserts in the chiasmus of the last stanza which cleverly identifies both phenomena rhetorically and ideally, proof for Creation can be found in man's continued existence just as proof for God's appearances in Biblical times persists in our faith; both impulses, life and faith, emanate from mystery, and the persona, an ordinary man sitting by an ordinary bush in broad daylight and seeing neither God nor the act of creation, can still affirm his spiritual origins through the facts of his existence and his faith. Here faith as it pertains to the nature of belief is clearly perceived as a rejection of the constraints of the material world.

While "Sitting by a Bush in Broad Sunlight" treats incarnation directly and pietistically, "West-Running Brook" (1928) deals with the subject by means of an ironic mixture of reason and faith, and indeed through this poem Frost considers the issue of belief in Divine Cause and the problem of accepting man's condition and destiny with greater complexity than in any of his other poems. The setting is a New Hampshire farm, the characters a newlywed couple assessing the farm upon which they are to live. The wife notes that the brook passing in front of their farmhouse goes west rather than east like the other brooks in the area. The brook becomes the occasion for reflections on the nature of life, the wife's intuitive and the husband's apparently more logical. Almost casually, the poem reveals some essential conflicts in the poet that are deftly resolved through his use of imagery. The poem can be easily misunderstood, as this comment by Yvor Winters shows: "The theology of this passage, if we may call it theology, is tenuous and incomplete; it is what a certain kind of critic would call suggestive, rather than definitive; there is, in brief, very little to it. Frost seems to have suspected this, for he did not let his meditation on the ripple stand alone on its merits; he framed it in the dialogue I have mentioned and made his young people responsible for it. Yet the people are not depicted as characters, and their remarks lead to no dramatic action; the meditation gives the momentary illusion that the characters are more important than they are; the conversational framework gives the momentary illusion that the meditation is more important than it is. Thus the structure of the poem is actually a piece of deception, and the substance of the poem is negligible."[1] Winters denigrates the poem because it does not conform to his conception of what the poem should be: dramatic rather than lyrical, discursive rather than intuitive, comprehensive rather than unique. Frost never intended the poem as a theological disquisition; he intended to show that two apparently contradictory points of view, though poetically depicted as male and female, could paradoxically be entertained in the same person and that these differences could indeed be mystically transcended. Examined closely, the poem is found to contain Frost's doubts, fears, and hopes for the human spirit. In the background is the question of "design . . . in a thing so small" (p. 302), of "what to make of a diminished thing" (p. 120). The work raises the issues of man's origins, of the evolution into consciousness (spirit investing matter), of the seeming diminution of matter and spirit, and of a faint hope for man's destiny. Lawrance Thompson has pointed out that "West-Running Brook" is Frost's most concentrated use of Bergson's images and ideas, particularly those from *Creative Evolution* (1911): "Frost particularly liked Bergson's gathering metaphors: the flowing stream of matter moves ever downward, but the life force resists and tries always to climb back upward, through matter, toward the Source" (I, 381–2). While Bergson's influence upon the poem is clear, his optimistic belief that human consciousness "in an overwhelming charge [is] able to beat down every resistance and clear the most formidable obstacles, perhaps even death"[2] is not apparent. The poem is built upon a principle of contraries which suggest an unequal dualism of uncreation and creation, one in which uncreation appears to dominate. Fred, the male persona, is impressed by the diminishing nature of the universe: the entire stream of existence is linked by a destruction-creation chain. Frost has modified the physical law that every action has an equal and opposite reaction to the principle that every action has a contrary (opposite) reaction which may not be equal. This principle, the persona tells us, transcends the physical and extends into the metaphysical.

He begins his explanation by alluding to the principle of contraries and citing the example of the brook and the wave: "Speaking of contraries, see how the brook/In that white wave runs counter to itself" (p. 259). The wave in the brook moves in a direction counter to the flow. From this example, Fred moves to a generalization about the stream of existence and the movement counter to the downward flow of the stream. He then goes on seemingly to discuss man's evolutionary movement from water-life:

> It is from that in water we were from
> Long, long before we were from any creature.
> Here we, in our impatience of the steps,
> Get back to the beginning of beginnings,
> The stream of everything that runs away.

The impatience to "Get back to the beginning of beginnings" is not just the couple's "return" to West-Running Brook as an analogue for the return to the stream of life that is constantly diminishing, but it also suggests the search for and intuition of a metaphysical, spiritual origin beyond "substance lapsing unsubstantial." Man is evolved not so much from a substance as he is from a principle, for "that in water we were from" alludes to the resistance to the downward flow of "The stream of everything that runs away." As Fred observes that all that is substantial will lapse "unsubstantial," "The universal cataract of death/That spends to nothingness," he fastens onto a mysterious creative principle of resistance immanent in this diminishing universe and with divine origins:

> —and unresisted,
> Save by some strange resistance in itself,
> . . . .
> As if regret were in it and were sacred.

All existence appears to be vitalistic and teleological, or so he wishes to believe when he speaks of the paradoxical resistance as "regret" and as "sacred." The resistance is small in proportion to the downward fall of existence, yet it exists:

> It has this throwing backward on itself
> So that the fall of most of it is always
> Raising up a little, sending up a little.

He then goes on to note the loss that takes place in the process of creation; he appears to subscribe to the theory that matter and energy can be destroyed (but, as a corollary, that they can be created), as he traces creative processes, resistive processes that, like the wave of consciousness, are "sendings-up." He begins with time and works back to the sun in a countermovement to larger sources of energy that have diminished in the creative process:

> Our life runs down in sending up the clock.
> The brook runs down in sending up our life.
> The sun runs down in sending up the brook.
> And there is something sending up the sun.

At this point, however, the persona and the poet encounter a metaphysical question about which one can only speculate: What sends up the sun? Obviously a force of cosmic proportions, God Himself. Is the force spiritual? In "Cluster of Faith," in his last collection (*In the Clearing*), Frost states clearly that spirit and matter are one, so man's source is unitary, both spiritual and material. Does this source for the sun Itself diminish like the rest of the stream of existence, or is It outside of the stream which It has created? Neither poet nor persona answers this question. Suffice to say, the persona acknowledges a divine source and implies a desire to return to its source:

> It is this backward motion toward the source,
> Against the stream, that most we see ourselves in,
> The tribute of the current to the source.
> It is from this in nature we are from.
> It is most us.

Once again, Frost through his persona reaffirms the divine origins of man; man's destiny or survival, the possibility of his extinction, is left in doubt.

In this poem, more than in many others, Frost appears to take sides; and the side he chooses is not the side of scientific logic, which, however, he does not attempt to refute. Science he queries back to its origins, back up the evolutionary ladder till it reaches God.

The rhetoric of the poem is rather deceptive, since a great part of the poem is given over to reflecting on the diminishing nature of existence. However, if one recalls the structure of "The Trial by Existence" which presented an answer before stating the problem, then the argument of this poem becomes clearer. The poem begins with the reconciliation, or at least acceptance, by the personae of the fact of resistance. The husband describes the wave in the brook:

> (... like a bird
> White feathers from the struggle of whose breast
> Flecked the dark stream and flecked the darker pool
> Below the point, and were at last driven wrinkled
> In a white scarf against the far-shore alders.) (p. 258)

adding, "It wasn't waved to us." The wife responds in contradiction: "It wasn't, yet it was. If not to you,/It was to me—in an annunciation." Yet she provides the image complementary to the white wave which is like a bird struggling, resisting the flow of the stream, "not gaining but not losing," and attempting to break free. The composite image is one of an annunciation or revelation; the wave/bird bears this message to the lady: that they are one with the stream, that life must be accepted, but that love like theirs can "bridge across" or transcend the stream of life. She says:

> As you and I are married to each other,
> We'll both be married to the brook. We'll build
> Our bridge across it, and the bridge shall be
> Our arm thrown over it asleep beside it.

Apparently the wife has already reconciled herself to the prospect of "The universal cataract of death" before the husband's long reflection upon the course of the stream. She accepts the paradoxical nature of existence just as she accepts the contrary direction of the stream's flow: "It must be the brook/Can trust itself to go by contraries/The way I can with you—and you with me." Contradiction is a basic principle of existence, and though the husband later ex-

pands on this principle, he does not lessen her belief. The problem
in belief is to "trust . . . to go by contraries," and though she resolves
the problem intuitively and with more conviction than her husband,
interpreting the wave from the brook as the sign of an approving
intelligence, the husband with his logical and orderly reflection,
seeing the wave more forcibly as a white bird struggling to free
itself from the encumbering surface tension in the failing stream of
existence, is himself forced to "trust . . . to go by contraries," to
accept that just as a diminishing universe emanating from a divine
source has created consciousness, so also can human consciousness
go counter to the downward motion of existence in the hope of
ultimately transcending matter (perhaps death). The wife takes
note of this hope for acceptance, for when Fred says:

> It is this backward motion toward the source,
> Against the stream, that most we see ourselves in,
> The tribute of the current to the source.
> It is from this in nature we are from.
> It is most us" (p. 260)

she acknowledges his "trust . . . to go by contraries," saying, "Today
will be the day/You said so." Like the other incarnation poems,
"West-Running Brook" affirms a belief in man's divine origins and
a hope for his destiny, a return to the divine.

Again in "Kitty Hawk" (*In the Clearing*, 1962), Frost treats the
incarnation theme in as heroic a fashion as he did in the early "Trial
by Existence." The poem, a little American folk epic, is meant to
celebrate both the town of Kitty Hawk, North Carolina, and the
flight of the Wright brothers. The heroic daring of the first aviators
is compared to God's daring act of incarnation which risks man's
disbelief:

> But God's own descent
> Into flesh was meant
> As a demonstration
> That the supreme merit
> Lay in risking spirit
> In substantiation. (p. 435)

Implicit in God's special Incarnation is the spiritual origin of man.
Frost goes further to imply a cosmic design and man's accommoda-

tion to his condition. Through risk in his attempt at flight, man comes partially to terms with life and appears to fulfill some part of the cosmic design. Man's daring, as exemplified in this flight, is ultimately a striving toward his obscure destiny:

> Though our leap in air
> Prove as vain a hop
> As the hop from grass
> Of a grasshopper,
> Don't discount our powers;
> We have made a pass
> At the infinite,
> Made it, as it were,
> Rationally ours,
> To the most remote
> Swirl of neon-lit
> Particle afloat. (p. 439)

The elements of Frost's view emerge in their familiar pattern: belief in man's spiritual origin and an ordered universe but a sense of mystery concerning the human condition and destiny. The human condition is shrouded in mystery: one may seek for answers but find only that he must face up to mystery. Still, risk is a condition of life; belief involves risk but may lead "substantiated" man back to his origins and destiny in the infinite or spirit.

The incarnation theme is again treated in "A Never Naught Song" (*In the Clearing*), but here Frost's argument takes an unusual and provocative tack. He begins by rejecting the existentialist concept of "creation" as the movement from nonexistence into existence. But he does not stop here. He also proceeds to dismiss the traditional dualism of spirit and matter, denying the limits of materialism or the finite.

> There was never naught,
> There was always thought.
> But when noticed first
> It was fairly burst
> Into having weight.
> It was in a state
> Of atomic One.
> Matter was begun—
> And in fact complete,

> One and yet discrete
> To conflict and pair.
> Everything was there,
> Every single thing
> Waiting was to bring,
> Clear from hydrogen
> All the way to men. (p. 426)

The claim made is that thought (spirit) and matter are essentially one, that the universe is unitary, and that the distinction of matter from thought is one imposed by human consciousness:

> There was always thought.
> But when *noticed* first
> It was fairly burst
> Into having weight.

Frost reaffirms man's origins once more, in the nonmaterial, and his comment upon the poem alludes to the teleological nature of life: "And my extravagence would go on from there to say that people think that life is a *result* of certain atoms coming together, instead of being the *cause* that brings the atoms together. There's something to be said about that in the utter, utter extravagant way."[3] Matter derives from spirit, the poet says, because they are simply one.

In "One More Brevity" (*In the Clearing*), Frost treats the incarnation theme in a homely fashion reminiscent of classical myths, but the myth created is a paradigm for his beliefs. The poem begins with a suggestion of valediction:

> I opened the door so my last look
> Should be taken outside a house and book.
> Before I gave up seeing and slept
> I said I would see how Sirius kept
> His watchdog eye on what remained
> To be gone into if not explained. (p. 419)

In casual, characteristically sly understatement, Frost suggests approaching death, a last look at the heavens, and a final consideration of mysteries ineffable. As if in answer to his thoughts, a stray dog appears, seeking refuge for the night:

> Not a heavenly dog made manifest,
> But an earthly dog of the carriage breed.

Next morning, before the persona can establish a friendship with the animal, the dog leaves, occasioning this reflection:

> I was to taste in little the grief
> That comes of dogs' lives being so brief,
> Only a fraction of ours at most.
> He might have been the dream of a ghost
> In spite of the way his tail had smacked
> My floor so hard and matter-of-fact. (pp. 420–21)

The brevity of the visit, the brevity of a dog's life—and the brevity of human life. To reconcile himself to yet "one more brevity," life itself or this short respite before death, the persona muses:

> I might even claim, he was Sirius
> (Think of presuming to call him Gus),
> The star itself—Heaven's greatest star,
> Not a meteorite, but an avatar—
> Who had made an overnight descent
> To show by deeds he didn't resent
> My having depended on him so long,
> And yet done nothing about it in song.
> A symbol was all he could hope to convey,
> An intimation, a shot of ray,
> A meaning I was supposed to seek,
> And finding, wasn't disposed to speak.

As an avatar, if only in a myth of the poet's creation, Dalmatian Gus confirms the correspondence between the celestial and the earthly. The dependence alluded to is not merely to Sirius as the brightest star in the sky by which one guides his voyaging but also as a confirmation of influences other than earthly. Incarnate as Dalmatian Gus, the August One, the avatar is a symbol, "an intimation of immortality."

Intimations are all that Frost perceives in his poetry, and these occur only in myths he creates which fix man's origins in the spiritual or divine, speak of his troubled existence, and hint at the possibility of return to the divine or spiritual. One can see what Frost wishes to believe in: creative spirit, meaningful existence, and transcendence. However, his poetry contains no allusions to a benevolent or communicating God. Man's role is to speculate, but God is not obliged to resolve his speculations; Frost is never impertinent enough to assume divinity's point of view in any of his poems but always looks with the eyes of baffled humanity. Frost's belief is that life is an act of faith, for it begins in mystery and ends in hope; the span between is paradox, to "trust . . . to go by contraries" that are true.

Notes to *"Trust . . . to go by contraries": Incarnation and the Paradox of Belief in the Poetry of Frost* by JOSEPH KAU

1. "Robert Frost; or, The Spiritual Drifter as Poet," in *Robert Frost: A Collection of Critical Essays*, ed. James M. Cox (Englewood Cliffs: Prentice-Hall, 1962), p. 70.
2. Trans. Arthur Mitchell (New York: Henry Holt and Co., 1911), pp. 270–71.
3. "On Extravagence," in *Robert Frost: Poetry and Prose*, ed. Edward Connery Lathem and Lawrance Thompson (New York: Holt, Rinehart and Winston, 1972), p. 453.

Frost's Theodicy:
"Word I Had No One Left But God"

THOMAS McCLANAHAN

A critical inspection of Robert Frost's canon reveals the poet's decided tendency to subjugate Emersonian assurances in benevolent nature and man's instinctive capabilities to the pragmatic concerns of William James. One such concern is for the problem of evil. James's theodicy, explicitly formulated in *Pragmatism* (1907), offers Frost a model for a pessimistic view of God's nature. From the stance in "The Trial by Existence" to the enigmatic poems of *In the Clearing*, Frost is concerned with the need to justify the ways of God to man. The outcome of this vindication and the manner in which it is accomplished mark Frost as a sophisticated philosophical poet who develops a theodicy which builds on that of William James. Thus, Frost is a significant figure in the development of twentieth-century thought because he reflects some of the primary tenets of the most influential philosopher in American history. Frost's theodicy poems are literary landmarks on a map of the desert places of the twentieth century. They are important elements in modern intellectual history because they document the movement in the American sensibility from the metaphysical optimism inherent in the work of Emerson to a darker turn of mind manifesting itself in the writings of such disparate writers as Pound, Eliot, Cummings, Hemingway and Dos Passos. In his most philosophical poems, Frost's religious doubt surfaces to reveal his skeptical leanings, and these, in turn, mark him as one of the two or three most important modern, intellectual poets.

Until the publication of William James's *Pragmatism* in 1907, the American philosophical treatment of the problem of evil was restricted largely to queries from postCalvinist pulpits and explications from Transcendentalist thinkers. The most important philosophic treatise dealing in detail with the dimensions of the concern was Henry James Sr.'s *The Problem of Evil* (1885). However, James

Sr. was saturated with the Calvinist notion of original sin; and as much as he tried to rid man of guilt, he was unsuccessful in coming to terms with the paradoxes of what Cotton Mather had termed "God's inscrutable will." It remained for Emerson to declare in the "Divinity School Address" (1838) that "Good is positive. Evil is merely privative, not absolute: it is like cold, which is the privation of heat. All evil is so much death or non-entity. Benevolence is absolute and real." Hence, Pope's classic need to "justify the ways of God to man," a conscious echo of Milton's attempt at vindication, becomes for Emerson an exercise in rhetoric and simple faith. The notion of progress had manifested itself in such a way that concern for real human suffering changed to a justification for man's divinity. The nineteenth century focused on trying to make evil intelligible and minimize its importance; and Emerson was the personification of the optimism regarding man's potential perfection. Emerson's Adam was not banned from the Garden of Eden, and the Fall of Man was relegated to the realm of myth.

For Frost, the traditional dilemma of the problem of evil remains intact: how can an omniscient, omnipotent and beneficent deity allow the presence of evil in the world? The "optimistic" answer, formulated by Plato, perpetuated by Augustine, revitalized by Descartes and Leibniz, reveals a decided tendency to underplay the human suffering that results from evil. In so doing, it exalts the notion of final cause by arguing in one of two ways: either (1) evil is essentially privative, i.e., it has no positive existence, or (2) good is ultimately dependent on the necessity of evil. The latter argument, far from asserting the unreality of evil, opts for the need of human grief. The only logical implication of Leibniz's claim that "this is the best of all possible worlds" is that any other metaphysically conceivable universe would be worse. The optimists' fundamental premise is that the perfection of the whole not merely depends upon but also consists in the existence of every possible degree of imperfection in the parts. A humorous echo of this explicit reasoning occurs in Frost's poem from *In the Clearing* (1962) entitled "Quandary":

> Never have I been sad or glad
> That there was such a thing as bad.
> There had to be, I understood,

> For there to have been any good.
> It was by having been contrasted
> That good and bad so long had lasted. (p. 467)

But the humor becomes ironic sarcasm when Frost satirizes prayer in a couplet from "Cluster of Faith" (*In the Clearing*):

> Forgive, O Lord, my little jokes on Thee
> And I'll forgive Thy great big one on me. (p. 428)

For Frost, of course, man is in no position to "forgive." He must "bow and accept" whatever evils are visited upon him. When he does attempt to question God's judgments, he generally finds them to be capricious and often whimsical. The arbitrariness of Frost's deity occasions a typically twentieth-century fear that no guiding power instigates and preserves order. Faced with "an arbitrary God," one whose makeshift throne collapses, man must retreat from the terrifying forces of confusion and order his own existence.

For William James, recognition of the lack of perfection in the universe initiates the need for philosophical and religious inquiry. He answers the question "why do they [philosophers]philosophize at all?" by saying that "the existence of evil forms a 'mystery'—a problem."[1] Thus, philosophy owes its being to human distress, to the confronting of thought with difficulties. Although on the surface James tries to maintain that a "golden mean" separates "inane optimism" and "stupid pessimism"[2] he is tortured by thoughts of suicide and death during the winter of 1865. Like the man in Frost's "Old Man's Winter Night," James tries to limit the power of evil by means of a whistling-in-the-dark kind of assurance.[3]

James's refusal to accept the optimistic premise that evil is, by definition, merely privative, marks the empirical nature of his examination. Like Frost, who recognizes that Emerson's concept is "too Platonic" (*SP*, p. 118), James cannot bring himself to gloss over the problem of human suffering. He formulates his solution to the problem of evil in pragmatic fashion, and the result is a belief in a God who is finite not only in power but also in wisdom. The god James describes is neither perfect nor infinite; rather, he is simply a hypothesized answer to man's moral and practical wants. James's "Power not ourselves" parallels the "non-human otherness" which manifests itself through nature in Frost's poems, although Frost's God is more whimsical and more vindictive.

Frost's "original response" to James's insights regarding evil marks him as a poet who is intellectually, if not emotionally, at home with pragmatic thought. The genteel view of the wise old crackerbarrel farmer who writes verse about New England landscapes becomes anachronistic when the reader is confronted by lyrics which rival Gerard Manley Hopkins' terror sonnets in intensity of despair and fear. Emersonian design becomes for Frost a "design of darkness," appalling as much for the answers it holds back as for those it offers. The God of the Christian tradition is no longer the dominant power. Nor can Frost fall back on the amorphous assurances of the Oversoul or Nature for his spiritual and psychological sustenance. Instead, Frost feels man must make his own order if he is to avoid the chaos of a mountain avalanche ("One Step Backward Taken"), a threatening storm ("An Old Man's Winter Night," "Bereft," "Once by the Pacific") or the frightening implications of "progress" ("The Egg and the Machine"). For the poet, confrontation with the sense of futility in human effort can, at worst, lead to insanity ("A Servant to Servants") or death ("Out, Out—"); at best, confusion can be stayed for brief periods only ("Directive").

Unlike Emerson, Frost sees nature's "laws" as vague manifestations of a power both fierce and inexplicable. The "something there is" that is responsible for crumbling man's artificial forms, whether walls or poems, is never fully defined. The ambiguity of nature's character contributes to the feeling of terror occasioned by a poem like "Design" in which Frost is concerned chiefly with depicting the malevolent qualities of a reigning force which disallows comprehension. A close examination of the poem reveals Frost's intellectual kinship with James.

The poet figure of "Design" is aware of the tragic implications of Darwin's theory of natural selection; thus he is forced to opt for a Jamesian explanation of man's place in the natural scheme. The pragmatic justification of man's concern for nature is that he cannot divorce himself from its effects. Ironically, this is the same justification which serves as a basic premise in Emerson's work. A comparison of "Design" and "The Rhodora" illustrates the distance between the two poets' conceptions of man's place in the workings of nature.

In "Design," a poem which Randall Jarrell says "makes Pascal's 'eternal silence of those infinite spaces' seem like the hush between the movements of a cantata" (p. 91), the speaker begins conversationally. There is a tone of ambivalence about the situation, a tone supported by the poet figure's use of ironic humor and images. He informs the reader merely of the facts he confronts, offering no judgment about the significance of what he sees:

> I found a dimpled spider, fat and white,
> On a white heal-all, holding up a moth
> Like a white piece of rigid satin cloth—(p. 302)

Emerson's poem begins on much the same note:

> In May, when sea winds pierced our solitudes,
> I found the fresh rhodora in the woods,
> Spreading its leafless blooms in a damp nook. . . .

But the images in Frost's poem quickly begin to take on an ominous significance. They become "Assorted characters of death and blight," suggesting a bizarre and unnatural situation. The heal-all is an innocent enough backdrop for the drama until the reader realizes it is discolored. The spider, an ancient symbol of death, becomes an active agent of destruction. It seems to flaunt the remains of its prey. The intended humor of the childlike images is sustained when all become a kind of halloween potpourri. They are:

> Mixed ready to begin the morning right,
> Like the ingredients of a witches' broth—
> A snow-drop spider, a flower like a froth,
> And dead wings carried like a paper kite.

All these natural elements are mingled in a supernatural "rite." Demonic and malevolent forces (witches) are creating a terrifying mixture from innocent ingredients, and fear is now the predominant tone. The final sestet assures the reader that design, if it indeed controls the universe, is nothing from which to gain assurance. If anything, it is as frightening as the idea of chaos itself. The poem concludes:

What had that flower to do with being white,
The wayside blue and innocent heal-all?
What brought the kindred spider to that height,
Then steered the white moth thither in the night?
What but design of darkness to appall? —
If design govern in a thing so small.

In "Design" Frost offers no real alternative to pessimism. Superficially, one can argue that he hints at the possibility of potential order, but the equivocation of the final couplet undermines such a stance. In fact, the reader is left with no choice at all; he is (like the moth) faced, purely and simply, with a design of darkness. Ironically, the disorder is brought about in part by a concentrated attempt at too much form. The rigidity of the syllogistic structure is a poetic device used to point up the inevitability of the final question. But, for all the form, the speaker's terror cannot be avoided. The simple logic of the poem is too clearcut to allow for an optimistic conclusion. Schematically, one can see that if the "if/then" proposition means anything at all, it is that design (D) and design of darkness (chaos (C)) are one and the same. The argument of the poem—if design governs, then design of darkness (chaos) governs—can be schematized as $D \supset C$. Applying the rule of contraposition, the conclusion reduces to $-C \supset -D$. Therefore, if it is *not* the case that chaos rules, then it is also *not* the case that design rules.

The argument in "Design" is part and parcel of the Jamesian dilemma in the opening pages of "What Pragmatism Means" (1907) when the philosopher deals with the "metaphysical" dispute about a squirrel and a tree. James solves the problem by use of the "pragmatic method" of interpreting each notion by tracing its respective practical consequences. In the case of the squirrel and the tree, James sees no real metaphysical problem because each man is arguing for practically the same thing. Likewise with the conclusion of "Design." The basic possible alternatives implied by the logic of the poem have essentially the same consequences for man's existence.

In "Some Metaphysical Problems" James deals explicitly with the cognate problems of God and the "question of design in nature." James first points out that: "God's existence has from time imme-

morial been held to be proved by certain natural facts. Many facts
appear as if expressly designed in view of one another. Thus the
woodpecker's bill, tongue, feet, tail, etc., fit him wondrously for a
world of trees, with grubs hid in their bark to feed upon. . . . Such
mutual fitting of things diverse in origin argued design, it was held;
and the designer was always treated as a man-loving deity."[4]

Frost also begins with natural facts, even going so far as to employ
the "stalking" motif, though he substitutes a spider for James's woodpecker and a moth for the philosopher's grub.

James's "diabolical designer" suggests a deity divested of traditional Christian characteristics, void of benevolent aspects: "The
designer is no longer the old man-like deity. His designs have grown
so vast as to be incomprehensive to us humans. The *what* of them so
overwhelms us that to establish the mere *that* of a designer for them
becomes of very little consequence in comparison. We can with
difficulty comprehend the *character* of a cosmic mind whose purposes are fully revealed by the strange mixture of goods and evils
that we find in this actual world's particulars. Or rather we cannot
by any possibility comprehend it. The mere word 'design' by itself
has no consequences and explains nothing. It is the most barren of
principles" (p. 49). According to James, the question of *whether*
there is design becomes idle because, no matter what it produces,
the means must necessarily be adequate; in James's words, the means
"must have been *fitted to that production*" (p. 51). Consequently,
the argument from fitness to design applies always, "for the parts of
things must always make some definite resultant, be it chaotic or
harmonious" (p. 51). James's "design," which "explains nothing,"
offers a "strange mixture of goods and evils." This mixture translates
into Frost's "Assorted characters of death and blight/Mixed ready
to begin the morning right."

On the pragmatic plane, the abstract word *design* becomes mean-
ingless because, in James's words, "it carries no consequences, it does
no execution. *What* design? And *what* designer? are the only serious
questions" (p. 52). Likewise for Frost the important consideration
is of the *kind* of cosmic force which rules. But the poet's vision is
more pessimistic even than James's conclusion. Whereas Frost's
alternatives are "design of darkness" or no design at all, James

chooses to juxtapose "blind force" with "seeing force." The latter is a "term of promise," says James, capable of instilling the feelings of calm and order. That there is no such promise in "Design" evidences the poet's more skeptical leanings.

One Frost sonnet which rivals "Design" for its suggestion of terror is "Once by the Pacific." As in "Design" there is the suggestion of some malevolence directed against man, a power closely resembling in degree of intensity the vengeful Puritan God. Unlike the Puritan deity, however, the force which acts against man in "Once by the Pacific" acts directly through nature. Nature is seen not as chaotic otherness which runs by random energy; rather, it is characterized by malicious intention. The speaker is convinced throughout the poem that, along with the rest of mankind, he is the object of an attack by an incomparably powerful force. He resembles the figure in "An Old Man's Winter Night" who must stand alone with only the pitiful defense of "barrels round him—at a loss." Too, like the "out-of-doors" that peers in on the old man, the force in "Once by the Pacific" is personified: it is given eyes and hair; it sees and thinks. Having given human characteristics to nature, the speaker attempts to ward off the terror by building up defenses through the use of equivocation (employing phrases like "as if" and "could not tell"), to avoid facing what he knows is there.

> You could not tell, and yet it looked as if
> The shore was lucky in being backed by cliff,
> The cliff in being backed by continent;
> It looked as if a night of dark intent
> Was coming, and not only a night, an age.
> Someone had better be prepared for rage.
> There would be more than ocean-water broken
> Before God's last *Put out the Light* was spoken. (p. 250)

The attempt at humor in the final line purposely fails, just as all the equivocating has failed in the preceding lines. The cliff and even the continent become puny "momentary stays" for the speaker, the more terrifying because of the suggested duration—not only a night, but an age.

Another theodicy poem, "Bereft," opens on much the same note as "Once by the Pacific." The poet figure is standing in his doorway listening to the roaring wind and gazing at the "frothy" shore. The use of *frothy* suggests madness and invites comparison with the flower in "Design." The questioning stance points up the poet figure's doubts concerning his safety:

> Where had I heard this wind before
> Change like this to a deeper roar?
> What would it take my standing there for,
> Holding open a restive door,
> Looking down hill to a frothy shore?

The traditional "stays," summer and day, are no longer present to offer strength to combat his fear; hence, he begins to view the natural elements as antagonisic forces.

> Summer was past and day was past.
> Somber clouds in the west were massed.
> Out in the porch's sagging floor
> Leaves got up in a coil and hissed,
> Blindly struck at my knee and missed.

The fear is heightened with the poet's realization that the satanic (snake image) enemies are not organized against him, but "blindly" strike:

> Something sinister in the tone
> Told me my secret must be known:
> Word I was in the house alone
> Somehow must have gotten abroad,
> Word I was in my life alone,
> Word I had no one left but God. (p. 251)

The dimensions of the poem's theme begin to expand, from "house," through "life" to "God." When the poet figure senses his fear of meeting with God, his isolation suddenly seems preferable. Whereas in "Once by the Pacific" the speaker's primary defense is his ability to step back from the brute force which threatens mankind, the poet figure of "Bereft" must face God directly. One recognizes a particularly dark side of Frost's vision: the natural world seldom forestalls, and often accompanies, the most frightful and immediate circumstance of metaphysical fear. It is the unavoidable confrontation with God that causes Frost's personae to lose faith in the traditional attributes of the Christian deity.

Frost's fear is not of the deity of Jonathan Edwards and those Puritans who expected that they were, and should be, sinners in the hands of an angry God. Rather, Frost's fear is of a force whose power is uncontrolled, the "arbitrary God" who surfaces in *Steeple Bush* (1947) to offer success or failure without regard for reason. In "The Fear of God" the poet warns:

> If you should rise from Nowhere up to Somewhere,
> From being No one up to being Someone,
> Be sure to keep repeating to yourself
> You owe it to an arbitrary god
> Whose mercy to you rather than to others
> Won't bear too critical examination.
> Stay unassuming. (p. 385)

The whimsicality and arbitrariness which characterize Frost's "god" are the primary reasons for the fear which ensues. The spiritual longing in a poem like "Revelation" becomes a kind of bravado. The assurance that those who "play/At hide-and-seek," including God, must "speak and tell us where they are" (p. 19) evolves into the fear that such revelation might not occur and that if it does occur, it is nothing to be welcomed.

Frost's religious concern reaches its climax in *A Masque of Reason* and *A Masque of Mercy*. Although only a limited amount of critical material exists on the *Masques*, they are undoubtedly important focal points for the study of Frost's thought. *A Masque of Reason* is an ironic and skeptical farce of the story of Job. Frost updates the drama, having it take place in a quasimodern world in which the characteristics of God are altered to make him fit into a world where his image has been debased. The majesty of Yahweh's throne of judgment becomes "a plywood flat, prefabricated,/That God pulls lightly upright on its hinges/And stands beside, supporting it in place" (p. 474). The artist in Frost's Job "cries out for design" (p. 482), but God is incapable of or unwilling to explain the "reason" behind events. Job's initial hope that he can "lay aside/My varying opinion of myself/And come to rest on an official verdict" (p. 474) is shattered. He soon learns that he has been an active agent in the establishment of the principle of cosmic injustice. God even thanks man for his cooperation:

> Yes, by and by. But first a large matter.
> I've had you on my mind a thousand years
> To thank you someday for the way you helped me
> Establish once for all the principle
> There's no connection man can reason out
> Between his just deserts and what he gets. (p. 475)

The pun on "deserts" in the last line suggests a number of possible meanings. Literally, of course, Job and Thyatira are in a desert. Presumably Frost wants to make it clear that to a large degree man's existence is religiously arid. Their oasis, like the one called up by the narrator in "The Black Cottage," seems confining, as if it were a kind of prison.

Another meaning for "desert" is abandonment. Job and his wife have been left for "a thousand years" to ponder the metaphysical questions which are never answered. They are like those persons in "The Trial by Existence" who are denied the memory of choice. For this, God is apologetic:

> I have to wait for words like anyone.
> Too long I've owed you this apology
> For the apparently unmeaning sorrow
> You were afflicted with in those old days.
> But it was of the essence of the trial
> You shouldn't understand it at the time.
> It had to seem unmeaning to have meaning.

But the possibility of metaphysical meaning immediately evaporates as God confesses his own lack of freedom:

> My thanks are to you for releasing me
> From moral bondage to the human race.
> The only free will there at first was man's,
> Who could do good or evil as he chose.
> I had no choice but I must follow him
> With forfeits and rewards he understood—
> Unless I liked to suffer loss of worship. (pp. 475–76)

The "reason-hungry mortals" (p. 478) continue to question the motives of Frost's all-too-human deity, however, and they meet with more disappointing revelations. They learn that there is not only an absence of universal, Platonic reason, but also a lack of momentary intellectual stays. Thyatira vainly attempts to force God to offer the limited "scraps of palliative reason":

> Of course, in the abstract high singular
> There isn't any universal reason;
> And no one but a man would think there was.
> You don't catch women trying to be Plato.
> Still there must be lots of unsystematic
> Stray scraps of palliative reason
> It wouldn't hurt You to vouchsafe the faithful. (p. 478)

"The faithful," however, are made to beg for answers from a God whose "forte is truth,/Or metaphysics" (p. 480). They want his ways justified to them, even if the justification is weak and unconvincing. Job begs for reason while flatly refusing to believe in God's arbitrary nature; he is "reduced/To asking flatly for the reason—outright" (p. 483):

> Because I let You off
> From telling me Your reason, don't assume
> I thought You had none. Somewhere back
> I knew You had one.
>
> . . . .
>
> You'd be the last to want me to believe
> All Your effects were merely lucky blunders.
> That would be unbelief and atheism.
> The artist in me cries out for design. (p. 482)

All of Job's and Thyatira's begging is useless. Like James when he calls Leibniz's *Theodicy* "superficiality incarnate," Job becomes "sick of the whole artificial puzzle" (p. 484). God's laughter causes him to sense the "nothingness" which underlies human experience; he realizes that "The chances are when there's so much pretense/Of metaphysical profundity/The obscurity's a fraud to cover nothing." And even the faint suggestion of knowledge in a poem like "For Once, Then, Something" is replaced by skepticism:

> Get down into things,
> It will be found there's no more given there
> Than on the surface. If there ever was,
> The crypt was long since rifled by the Greeks.
> We don't know where we are, or who we are.
> We don't know one another; don't know You;
> Don't know what time it is. We don't know, don't we? (p. 483)

Job and Thyatira never gain the knowledge they attempt to find. Like the poet figure of "Design," they are forced to recognize the possibility of arbitrariness. The characters in *A Masque of Mercy*, however, unlike those in *A Masque of Reason*, find that they can at least begin to deal with such confusion—the blow of uncertainty can be softened. As Keeper says:

> . . . I can see that the uncertainty
> In which we act is a severity,
> A cruelty, amounting to injustice
> That nothing but God's mercy can assuage. (p. 520)

Although Paul still feels the need "to stay afraid deep in our souls" (p. 520), he recognizes too that injustice can be made just by mercy.

The fearful white imagery of "Design" is partially offset by the affirmation of *A Masque of Mercy* where "God's white light" is "refracted into colors" (p. 516). Still, however, the pilgrims have no assurance that they see the gate of salvation. They *want* to see it and sometimes they *think* they do, but it is never certain. Jonah says:

> You ask if I see yonder shining gate,
> And I reply I almost think I do,
> Beyond this great door you have locked against me,
> Beyond the storm, beyond the universe. (p. 513)

Like the man who *thinks* he sees "something" from the window of a train crossing Utah, and like the poet figure who *thinks* he discerns "something" "beyond" the surface of the well water, the characters of the *Masques* must content themselves with faith rather than fact. They are left with "an arbitrary god/Whose mercy to . . . [them] rather than to others/Won't bear too critical examination." Frost's advice still is to "Stay unassuming" ("The Fear of God," p. 385).

Ultimately, Frost's theodicy revolves around the recognition of both human and divine finitude. Unlike Emerson, Frost cannot accept the doctrine of a fortunate fall. Rather, his is, with James's, the realization that man must learn to accept his epistemological, religious and metaphysical limitations if he is to survive in a universe which grants him little in the way of certainty. Perhaps his most succinct poetic account of this realization is a poem from *New Hampshire* (1923) entitled "Nothing Gold Can Stay":

> Nature's first green is gold,
> Her hardest hue to hold.
> Her early leaf's a flower;
> But only so an hour.
> Then leaf subsides to leaf.
> So Eden sank to grief,
> So dawn goes down to day.
> Nothing gold can stay. (pp. 222–23)

For Frost, the Platonic "golden age" is gone. His Eden sinks to grief and fails to regain its Emersonian innocence. Consequently, man's happiness is brief, often illusory, and his glimpses at religious truth are short lived. Left alone with nature, Frost's personae are forced to seek shelter from "outer" weather. But left alone with "an arbitrary god," where shelter is not to be had, they are faced with chaos. There is no appeal to reason or intuition, to a covenant of works or one of grace, because Frost recognizes that religion "is merely consolation for what we don't know" (*SP*, p. 62). As such, it is, like nature, "a diminished thing"—"that other fall we name the fall." The pragmatic dimensions of Frost's theodicy poems indicate the poet's skeptical orientation toward traditional religious concerns. The significance of the poet's vision stems not only from the power of the individual poems but also from the realization that Frost's intellectual preoccupations parallel those of the most important figure in American philosophy, William James. Thus, Frost's canon deserves a high rank as a sophisticated document in modern intellectual history.

Notes to *Frost's Theodicy: "Word I Had No One Left But God"*
   by THOMAS McCLANAHAN

   1. William James, "The Sentiment of Rationality," *Collected Essays* (New York: Longmans, Green and Co., 1920), p. 25.

2. William James, *The Letters of William James*, ed. Henry James (Boston: Atlantic Monthly Press, 1920), p. 7.

3. Ibid., pp. 127–8.

4. William James, "Some Metaphysical Problems," *Pragmatism and Other Essays* (New York: Washington Square Press, 1963), p. 50. Following page numbers in the text are to this volume.

METHOD
AND THEORY

While this section is a miscellany, it is one of the most interesting in this collection. Even prosody deals with Frost's theory as well as with his technique. David Wyatt concentrates on "The Road Not Taken" both to reply to the famous strictures of Yvor Winters and to discuss a major aspect of Frost's technique, not merely in the poem discussed but also in the poetry. He finds that "The Figure a Poem Makes" presents an aesthetic substantiating his discussion of the relationship of poet, reader and poem. The concept of surprise is yet another insight into Frost—as both man and poet—and yet another indication that Frost must be studied—and studied.

David Miller takes up again the question of Frost's relationship to the English Romantics. (His remarks about play are coincidental compared with those essays deliberately treating the subject.) His thesis sets his paper apart from most of the other essays, yet the distinction he makes in stating his intent has a revealing parallel in the distinction Thomas McClanahan makes in discussing Frost's relationship to Emerson and James. The essay is, however, mainly concerned with aesthetics, both in the word's original meaning as perception and in its present meaning as a discipline in philosophy. The concept of surmise, central to the essay, refers to the method of artistic creativity. The essay concludes that Frost is distinctly unlike the earlier lyricists in his view of the poetic imagination and of the creative process.

Richard Reed's discussion of the animals in Frost's poetry shows a change in Frost's view, which Professor Reed notes at the end of his brief discussion of *A Boy's Will*. The somewhat romantic and of course youthful poet who glossed his first volume apparently began to find animals less than the live properties of a harmonious pastoral

127

nature. Of particular interest is the idea that the changed view of animals indicates a changed view of nature—of man's relationship to nature—a theme that would dominate Frost's poetry, without—as more and more studies indicate—making him a nature poet. And as Professor Reed notes pertinently, this changed view of animals and nature shows in one way Frost's move from being a poet of the nineteenth century to one of the twentieth.

Stearns Morse discusses the intriguing "Subverted Flower" that, as he says, appears unFrostian in seeming to deal openly with sex. Suggesting that autobiography can hardly account for the poem—at least in referring only to Frost's courtship—the essay learnedly moves among various aspects of love and concludes with the suggestion that the poem is to some extent explained by its placement among other poems in the volume. The essay not only provokes speculation about other possibilities of poems dealing with sexual love but also about the care Frost took in arranging his poems in the various separate volumes.

Karen Rood's essay (like a portion of Walton Beacham's in PLAY) concentrates on craftsmanship. Yet, as indicated by the title, "Robert Frost's 'Sentence Sounds': Wildness Opposing the Sonnet Form," the study of technique is involved not only with content but also with poetic theory and poetic accomplishment. Some of the author's observations should also be compared with those of David Wyatt. Both critics are, among other things, by implication using aesthetics to get tentatively at metaphysics in Frost's work and ultimately at the "real" Frost.

Patricia Wallace has fascinating observations about the relationship between Frost's women and the subtleties of his methods. The introduction shows the difficulties of explaining the intricacies of a man who may have done a great deal of artistic fooling by no means fully explored. The study of Frost's women goes far beyond the realistic to examine an aesthetic, found in "The Hill Wife," the "Two Witches" and "Paul's Wife."

J. T.

Choosing in Frost

DAVID M. WYATT

$\mathcal{S}$URPRISE: Robert Frost writes continually of it. As a disposition toward life it becomes a project for poetry, a way of moving through both. Even metaphor emerges as something come upon unawares. With a tenor firmly in mind, Frost can happen at any time upon a hidden vehicle. The pleasure is in falling for something one didn't expect to find, in a place one didn't know one was: "the pleasure of ulteriority."[1] So in the act of composition the poet remains absent from himself, waiting to surprise himself as he emerges onto the landing from which the climb into and out of the poem might be viewed. His "intention" is pleasantly ulterior, of "a particular mood that won't be satisfied with anything less than its own fulfillment. But it is not yet a thought concerned with what becomes it. One thing to know it by: it shrinks shyly from anticipatory expression. . . . A poem is the emotion of having a thought while the reader waits a little anxiously for the success of dawn." Unlike his forerunner Thoreau, Frost does not wish to prepare his own way, "To anticipate, not the sunrise and the dawn merely, but, if possible, Nature herself!" This is Frost's greatest fear: that he might anticipate himself and the unforeseen destiny of his poem.

Frost's anxiety that he might sacrifice wonder to order becomes his motive for metaphor. To preserve the "Order of Wonder" he follows a radically Emersonian impulse: "If you desire to arrest attention, to surprise, do not give me facts in the order of cause and effect, but drop one or two links in the chain, & give me with a cause, an effect two or three times removed."[2] Nowhere in Frost is the tension between surprise and anticipation, wayward experience and the form into which it is cast or forecast, more acute than in "The Road Not Taken":

> Two roads diverged in a yellow wood,
> And sorry I could not travel both
> And be one traveler, long I stood

And looked down one as far as I could
To where it bent in the undergrowth;

Then took the other, as just as fair,
And having perhaps the better claim,
Because it was grassy and wanted wear;
Though as for that, the passing there
Had worn them really about the same,

And both that morning equally lay
In leaves no step had trodden black.
Oh, I kept the first for another day!
Yet knowing how way leads on to way,
I doubted if I should ever come back.

I shall be telling this with a sigh
Somewhere ages and ages hence:
Two roads diverged in a wood, and I—
I took the one less traveled by,
And that has made all the difference.

Reuben Brower advances the traditional reading of this poem: "Although 'The Road Not Taken' lends itself like some of Shakespeare's sonnets to over-easy identifications with the youthful self of the poet or the reader, it is still a powerful image of the choice of life."[3] I will argue that the much crankier response of Yvor Winters to the poem as written by "a man whom one might well call a spiritual drifter"[4] more accurately describes it. In surrendering to the "rightness of impulse," Frost is seen by Winters as conferring the active role in the poem upon the reader, who must assume the "burden of critical intelligence which ought to be borne by the poet." This is true, although it need not be lamented. Nor need we cringe when Winters pejoratively labels such impulses "Emersonian." The critic reveals his deep grasp of the Emersonian tradition even in the very act of trying to belittle it. For all of his unwillingness to honor it, Winters has correctly identified this tradition, and we should pause to outline its essential dimensions before going on to read Frost's central poetic extension of it.

The full force of Winters's objections to Frost has never been met. His attack begins to surface in *Maule's Curse* and adumbrates the later complaints—by Cowley, Pearce, Nitchie—that Frost fails of being a "serious" or a committed writer. While it took Winters twenty years to accuse Frost openly of being a spiritual drifter, any reader of *Maule's Curse* could have predicted that Frost would one day join Hawthorne, Emerson, Melville and James in the "History of American Obscurantism." Winters's argument is historical; his theme is the crisis of the will. By "obscurantism" he really means the abandonment, by major American writers, of belief in a world of clear moral options. He sees this problem devolving inevitably from a conflict between Puritan theory and practice: "They may have denied the freedom of the will and the efficaciousness of good works by lip, but by habit, and without really grasping the fact, they believed in them and acted upon them."[5] While Perry Miller has given this conflict its most careful exposition, Winters can lay claim to having first lamented it as afflicting, through numerous transformations, our greatest literature. And he was also inspired in locating Emerson as the crucial vortex in which this conflicted experience of the will was concentrated and passed on: "In Emerson the exercise of the will is as active as ever, and his moral judgments are frequently made with force and with accuracy; but his central doctrine is that of submission to emotion, which for the pantheist is a kind of divine instigation: an inadmissable doctrine, for it eliminates at a stroke both choice and the values that serve as a basis for choice, it substitutes for a doctrine of values a doctrine of equivalence, thus rendering man an automaton and paralyzing all genuine action, so that Emerson's acceptable acts of expression are accidental poems or epigrams drawing their only nutriment from the fringe or from beyond the fringe of his doctrine." In the tradition flowing through Emerson attention shifts from the free exercise of choice to the difficulty of ever approaching it. "Maule's Curse" is to feel the will stimulated to no *end*.

Winters is more convincing as a literary critic than an historian of ideas. Yet however questionable his analysis of the origins of "Maule's Curse," he does prove that choosing rarely happens in the works he reads. Unfortunately the violence of Winters's judgments has obscured the accuracy of his descriptions. He complained of his book that it "was attacked . . . because it found obscurity where the reviewer found none." Yet the book very likely aroused more resistance because of its method and tone than its theme. On every page one encounters a sensibility unwilling to accept the demands this literature makes upon us. When Winters claims that "a work of art, like each detail comprising it, is by definition a judgment," he advances a definition none of these artists would recognize. They are by Winters's own persuasive description unwilling or unable to embody "judgment." Yet Winters's way of reading sheds just that negative light upon this literature which illuminates what it decidedly is not. Our debate with him should not be over whether such a tradition exists, but how to value it. These writers were not victims of a failure of nerve. They were intent upon creating a new way of being in the world. One thing they appear to have agreed upon: selves are not shaped through traditional acts of volition. So when Winters eventually includes Frost within this line and says of "The Road Not Taken" that it deals with "what in the hands of a more serious writer one could call the theme of moral choice,"[6] he proves himself of Frost's party without knowing it. This is just the response Frost's poem should encourage: the realization that the choice the poem appears to promise is not actually delivered. Winters writes as if he were Frost's "Escapist—Never," that aggressive self-seeker for whom "All is an interminable chain of longing." The curse of his morality is to find identity the more receding as it is the more ambitiously sought. Frost inducts us into a contrary discipline: in his poetry identity is not pursued, but allowed spontaneously to emerge. He questions the narrow fiction that selves are formed only in the clash between the will and the world. People are, no more than poems, preconceived. Frost redeems "Maule's Curse" by initiating us into a world where the wonder of order has been superseded by the order of wonder.

The title of "The Road Not Taken" promises an anatomy of choice. We look forward to further dealings with a way not abandoned to. Most readers fail to relinquish this initial expectation, reading the poem as if it were of a fateful taking and a not-taking. The first stanza encourages this reaction by giving us the "facts in the order of cause and effect." We start by coming upon "two roads" diverging. As a literary situation, this could hardly be less original. As a moment bearing the burden of choice, the Western imagination knows few more compelling. The lines begin therefore to generate an anxiety so deep as to be obscure. Precisely because this possible divergence confounds so broad a range of fears, so many modes of loss, we are not sorry to linger "long" with the speaker at the fork. The necessary process of examination leading up to choice seems well underway as we complete the first stanza. At least "one" road has been "looked down" as far as we can look. Thus the semicolon after "undergrowth" prepares us for a turn of the head, a further gazing down the other road:

> Then took the other, as just as fair,
> And having perhaps the better claim,
> Because it was grassy and wanted wear;
> Though as for that, the passing there
> Had worn them really about the same,
>
> And both that morning equally lay
> In leaves no step had trodden black.

These seven lines complete the first sentence in the poem, though in ways wholly unexpected. Just as we begin to get lost in the undergrowth, the poem asks us to make a stylistic and experiential leap. That we expect merely a turn measures the surprising motion made between the two stanzas. For surely with "Then took the other" we are given an "effect two or three times removed" from a "cause." We seem to have jumped from stanza one to stanza three. The moment of choosing has been overshot—stanza two is missing—and we are already on the road. Why do so many readers fail to experience this surprise? What devices work to mask it? The most profound answer evades literary analysis, since the device is deeply hidden within each reader. The poem triggers an anxiety we all feel in separating ourselves from our first source, in growing into division and maturity. Faced squarely with the crisis of separation, avoidance may be preferable to choice. In the moment of decision we leave as much behind as we find to carry with us. So the poem grants an impression of such a moment while actually shielding us from a true experience of it. By helping us to avoid the threat of self-division, Frost allows us to preserve an illusion of wholeness and eases us through a boundary situation in which it is barely possible to gather the reasons for moving:

[handwritten marginal notes: "it really is a choice / not fateful" "joking"; "did he want to choose?"]

> Wherever I am
> I am what is missing.
>
> . . . .
>
> We all have reasons
> for moving.
> I move
> to keep things whole.[7]

Whatever our reasons for moving, we need not balk at a more practical analysis of how Frost makes us pass on. To describe this strategy an elaborate formula might be advanced: in lines six through twelve, the syntax of deliberation masks the rhetoric of equivocation. How different, really, are the two roads? Having missed our chance to examine them both, can we justify our course on the run?

We first find ourselves taking a rather undifferentiated road: "the other." Backing up, it seems as if "then took" carries a greater portentousness than "the other" can satisfy. This opening phrase certainly preserves our ignorance as to how or why we came here. The next equates both roads: this other is taken "as just as fair." But how are we to take the first "as"? Does it have the force of *since* or *though*? That is, does it signal a choice made, or a chance taken? The question passes as fleetingly through our minds as we do through the stanza, where we move on to a qualification in favor of the taken road. "Perhaps" scarcely works as self-congratulation, so the speaker goes on to shore it up with a "because." Hard evidence of "difference" seems to be at hand, if not underfoot. The frivolity of the claim—that being "grassy" and wanting "wear" are the necessary attractions of a road—may be overlooked in our relief at being granted some reasons for moving. But even this shaky rationale gets trodden down by a counter-qualification. "Though" in line nine initiates, for the attentive reader, the most disturbing revelation in the poem: as for "passing," it has "worn them really about the same." All the stanza's carefully measured phrases and counter-phrases finally contain no more capacity to differentiate the two roads than this.

The opening two lines of stanza three ask us to continue the process of equating the two roads through the agency of the poem's climactic, if often overlooked adverb—"equally." By the time we reach the first period in the poem, the two roads have registered themselves as the same and different, worn and untrodden. Frost has gone a good distance toward making "both" seem like "one" while preserving for the overeager reader the illusion of being on a unique course. The poem presents two roads through itself: one, the wide road toward easeful differentiation; the other, the straight and narrow way toward discovery of its choice as a hoax. Frost continues to play more upon our desire to master options than upon any reluctance to force our will onto our way. The exclamation in "Oh, I kept the first for another day!" sustains the illusion about some loss to regret. The resigned, forward-looking tone of the next two lines asks us to join in a manly acceptance of the consequence of choice. But the speaker undermines himself by being too knowing. He describes a choice becoming a fate. The "way" is to become what "leads" him. This fate might be the source of some concern had it not been his from the beginning of the poem. If "way leads on to way," doubts lead back to the self. The process of rationalization culminates in "I doubted if I should ever come back." Here we stumble over an extra half-foot; too many "I's" figure in this line. The speaker crams in an extra one at the beginning to throw off the rhythm of our stride through the poem. Nowhere do the anxieties of self-division, of being "one" and yet "both," surface more stubbornly than in this doubtful line, overfull of the reiterated singular self.

From a spurious resignation to the future in the third stanza we move in the fourth to a realization of that time. The burden of self-consciousness has become so great for the speaker that he projects the present into the future to think about it as the past. The main difficulty for the reader is in making out what "this" is. Does it refer to the choice (not made) or to the poem itself (still being said and read)? "This" usually testifies to the presence of a thing just as "that" does to its absence. Frost is fond of creating a sense of presentness by using *this*. But here the speaker is only present to his poem—not to the lived experience upon which it is based. He has already worked up this interval as a tale to tell, and one with a rhyme scheme so intricate as to challenge any notion that the end of each line remains unforeseen. "This" reduces and abstracts the poet's experience into portable content. As an abstraction, it distances us even further from the concrete immediacy of a moment of choice. It begs the question, as has the entire poem, of what did happen at the fork, while leaving the speaker (and willing auditors) free to point a moral and adorn a tale.

Thus the voice speaking the last stanza grows increasingly elegiac. It recapitulates the poem's first line—it recommences to tell the tale—with a revealing distortion. "Two roads diverged in a wood, and I—" introduces a momentary stay into a process where none had been before. As we—now become a future audience—hover at the end of the line in wait for the choice to come, we get "I." Can we have expected anything else? Here "I" literally gets split from "I" to suggest the inevitable self-division consequent upon the failure to acknowledge the impossibility of choice. While the speaker misleads his listeners with "I took the one less traveled by," the attentive reader remembers that a moment of choosing between more and less never existed. This poem not only refuses to grant the time in which to choose; it presents a world void of difference which we might contemplate in such an interval. The crucial deception at the end turns upon "and." While we can understand that from a future vantage point any speaker might perceive "all the difference" between his past and his present self, we cannot agree that this particular difference flows from a fateful taking. The fictions of order a self projects back onto experience, even while that experience is still to be completed, here supplant the moment it actually lived. Overcome by what he has missed, the speaker tries to recreate the moment of choice and a world of alternatives "ages and ages" later. He has failed his trial by existence, but the watchful reader will not be unaware that the pure fate through which he has just gone "Admits no memory of choice" ("The Trial by Existence," p. 21).

Frost spells out the poetic strategies appropriate to this view of experience in "The Figure a Poem Makes." This essay does not so much announce as embody Frost's aesthetic of surprise. Reading the essay is like reading the poem. Its initial question—"Why can't we have any one quality of poetry we choose by itself?"— is, at the end, still asking to be answered. Every time Frost seems to define in poetry a set of distinct qualities between which a poet must choose —"sound" and "soundness," "wildness" and "subject," "delight" and "wisdom"—he deftly whisks them away. To say of a poem that "It begins in delight and ends in wisdom" may satisfy our desire for formulaic symmetry. But it also breaks our experience of a poem into so discrete a series of steps as to advertise its inadequacy. Where does the transition between one mode of response and the other occur? This is a definition of an effect without a middle—no definition at all. And of poems, as of life, Frost says:

> "Ends and beginnings—there are no such things.
> There are only middles." (p. 116)

Poems written by such formulas would have the reader meet himself coming from delight and going toward wisdom while remaining incapable of bridging their intervening confusion. No less aware of this compromise than his reader, Frost quickly takes refuge in a patent enigma: "The figure is the same as for love." Given this aesthetic, anything is a poem if you say it is. No one will object to this formulation—it is unarguable—just as no one will be able to agree as to its particular consequences. We must love a poem, as we love anything, of and for itself. And we take it, like this sentence, like a loved one's love, on faith.

As quickly as he broadens the range of belief in whatever poetic quality we will, Frost begins to narrow it: "No one can really hold that the ecstasy should be static and stand still in one place." And standing still is the last thing this prose permits us. Having affixed the poem through two figures, Frost now sets them moving. He substitutes "ecstasy" for the figure of love, motion for the object of emotion. To preserve the illusion of choice, of an argument discovered and agreed to by the reader rather than imposed by the poet, he inducts us through an "is" expressed as an "ought." For it is not possible, once we entertain the notion of poem as ecstasy, to "hold" that it should only stand and wait for us. So the next sentence unfolds the consequent stages of ecstasy: "It begins in delight, it inclines to the impulse, it assumes direction with the first line laid down, it runs a course of lucky events, and ends in a clarification of life—not necessarily a great clarification, such as sects and cults are founded on, but in a momentary stay against confusion." This is Frost's essential poetic. As each phrase advances our steps a little further, we remain in an ongoing present—it begins, inclines, assumes, runs, and ends—which can barely be glimpsed before it runs away. The sequence itself is stayed as its end proves not an end. Frost's most famous formula intrudes as an afterthought—a surprising stay against the sentence's gathering confusion. As we spiral through the sentence we are stayed by "momentary stay against confusion." During such moments it is ourselves we surprise in the act of figuring forth (not figuring out) a poem. The reader is the figure a Frost poem makes.

Such poetry asks us to focus on either the movement toward or the moment of staying. In his most authentic poems, Frost remains true to the discipline of surprise embodied in "The Figure a Poem Makes." Where "Form is for Frost identical with the act of creation and every poem is by virtue of its form a deed,"[8] the reading act becomes isomorphic with the ongoing creative one. Where form is imposed as an afterthought, the poem ceases to be a deed, and reading, instead of demanding existential readiness, dwindles into detached observation. Where wonder is not sacrificed to order Frost continues to fulfill an Emersonian bequest: "The one thing which we seek with insatiable desire is to forget ourselves, to be surprised out of our propriety, to lose our sempiternal memory and to do something without knowing how or why; in short to draw a new circle. Nothing great was ever achieved without enthusiasm. The way of life is wonderful; it is by abandonment."[9]

For what Leslie Brisman has called the "Poetry of Choice,"[10] Frost substitutes the Poetry of Surprise. When his speaker stops to stand at the convergence of two roads, he does not, like Oedipus, or Milton's Adam or Wordsworth's Luke, experience "The moment of turning, when motion in one direction is about to begin" as "the still point at which the present is captured and alternatives are real." For no moment of presentness emerges in the poem during which the speaker and the reader might so choose. It is the entire process of conscious decision-making, the reality of a world of foreknown options, which Frost calls into question through his intentional strategies. Can poems get us to enact a life containing moments intersected by a conscious will? They may for some: "To those who fix today a point through which from earlier years they draw a line of life projected far into the future, this hour is of deep significance."[11] Frost's life in his poetry cannot be reduced to such a time-line. It is not the future that creates his present.

In "The Road Not Taken," so fully in control of the experience he offers, Frost chooses to enact a mode of being he seems elsewhere merely to suffer. Through this very self-conscious performance he reveals the prevailing mode of his poetry: Frost does not choose form so much as find himself chosen by it. The surprise of the writer becomes the surprise of the reader. Reading Frost we acquire Coleridgian prejudices: "Remember there is a difference between form as proceeding, and shape as superinduced;—the latter is either the death or the imprisonment of the thing;—the former is its self-witnessing and self-effected sphere of agency."[12] Once inside a strong Frost poem, we find ourselves more chosen than choosing, doomed to anticipate only surprise. In this way we perhaps reenact the kind of life the poet himself seems to have lived, where devising surprise became his way of redeeming human time. The waywardness of poetry serves as consolation for a life otherwise impossible to bear, a release from the burden of the wholly fated. After the first choice, there is no other:

> 'Tis of the essence of life here,
>   Though we choose greatly, still to lack
> The lasting memory at all clear,
>   That life has for us on the wrack
> Nothing but what we somehow chose;
>   Thus are we wholly stripped of pride
> In the pain that has but one close,
>   Bearing it crushed and mystified.
>   ("The Trial by Existence," p. 21)

Notes to *Choosing in Frost* by DAVID M. WYATT

1. *Robert Frost: Poetry and Prose*, ed. E. C. Lathem and Lawrance Thompson (New York: Holt, Rinehart and Winston, 1972), p. 401. The following quotation is from pp. 402–3.

2. *The Journals and Miscellaneous Notebooks of Ralph Waldo Emerson*, ed. A. W. Plumstead and Harrison Hayford (Cambridge, Mass: Harvard University Press, 1967), VII, 90.

3. Reuben E. Brower, *The Poetry of Robert Frost: Constellations of Intention* (New York: Oxford University Press, 1963), p. 231.

4. Yvor Winters, "Robert Frost; or, the Spiritual Drifter as Poet" in *Robert Frost: A Collection of Critical Essays*, ed. James M. Cox (Englewood Cliffs, N.J.: Prentice-Hall, 1962), p. 2.

5. Yvor Winters, *Maule's Curse*, in *In Defense of Reason* (New York: Swallow Press, 1947), p. 161. The following three quotations are from pp. 267, 153, and 227.

6. Winters, in Cox, p. 61.

7. Mark Strand, *Reasons For Moving* (New York: Atheneum, 1968), p. 40.

8. James M. Cox, "Introduction," in Cox, p. 2.

9. Emerson, "Circles."

10. See Leslie S. Brisman, *Milton's Poetry of Choice and Its Romantic Heirs* (Ithaca: Cornell University Press, 1973). The following quotation is from p. 61. Roy Harvey Pearce does not find in Frost's work a pattern of experience opposed to Brisman's poetry of choice: "Thus Frost has made his choice. He wills himself and his protagonists to choose, whereas Emerson willed himself to be chosen—unlike Frost, running the risk of losing control not only of his poems but his sense of himself. Frost has always known where he is going; or he says he has" (*The Continuity of American Poetry*, p. 281). This observation seems to invert the case. Emerson as writer chooses or is chosen by experience, depending upon the line or sentence one chooses to quote. Frost is manifestly denied the possibility of choice except as a retrospective imposition of form upon the flow of ongoing time. But Pearce comes close to admitting this, adding, as an afterthought, that when it comes to choosing, Frost only "says he has."

11. Lathem and Thompson, p. 206.

12. Coleridge, "On Poesy as Art."

Dominion of the Eye in Frost

DAVID L. MILLER

Five windows light the cavern'd man.
Blake
("Europe a Prophecy")

Ⅰ N a familiar passage from *The Prelude* (1850), Wordsworth remembers a time in his youth

> When the bodily eye, in every stage of life
> The most despotic of our senses, gained
> Such strength in *me* as often held my mind
> In absolute dominion. (XII. 128–131)[1]

It may seem strange to speak of such "dominion" in Frost. I think
we tend to regard the idea of an opposition between "the bodily
eye" and the powers of the mind as belonging to the poetry of High
Romanticism—Blake, Shelley, Wordsworth when he rises to the
prophetic strain—perhaps because it is these poets who express the
idea in its extreme form, as a belief that the imagination must either
transform the world of experience from within or be enslaved by
sense perceptions. Recent interpretations[2] of Wordsworth, for example, very often turn to the Simplon Pass episode of *The Prelude*,
where Wordsworth's poetic vocation is confirmed for him by a
moment of full visionary "blindness" in which the imagination
simply takes over the mind:

> . . . in such strength
> Of usurpation, when the light of sense
> Goes out, but with a flash that has revealed
> The invisible world, doth greatness make abode. (VI. 599–602)

The opposition between vision and ordinary seeing is presented in
such passages with the arresting clarity of an absolute.

The same opposition appears generally in more mixed and various
forms, however, and not only in Wordsworth or the other Romantics. I propose to follow a less radical form of the "visionary blind-

ness" theme into the work of a very unRomantic modern poet, borrowing passages along the way from Wordsworth and from Keats to set off Frost's more skeptical attitude toward the powers of the imagination. The historical reasons for this difference, including Darwin, Freud, and the increasingly moribund state of philosophical idealism, are certainly not to be discounted, but I am mainly interested in exploring the contrast between Frost and Romanticism from a more nearly phenomenological point of view, as a contrast between two kinds of imaginative temperament. Although this approach may slight the genuine skepticism of the Romantics, especially Keats, my final aim is nevertheless to clarify not only the differences in temperament or belief that set Frost against Romanticism but also, and more important, the continuity that joins him to the Romantics and provides the real grounds of comparison. Both aspects of his work show themselves in the way he dramatizes the relation of the imagination to empirical reality, which is the relation of the mind to the bodily eye.

Eighteenth-century writers on the sublime, who often speak of obscure vistas as a promising source of sublime feeling, had a definite influence on the Romantic theme of "visionary blindness," especially in Coleridge and Wordsworth.[3] The overriding literary influence, however, was *Paradise Lost*, particularly the invocation to light in Book III, where Milton transforms his lament for the phenomenal world ("to me expung'd and ras'd") into a prayer for visionary power: "So much the rather thou Celestial light/Shine inward. . . ." Since Milton's time, however, various trends of "enlightenment"—the growth and prestige of scientific rationalism, the epistemological skepticism of Locke, Hume, and Hartley, the disparagement of religious revelation—had considerably altered the status of imaginative vision; a Romantic poet could hardly claim divine inspiration, as Milton had done, and the absence of any strong idealistic tradition in English philosophy comparable to the German meant that the Romantics had no powerful sanction to bring against the depredations of empiricism. It was much more difficult for them to assume the special value or powers of the imagination.

It is for this reason that Geoffrey Hartman stresses the importance of what he calls "surmise," the opportunities of supposition that open to the mind in specific dramatic settings where something important is unseen or somehow withheld. "Surmise" reconciles vision to epistemological skepticism—although it is rather a phenomenological than a metaphysical accommodation—by creating a kind of provisional release from empirical facts which allows for a momentary flight of the imagination *toward* reality instead of away from it, a brief "trembling of the imagined," in Hartman's phrase, "on the brink of the real" (*Wordsworth's Poetry*, p. 11). One of Keats's best-known descriptive passages, for example, is a catalogue of things he "cannot see" on a dark night:

> I cannot see what flowers are at my feet,
>   Nor what soft incense hangs upon the boughs,
> But, in embalmed darkness, guess each sweet
>   Wherewith the seasonable month endows
> The grass, the thicket, and the fruit-tree wild;
>   White hawthorn, and the pastoral eglantine;
>   Fast fading violets cover'd up in leaves;
>   And mid-May's eldest child,
> The coming musk-rose, full of dewy wine,
>   The murmurous haunt of flies on summer eves.

The poet's simple inability to see releases his visual imagination, which recreates the physical space that surrounds him and thereby releases *him* from the isolation of the "sole self." Such moments are by their very nature temporary, not to say precarious, as the rest of the poem so clearly shows; but their value is real, and the value of this moment derives from the union it allows of imagination with reality, of mind with place: the poet reaches not for "things invisible to mortal sight" but for the unseen fact, the flowers really there at his feet.

Hartman compares this stanza from Keats to the flower-passage in "Lycidas": "Milton resorts to surmise when he wishes to 'interpose a little ease' during his lament for Lycidas. To make death seem less deadly he turns first to the old pastoral myth of sympathetic Nature . . . to bid all flowers mourn his friend. A gorgeous *anthology* follows, in which each flower is evocatively invoked (lines 133–151), but Christian honesty compels Milton to dismiss this consoling picture as a dallying with 'false surmise' (line 153) and to proceed to . . . the truer 'ease' of Resurrection" (*Wordsworth's Poetry*, pp. 9–10). Like Milton, Keats is unable to rest with the old pastoral myth; but unlike Milton he cannot proceed to the "ease" of Christian doctrine. For him, "surmise" provides a way of forestalling this dilemma.

A number of Frost's poems of imaginative "play" are also poems of surmise. Frank Lentricchia has recently demonstrated the importance of the brook in Frost as a symbol of the imagination and as the specific dramatic occasion, in poem after poem, for imaginative visions.[4] Many of the brook poems depend for their visions on the fact that the brook itself isn't *seen*: "The Mountain," "The Generations of Men," "Hyla Brook," "A Brook in the City," "Going for Water." As Lentricchia argues, however, the visions in these poems are unRomantic in that they never surrender, even for a moment, the ironic awareness of their merely fictional status, which is exactly the kind of self-consciousness that Romantic surmise was trying to go beyond.

Moreover, in his explicit treatment of the idea that the imagination may need a kind of "blindness" to create, Frost displays all the witty skepticism that might be expected of a modern positivist: "Heaven gives its glimpses only to those/Not in position to look too close." The Romantic association between vision and an inability to see things clearly remains constant here, but the values are completely reversed: the implication is that the visions of Endymion-types are compounded of myopia and wishful thinking. The quoted couplet ends "A Passing Glimpse" and may be taken as representing the limit of skepticism in Frost—in fact the whole poem can almost be taken as his answer to the flower-passages in Milton and Keats. The situation is precisely that of surmise: the speaker has seen a clump of flowers from the window of a moving train, but not very clearly, and so a sort of gap remains in experience which the mind has to fill. The speaker is no Romantic, however, for his initial impulse is to verify with the senses: "I want to get out of the train and go back/To see what they were beside the track." Then when reduced to surmise, he proceeds not by guessing what the flowers he saw *might* have been, but by listing all the things he *knows* they were not:

> I name all the flowers I am sure they weren't:
> Not fireweed loving where woods have burnt—
>
> Not bluebells gracing a tunnel mouth—
> Not lupine living on sand and drouth. (p. 248)

The bias of this catalogue is pointed up in the odd rhyme on "weren't." And instead of giving literary tags to the kinds (cf. Milton's "cow-slips wan that hang the pensive head"), the speaker here lists real traits that bespeak a shrewd eye for nature. He may seem to accede briefly to the possibility of supernatural vision when he asks "Was something brushed across my mind/That no one on earth will ever find?"—but the question is very carefully worded so as *not* to imply that the "something" was really out there; and the poem ends, as we have seen, by placing the imagination's vision of heaven on par with optical illusion.

Frost has many other poems of surmise, and while skepticism is always the controlling attitude, some poems accord a certain dignity to the "something" that may brush across the mind in a moment when the senses are baffled.

> He halted in the wind, and—what was that
> Far in the maples, pale, but not a ghost?
> He stood there bringing March against his thought,
> And yet too ready to believe the most.

The opening lines of "A Boundless Moment" reveal a man "halted in the wind" on the border between imagination and reality. The "something" he sees is really there—obscure, perhaps, "but not a ghost." Not flowers, surely? But he can't see clearly enough to be sure—like the man in the train, he can only surmise. Nevertheless, to think of Keats when reading these lines is to realize that the poem never gives itself up to the breathless feeling of a mind poised before reality in the attitude of discovery—a feeling Keats yields to completely in, for example, the image of Cortez and his men exchanging glances "with a wild surmise" when they first catch sight of the Pacific Ocean. Instead the point of view in Frost's poem is retrospective, located after and therefore outside the boundless moment of surmise, and quietly distant, so that the man in the wind is seen as being "too ready" to believe.

This distance and control are sustained in the second quatrain of the poem:

> "Oh, that's the Paradise-in-Bloom," I said;
> And truly it was fair enough for flowers
> Had we but in us to assume in March
> Such white luxurance of May for ours.

Even as Frost identifies the "wild surmise" of line five with a return to paradise (where plants of all climates and seasons grew side by side), he nevertheless withholds assent by adopting the conditional tense (line seven) and returning, finally, to his knowledge of the fallen world, where May is never March. The easy transition from actual mid-May to hypothetical mid-summer takes place in the flower-passage from "Ode to a Nightingale": there surmise is the governing point of view, and the whole passage moves in the free-fall of purely mental space, where "true" violets have no more weight or substance than "false" roses; as a result, the speaker moves forgetfully from an image of the "fast fading violets" really there at his feet to an image of musk-roses in full bloom "on summer eves." He has it in him to assume in May such red luxurance of June for his, and by assuming to possess it.

The two observers in "A Boundless Moment" do not quite have it in them to forget that flowers never bloom in March in the cold woods of New England:

> We stood a moment so, in a strange world,
> Myself as one his own pretense deceives;
> And then I said the truth (and we moved on).
> A young beech clinging to its last year's leaves. (pp. 233–34)

For the space of a moment, a single line, Frost really entertains the *fiat* of the imagination—a "strange world" that is truly "ours"—but then the poem moves on, ending in the world of empirical facts (where "little we see in nature that is ours"). Still, the vision is not mocked. The talk about pretense, deception, and truth, the final gesture of moving on—these are very firm, they define the poem, but "the most" here is still more than it was in "A Passing Glimpse." The reference to paradise doesn't serve the wit of a disclaimer the way the reference to heaven does in the other poem. The "boundless moment," although bounded very narrowly by "the truth," is not flatly dismissed.

Both poems, despite the ironic and unRomantic attitudes they express, confirm the Romantic insight that moments of blurred perception are an opportunity for the imagination. The mind actively constructs the phenomenal world from the data of the senses, and its constructive impulse has wider latitude where sense impressions are obscure or ambiguous. E. H. Gombrich has explored this principle thoroughly from the point of view of the visual arts in *Art and Illusion*; he finds, for example, that the eighteenth-century technique of deliberate blurring lets the eye of the viewer participate in the composition of a painting, "draw[ing] him into the magic circle of creation and allow[ing] him to experience something of the thrill of 'making' which had once been the privilege of the artist."[5] This technique anticipated the even bolder experiments of the Impressionists.

Wordsworth believed that such creative perception becomes possible whenever the imagination wins free of the eye: then it can recreate the visible world "by innumerable processes; and in none does it more delight than in that of consolidating numbers into unity, and dissolving and separating unity into number,—alternations proceeding from, and governed by, a sublime consciousness of the soul in her own mighty and almost divine powers." Milton was England's mightiest poet of the sublime because he was a master of such alternations; and this mastery was made possible by his freedom from "the bondage of definite form," a bondage which is the poetic equivalent of "idolatry" ("Preface to the Edition of 1815"). Wordsworth's rhetoric in such passages reveals his preoccupation with the sovereign powers of the mind: by worshipping idolatrously at the altar of empiricism the mind falls into "bondage," and is held in "absolute dominion" by the "despotic" sense of sight; only the imagination can release within the mind its "strength of usurpation," its "mighty and almost divine powers," its "greatness." Opposition to Hartleyan psychology joins forces here with a sense of personal destiny: visionary poetry depends on a faith in the ability of consciousness to transfigure the phenomenal world from within.

Frost had no such faith in the powers of the mind, and when he dramatizes an opposition between the mind and the eye he does so only as a way of dismissing or at best narrowly circumscribing all claims for the visionary imagination. When he does approach the theme of subjective autonomy over sense experience, he approaches it entirely by way of the eye, manipulating ordinary perception to create a playful illusion of visionary power. In "The Freedom of the Moon," he pretends to work sublime alternations in the structure of the visible world:

> I've tried the new moon tilted in the air
> Above a hazy tree-and-farmhouse cluster
> As you might try a jewel in your hair.
> I've tried it fine with little breadth of luster,
> Alone, or in one ornament combining
> With one first-water star almost as shining.
>
> I put it shining anywhere I please.
> By walking slowly on some evening later
> I've pulled it from a crate of crooked trees,
> And brought it over glossy water, greater,
> And dropped it in, and seen the image wallow,
> The color run, all sorts of wonder follow. (p. 245)

The aesthetic effects he "creates" are striking, but the wonder that follows doesn't have much to do with "the sublime consciousness of the soul in her own mighty and almost divine powers." The real freedom in the poem is not that of the moon or even the imagination; it is, to quote one of Frost's own characters, simply the freedom to have fun with "how you say a thing" ("The Mountain"). An appropriate modesty appears in the metaphoric language that claims merely ornamental effects.

Frost approaches the theme of subjective autonomy over sense experience more imaginatively in an early sonnet from *A Boy's Will*, "The Vantage Point." It begins:

> If tired of trees I seek again mankind,
>   Well I know where to hie me—in the dawn,
>   To a slope where the cattle keep the lawn.
> There amid lolling juniper reclined,
> Myself unseen, I see in white defined
>   Far off the homes of men, and farther still,

> The graves of men on an opposing hill,
> Living or dead, whichever are to mind.

Initially the poem seems to be an ironic picture of seclusion: the speaker's approach to "mankind" is certainly reserved. But the title, with its implicit emphasis on the possibilities of visual perspective, connects "The Vantage Point" with "The Freedom of the Moon," and draws attention to the less prominent theme of subjective autonomy over the phenomenal world. If we ask what the real value of the vantage point is, the obvious answer will be that it suits the speaker's evident desire to avoid the human community: here the lawn is "kept" only by grazing cattle. But the vantage point also offers a range of visible objects that matches the speaker's inner range of meditations ("whichever are to mind"), thereby approximating the conditions of "visionary" imagination, in which the visible world is at the mind's disposal. This approximation takes place within the limits of ordinary perception, however, and without any loss of clarity or intensity in sense experience: the emblematic houses and tombstones are sharply "defined" (Latin, *finire*, *to limit*) against a background of natural green.

At first, the sestet seems to execute a number of surprising reversals:

> And if by noon I have too much of these,
> I have but to turn on my arm, and lo,
> The sunburned hillside sets my face aglow,
> My breathing shakes the bluet like a breeze,
> I smell the earth, I smell the bruisèd plant,
> I look into the crater of the ant. (p. 17)

Every effect set up in the octave is now thrown into relief by its opposite. The speaker was concealed; now he looms enormous over the crater of the ant. He was withdrawn into contemplation; now he is caught up in sensation. The octave ends with a relatively complicated sentence five lines long that slows the rhythm down; the rhythm of the sestet accelerates at the end in a rush of short emphatic clauses. And the flashiest effect of all is the shift in visual perspective, from panorama to extreme close-up.

At one moment the vantage point seems to offer a contemplative retreat, placing the dominion of the eye completely at the mind's disposal; at the next, an altogether unvisionary adventure in pure sensation. Its value, apparently, is to offer both. Yet what the octave really presents is only an approximation or mock-up, within the limits of ordinary experience, of the "visionary" ideal of subjective autonomy over the phenomenal world: the speaker arranges reality to serve his meditative purposes by manipulating the laws of perspective, like the speaker in "The Freedom of the Moon," not by working sublime alternations in the visible world through the power of imagination. Thus the sudden appeal to the senses in the sestet is only a more impetuous phase of the same empirical predisposition that governs the octave, and the conspicuous play of opposites between them resolves itself into a single underlying impulse to approach and confront the ordinary limits of sense experience without going beyond them. Frost is testing these limits in very different ways as he turns from meditation to sensation, but he clearly wants to feel them there. In the final lines of the poem "To Earthward" he says

> When stiff and sore and scarred
> I take away my hand
> From leaning on it hard
> In grass and sand,
>
> The hurt is not enough:
> I long for weight and strength
> To feel the earth as rough
> To all my length. (p. 227)

The speaker of "To Earthward" has learned, as he feels himself aging, to value pain itself for its very intensity, "The sweet of bitter bark/And burning clove" or the sting of sharp sand on his palm; by pressing up against the limits of sensation, and feeling their resistance, he has learned to revive and intensify a sense of the life those limits contain.

This figure of an old man grinding his palm in the sand to resist the approaching numbness of death recalls Wordsworth, who remembers grasping at a tree or wall, when he was very young, to recover a sense of the independent reality of nature (I. F. note to the "Intimations" Ode). In either instance the physical sensation of sheer otherness prompts a recovery of the sense of self. In the work of both poets, sharp sensations, including distinct visual perceptions, tend to reinforce self-consciousness, whereas indistinct sensations tend to foster self-forgetfulness. Albert Wlecke shows in some detail how Wordsworth found indefinite perceptions conducive to a "dissolution of the mind's sense of itself as a fixed and limited entity" (p. 71), a process of self-forgetfulness which let him commune with the objective world as if it were a part of him (I. F. note to the "Intimations" Ode). By contrast, Frost's very evident distrust of indistinct perceptions reflects an impulse to preserve "the mind's sense of itself as a fixed and limited entity." Harold Toliver points out that "if the poet cannot bear witness to things, he himself cannot be permanently defined by his place among them";[6] and Wallace Stevens describes the same relation between definite forms in nature and a definite sense of self when he says

> For so retentive of themselves are men
> That music is intensest which proclaims
> The near, the clear, and vaunts the clearest bloom,
> And of all vigils musing the obscure,
> That apprehends the most which sees and names,
> As in your name, an image that is sure. . . .
>   ("To the One of Fictive Music")

The image that is sure, seen and clearly identified, buttresses self-possession.

The motif of visual obscurity, on the other hand, reflects what might be called the romantic impulse toward self-transcendence. In later life Wordsworth came to celebrate the "dissolution" of self-consciousness that he had feared and sometimes resisted in his youth (I. F. note to the "Intimations" Ode). And Keats's unhappy wish to escape from being "fixed and limited" as a "sole self"—in other respects so different from Wordsworth's desire for transcendence—resembles it in finding expression as a yearning to escape from the dominion of the eye, to "leave the world unseen,/And with thee fade away into the forest dim:/Fade far away, dissolve, and quite forget." The contrast with Frost is complete because Frost so deeply values self-possession. In "Beech," the poem he placed at the front of his

1942 volume *A Witness Tree,* Frost explicitly identifies this anti-Romantic need to reaffirm the boundaries of the self with his prefer-ence for definite forms in nature:

> Where my imaginary line
> Bends square in woods, an iron spine
> And pile of real rocks have been founded.
> And off this corner in the wild,
> Where these are driven in and piled,
> One tree, by being deeply wounded,
> Has been impressed as Witness Tree
> And made commit to memory
> My proof of being not unbounded.
> Thus truth's established and borne out,
> Though circumstanced with dark and doubt—
> Though by a world of doubt surrounded. (p. 331)

In its closing lines the poem spells out an analogy between the cer-tainty of external truth and that of the self—an analogy, however, which has been quietly taken for granted all along in the speaker's way of referring to his property as if it were identical with himself ("my proof of being not unbounded"). The iron spine, the pile of real rocks, and the "deeply wounded" tree are visible marks, in-dividual acts of definition, which secure both inner and outer boundaries.

The poem also reveals a certain ambivalence toward the regions of "dark and doubt." In "A Boundless Moment," for example, it was the truth that hemmed in the strange world of Paradise-in-Bloom, whereas here the truth itself is shut in all around. Moreover the same two things, "dark and doubt"—the uncertain and the visu-ally obscure—seem to liberate the mind briefly in "A Boundless Mo-ment," while they threaten the mind and keep it limited here. And "A Boundless Moment" intimates paradise, finally, whereas "Beech" intimates chaos. Chaos and paradise are both conditions entailing a loss of personal identity, however, and the willingness to reach for paradise may in fact be very close to a death-wish. Keats acknowl-edges this in confessing how often he had been "half in love with easeful death," and Frost acknowledges it when he concedes that the "dark and deep" woods are also "lovely." He does so again in the personification of "Witness Tree," the one tree that has been marked—made to stand out "sure" from "the obscure" wild, and named with a proper name—to secure *his* identity:

> One tree, by being deeply wounded,
> Has been impressed as Witness Tree
> And made commit to memory
> My proof of being not unbounded.

In the emphasis on "memory" Frost openly confronts the Keatsian urge to forget, and the emphasis on wounding shows his implicit recognition of how attractive such forgetfulness can be. Nietzsche, in the *Genealogy of Morals*, said that all the savage cruelties inflicted on transgressors in primitive societies are a measure of how deeply men resisted acquiring memory. Memory endows man with the terrible responsibility of an identity, and gives him "the right to make promises."[7] Against the yearning for unconsciousness, against what Nietzsche calls "the faculty of oblivion," memory brings the strictures of the conscious self: "I have promises to keep." The insistence on driving things in and piling them up and carving them out is defensive in two ways, a response not only to the threats of darkness and doubt but to the attractions as well.

The poem "A Leaf-Treader" will serve as a final example. Autumn leaves, says the speaker, seem to fall "with a will to carry me with them to death." He responds by trampling on them all. There is humor in his brief misgiving—"Perhaps I have put forth too much strength and been too fierce from fear"—but the poem shows an underlying seriousness. The leaves themselves are no match for him, so his overkill is funny; but he is really responding not so much to their "threatening" as to their "invitation": "They spoke to the fugitive in my heart as if it were leaf to leaf." What he really fears is not just death, but his own incipient or "fugitive" death-wish.

In Frost, then, the clear-sighted "defining" of visual phenomena turns out to be an indirect means of self-definition. On the other hand, Coleridge himself recognized the tendency among his contemporaries to "affect the indefinite" as a sign of their reverence for "the infinite." In "The Eolian Harp" he acts out the terms of this paradigm very clearly: lying on a hillside with half-closed eyes, watching the blurred play of water-lights on the ocean, he passes into a visionary surmise; the content of this surmise is a sort of pantheistic monism involving the happy dissolution of all distinct entities, including the personal ego, into a higher reality, "the one Life within us and abroad," the one "plastic and vast . . . intellectual breeze" that animates all men and all things in nature like so many wind-harps.[8] By contrast, "the infinite" for Frost is a void, a desert place "where no human race is," and the very possibility of self-transcendence therefore presents itself to him under the fearful aspect of self-annihilation. The poems show him turning away from such "opportunities" again and again to reaffirm the boundaries of the self.

"West-Running Brook" is the poem in which Frost projects this vision of eternity most comprehensively. It is a vision of the universe as randomness in motion toward oblivion; this commits the mind to tactics of resistance, subjective acts which impose boundaries on the matter and energy in process all around us: the self is defined by its opposition to the universal flux, like the white wave that exists by virtue of its resistance to the dark westward current of the brook. The difference between the "universal cataract of death" that "flows between us, over us, and *with* us" and Coleridge's "plastic and vast . . . intellectual breeze" that sweeps over all of animated nature is the difference between two world views: however tentatively a poet like Coleridge or Wordsworth may have held his faith in "the one life," it was still *available* to belief. For Wordsworth in particular, the way to self-preservation lay only in self-transcendence. He could believe in "what Goethe calls *Dauer im Wechsel*, endurance within a pattern of change, . . . a metatemporal, stationary" realm beyond apparent mutability;[9] and part of the experience of sublimity was for him a sense of participation in the vision of eternity. Since the merely personal self is irretrievably lost to mutability, this sense of belonging to eternity could come only with self-transcendence, or, as Wlecke says, the "dissolution of the mind's sense of itself as a fixed and limited entity" (p. 71; see also pp. 114–28).

In the Simplon Pass episode of *The Prelude*, Wordsworth's visionary glimpse of an "invisible world" is followed by the declaration that "our being's heart and home,/Is with infinitude, and only there," and then by a magnificent descriptive passage filled with revelations of "endurance within a pattern of change" (ll. 604–5, 617–40). The passage is comparable in importance and in authority of tone to Fred's speech in "West-Running Brook," and its images of "woods decaying, never to be decayed" or "the stationary blasts of waterfalls" are precisely contradicted by the images of "substance lapsing unsubstantial," "the universal cataract of death," and "the stream of everything that runs away." It seems inevitable, given such a vision of the universe joined to a radical intuition of consciousness as embattled, that the prospect of surrendering his "proof of being not unbounded" should have appeared to Frost only as the prospect of annihilation.

What was not inevitable is the form this vision takes: the mind does finally locate and "define" its emblem in nature, the language rising in response to an impersonal grandeur and metaphoric intensity unlike anything else in Frost. The profound irony of the poem is that Frost takes up the prophetic voice, the unrestrained and committed eloquence of metaphysical vision, only to repudiate the metaphysical grounds of vision altogether: the final meaning of the emblem is that there are no emblems or meanings, except the ones we create and impose in our resistance to loss and decay. Elsewhere in the poetry vision is supplanted by imaginative "play"—in "Mending Wall," for example, "The Generations of Men," "The Mountain," or "Birches"—and Frost's need for self-possession reveals itself in a disengaged and ironic tone which always conveys the impression T. E. Hulme approved as proper to the "classical attitude": an impression of "standing outside it [the "extravagant thing"], and not quite believing it, or consciously putting it forward as a flourish."[10]

I began this essay with a discussion of "surmise" as a way of accommodating vision to skepticism by finding opportunities for the mind to imagine what may be empirically true—to create, in effect, what already exists, as the speaker in "Ode to a Nightingale" does when he imagines the flowers he cannot see. I would like to conclude by examining an early lyric in which Frost moves beyond "classical" decorum and gives himself up, for once, to a Keatsian surmise. "Surmise" *was* available and potentially attractive to Frost, implicit in "A Passing Glimpse" and "A Boundless Moment" as an opportunity resisted or dismissed, a road not taken that was, nevertheless, really there. More clearly than any of his later, more substantial poems, "Going for Water" illustrates how much Frost had in common with such poets as Wordsworth and Keats, who were, after all, very often skeptical of their own earnest faith in the imagination.

> The well was dry beside the door,
>   And so we went with pail and can
> Across the fields behind the house
>   To seek the brook if still it ran;
>
> Not loth to have excuse to go,
>   Because the autumn eve was fair
> (Though chill), because the fields were ours,
>   And by the brook our woods were there.
>
> We ran as if to meet the moon
>   That slowly dawned behind the trees,
> The barren boughs without the leaves,
>   Without the birds, without the breeze.
>
> But once within the wood, we paused
>   Like gnomes that hid us from the moon,
> Ready to run to hiding new
>   With laughter when she found us soon.
>
> Each laid on other a staying hand
>   To listen ere we dared to look,
> And in the hush we joined to make
>   We heard, we knew we heard the brook.
>
> A note as from a single place,
>   A slender tinkling fall that made
> Now drops that floated on the pool
>   Like pearls, and now a silver blade. (p. 18)

The title is slightly paradoxical, since water isn't really what the couple in the poem goes out for. They go, says the speaker, "because the autumn eve was fair," which makes sense, and "because the fields were ours,/And by the brook our woods were there," which doesn't quite make sense unless we attach a special significance to the repeated pronoun. Specifically, it suggests the kind of subjective, created value that the mind attaches to the things it cherishes—the phenomenological term for this is "valorization." (Compare the use of "ours" in stanza two of "A Boundless Moment.")

The theme of man's relation to nature enters the poem very unobtrusively in these lines. In the third and fourth stanzas, however, Frost starts to play with it openly, exaggerating the pretense of a rapport with nature by implying that the couple had a rendezvous with the moon, which was coming out to meet them. Up to this point he is still working well inside the limits of the "classical attitude," consciously putting his exaggeration forward as a flourish, keeping truth and fiction well clear of each other: "We ran *as if* to meet the moon."

The last two stanzas, however, are remarkable for the way they coopt ironies developed earlier in the poem. There has been a secondary and ironic sense, for example, in which the speaker and his companion could lay claim to the woods: they've had the barren scene to themselves, "without the leaves,/Without the birds, without the breeze." But here the question about "what to make of a diminished thing" finds an answer: the zero values of nature's absences are turned to fine effect as man and nature "join" to make a "hush"—no mere absence of sound, but something vibrantly *there*.

This brief hush becomes a moment of imagination, a very Keatsian "trembling of the imagined on the brink of the real" (in Hartman's phrase again). The couple has not yet seen the brook: they pause, and deliberately wait. The real physical presence of the brook is suspended. They stand "a moment so" in a strange world of their own making, but this time there is no pretense: the images give up their supposed reality. The "drops that floated on the pool" are no less imaginary than "pearls," the very emblems of rich and strange transformation. By the same token the "slender tinkling fall" of plain water is no more real than the "silver blade" it resembles: both are "made" by the mind in response to a disembodied sound. The heightening of mood which accompanies this moment—the quiet gesture of the "staying hand" complemented by the staying rhythm of the line "we heard, we knew we heard the brook"—tells us that we are beyond mere playful extravagance; and the repetition of "now" in the final lines,

> Now drops that floated on the pool
> Like pearls, and now a silver blade,

implies that we have left the world of ordinary experience, in which two people went for water, and entered fairyland, where ageless "gnomes" are finding hidden treasure in a time that is always the present. The treasure they find is a moment of surmise that emerges naturally from the action of the poem, a moment of pure imagination that transfigures the familiar brook without really changing it at all.

Notes to *Dominion of the Eye in Frost* by DAVID L. MILLER

1. *Selected Poems and Prefaces*, ed. Jack Stillinger (Boston: Houghton Mifflin, 1965) used for all citations.

2. My primary debt is obviously to Geoffrey Hartman, *Wordsworth's Poetry 1787–1814* (New Haven: Yale University Press, 1964); and "Romanticism and Anti-Self-Consciousness," in *Beyond Formalism* (New Haven: Yale University Press, 1970), pp. 298–310; see also chapter five of *The Unmediated Vision* (New Haven: Yale University Press, 1954).

3. See Albert O. Wlecke, *Wordsworth and the Sublime* (Berkeley: University of California Press, 1973), especially chapters three and four.

4. Frank Lentricchia, *Robert Frost: Modern Poetics and the Landscapes of Self* (Durham, N.C.: Duke University Press, 1975), chapter two; I am also indebted to Lentricchia's reading of "West-Running Brook," pp. 54–7; his comments on the "play" imagination in Frost, pp. 101–19; and his reading of "Going for Water," pp. 40–3.

5. 2nd ed., Bollingen Series XXXV, v. 5 (Princeton: Princeton University Press, 1961), p. 202.

6. *Pastoral Forms and Attitudes* (Berkeley: University of California Press, 1971), p. 355.

7. *The Birth of Tragedy and The Genealogy of Morals*, trans. Francis Golffing (Garden City, N.Y.: Doubleday, 1956), p. 189.

8. *Selected Poetry and Prose of Coleridge*, ed. Donald A. Stauffer (New York: Modern Library, 1951), pp. 57–8. Stauffer, p. xxiii quotes without reference: "The Greeks idolized the finite, . . . whatever, in short, is capable of being definitely conveyed by defined forms or thoughts: the moderns revere the infinite, and affect the indefinite as a vehicle of the infinite. . . ."

9. Paul de Man, "The Rhetoric of Temporality," in *Interpretation: Theory and Practice*, ed. John S. Singleton (Baltimore: The Johns Hopkins Press, 1969), p. 181.

10. "Romanticism and Classicism" (1913–14, pub. 1924), rpt. in *Critical Theory Since Plato*, ed. Hazard Adams (New York: Harcourt, Brace, Jovanovich, 1971), pp. 767–74.

The Animal World
in Robert Frost's Poetry

RICHARD REED

"The Pasture," that short poem which Robert Frost designated as the epigraph for editions of his collected poetry, not only stands as an invitation to his poetic world but also presents the figures that are central to that world: the poet, the reader, the natural setting, and the animals. While much has been written about the poet, about the responses of readers, and about the poet's view of nature, the animals in Frost's poetry—except the woodchucks—are rarely noticed. Yet, a survey of Frost's use of animals uncovers a dramatic change in the poet's attitudes and provides a way of both discovering and unifying his major ideas and dominant themes.

Although reviewers lauded the freshness and honesty of *A Boy's Will* when it was published in 1913, the book gave only a faint glimpse of what Frost was to become. When judged by modern standards, this early poetry is seen to be marred by several shortcomings, the most striking of which are a romantic belief in the innate purity and harmony of wild things, excessive sentimentality and subjectivity, and an unquestioning confidence in nature. All these deficiencies may be seen in Frost's references to the animal kingdom. The animals of *A Boy's Will* are idealized, romantically conventional creatures happily sufficient in their innocent partaking of God's bounty and inherently in harmony with their surroundings. Except for the dreaming of the wistful poet, human activity is, for the most part, absent from the book; apparent throughout is the belief that happiness for men can be achieved only when they emulate the animals. According to "A Prayer in Spring" (p. 12), human fulfilment can be attained only through an ignorant pleasure-taking in "happy bees" and "the darting bird." And implicit in "Waiting" (p. 14) is the speaker's belief that only his feelings for his beloved can provide anything akin to the harmony enjoyed by the wild creatures.

The sentimentality evident in so many of these early poems is often evoked through the presence or absence of animals. Typically, the speaker displays an acute sense of loss when animals are gone from the landscape or even when there is any possibility of their being gone. For example, in "October" (p. 27) the speaker hears the calling of crows and regrets that "Tomorrow they may form and go." The most intense concern for departed wildlife, as well as the grossest example of sentimentality in *A Boy's Will*, appears in "My Butterfly." Emphasizing that he is the sole mourner, the speaker bewails the death of a butterfly which, by the mere touch of its wing, had been capable of sustaining him when "once conspiracy was rife/Against my life." Moreover, the reader is asked to believe that the butterfly's death had not been caused by a simple accident, but by the "o'ereager, . . . ungentle grasp" (p. 29) of God, who feared that the butterfly would exceed his reach. In addition to the ludicrous claims made for the insect, the poem displays a selfish and deceptive view of death, a morose unwillingness to accept reality or proportion, and a disproportionate expense of and request for emotion.

While subjectivity is a dominant characteristic of the poems in *A Boy's Will*, in some pieces the poet's use of animals demonstrates a hermitlike distaste for other human beings. For example, in "The Vantage Point" the speaker claims that he is most comfortable at some midpoint between man and nature and that his closest association with other men is his mingling with their domesticated animals ("To a slope where the cattle keep the lawn," p. 17); however, even this distance affords too much of mankind, so he withdraws to the lazy solitude of nature and its creatures: "I smell the earth, I smell the bruisèd plant,/I look into the crater of the ant." As in many of these early poems, the speaker here is self-exiled from the realm of human activity. Even in "Pan With Us," one of the less subjective poems in *A Boy's Will*, the speaker regrets the world's discovery of "new terms of worth," and he prefers instead the apparent sufficiency of animal sounds: "the blue jay's screech/And the whimper of hawks beside the sun/Were music enough for him, for one" (p. 24).

Besides "Pan With Us," the only other poem in *A Boy's Will* that uses animals to express a concern for the humanity beyond self is "The Tuft of Flowers"; interestingly, it also contains the best use of animal imagery to be found in that volume. Lynen has said "The Tuft of Flowers" is one of the few early poems by Frost that "give premonitions of his mature style." But though its style and concern with humanity distinguish it from the other pieces in Frost's first book, "The Tuft of Flowers" nevertheless displays flaws not found in the later work. A butterfly, acting as the agent of truth, leads the dejected speaker to discover the tuft of flowers which a mower had spared; the insect's heartening "message from the dawn" evokes the concluding statement that "Men work together . . ./Whether they work together or apart." Although this final couplet stresses human brotherhood, the earlier lines recounting the discovery of the flowers give equal emphasis to humanity and animals: the message "made me hear the wakening birds around,/And hear his long scythe whispering to the ground" (p. 22). In addition, the butterfly is endowed with human qualities of mind and is described by such terms as *bewildered, memoried,* and *thought*; moreover, the insect's delivery of the message is depicted as a conscious, deliberate act. In much of *A Boy's Will* the poet seriously endows animals with human attributes and assumes that the life of animals is not merely simpler but also fuller, richer, and better than human life. Such assertions are never present in Frost's later work.

Between *A Boy's Will* and the later poetry occurs a striking change in Frost's uses of animals and in his poetic vision. While his early uses of animals serve primarily to celebrate the purity and rightfulness of the rural world and to bolster his advocacy of rustic virtues as ultimate goals, his later references to the animal world are employed in a variety of other ways, all of which support the major concern of his mature work: the wide range of human experience, endeavor, and emotion. After *A Boy's Will* animals are used to develop the personae of dramatic pieces, assist in the creation of plausible dramatic situations, depict the poet's view of the world in which man lives, define the limits of man's separation from the rest of nature, and describe a nobility of which only man is capable.

The earliest evidence of Frost's mature use of animals appears in "To a Moth Seen in Winter," which (according to Lathem, *Poetry*, p. 566) was written "Circa 1900" but which was not collected until 1942, in *A Witness Tree*. Its omission from *A Boy's Will* is both telling and understandable, for its pessimism about life and about animal-human relationships would have made it out of place in Frost's first book. Lacking the optimism and romantic assurance apparent in most of the other early work, the speaker in this poem does not know why the moth has sought him out; moreover, he asserts that the moth's endeavor "To make the venture of eternity/ And seek the love of kind" had been prompted by some "false hope." Recognizing the futility and inevitable fatality of the moth's imagined quest, the speaker is also aware of the tremendously wide gulf between them, and he concludes: "I cannot touch your life, much less can save,/Who am tasked to save my own a little while" (pp. 356, 357). Separating this poem from most of the others produced during this period in Frost's career are its lack of assurance about life, its recognition of the gulf between man and nature, and its clear focus on human life and human problems. These differences were to become major characteristics of the poetry published in and after *North of Boston*.

Although it appeared in London only a year after *A Boy's Will*, *North of Boston* displays a major change in Frost's poetic vision. That change was probably best described by the poet himself when he called the work "a book of people" (p. 534). While present in many of the volume's poems, the animals of *North of Boston* are unobtrusive, used only for defining and exploring the human dimension of the poetry. In this second volume and in the books that followed, a primary function of the animals is to create plausible dramatic situations for the human personae. In "The Black Cottage" (p. 55) the minister's sudden awareness of the bees in the wall provides a reason for terminating his reverie about a new world, and the poignant effect of his story is heightened by the contrast between the old woman and the insects' "fierce heads." The local man in "The Mountain" ends his conversation with the speaker by goading his oxen; had he been afoot, the termination of the discussion would have been much more difficult. The animals in *North of Boston* also serve to heighten the characterization of the human beings in the poems. For example, the speaker in "The Mountain," a man who is curious about the mountain itself, is contrasted with the local oxen-driver, who sees it only as a place for "Deer-hunting and trout fishing" (p. 42). In "A Hundred Collars" (p. 44) Lafe's lazy enjoyment of the landscape is made possible by his mare's ability to guide herself, and her habit of turning in at every gate provides an excuse for Lafe to lead the sociable life he loves so well. John, the irresponsible farmer of "The Housekeeper" (p. 81), is characterized by his misplaced kindness to his chickens, which stands in sharp contrast to the apparent cruelty of his ignorance of his mistress' feelings. And in "The Self-Seeker" (p. 92) the goodness of the girl is established by her act of leaving rare orchid seeds for woodchucks to eat.

In the poetry published after *A Boy's Will* Frost not only uses animals to create situations or develop character; he also employs them as a means of commenting on human behavior. For example, the central subject of "The Exposed Nest" (p. 109) is not the birds but the relationship between two persons. "The Runaway" (p. 223), a piece about a strayed colt, ends with a comment on human careless-ness. "Blue-Butterfly Day" (p. 225) and "Fireflies in the Garden" (p. 246) suggest that man should strive to discover more stable values or objects in which to place his faith. "At Woodward's Gardens" (p. 293), by hinting that the monkeys' use of a magnifying glass as a remedy for ennui might be as valid as any human employment of it, implies that man should occasionally reappraise his use of objects. "Fragmentary Blue" (p. 220) criticizes those persons whose over-zealous appreciation of the blue of birds and butterflies prevents their recognizing the more expansive blue of heaven. The speaker of "A Minor Bird" (p. 250) reveals that he, not the bird, is out of tune. And the speaker of "The Rabbit-Hunter" states that, like the hounded rabbit, neither the hunter nor the poet "have wit/To comprehend" (p. 360) death.

In Frost's mature poetry animals frequently appear as substitutes for human characters, in a manner reminiscent of the beast fable. The judgments in these poems are implicitly but clearly intended as criticisms of human, not animal, behavior. "The Cow in Apple

Time" (p. 124), ostensibly about a cow that has gorged herself on fermented windfall apples, actually describes a drunken stubbornness more human than bovine. The egotistical dandyism of the wasp in "Waspish" (p. 309) mirrors the narcissistic tendencies of human beings. "Departmental" (p. 287), which describes the businesslike manner in which a bureaucracy of ants accepts the death of one of its members, is deliberately and successfully comic; however, it is also a deadly serious commentary on human behavior. As Lynen has noted, the poem treats "such serious matters as the blinding effects of custom and the indifference of the group to the individual," and its effectiveness forces the reader "to see the absurdity of man's allegiance to an impersonal social order" (p. 160).

In addition to using animals to satirize the seemingly avoidable errors of human vanity and insensitivity, Frost also employs an animal to comment on what he saw as a fundamental inability of mankind to make a completely satisfactory adjustment to the limitations of the human situation. Based on an analogy between a caged bear and man seeking to understand his world, "The Bear" mocks mankind's clumsy attempts to define reality. Because instinct fulfills all his needs, an uncaged bear feels at home in the world: "The world has room to make a bear feel free" (p. 269). On the other hand, just as a bear is cramped by a cage, so is man cramped by a heightened consciousness; just as the caged bear stupidly sways from buttock to buttock, so does man sway between two explanations of himself—the empirical explanation provided by science and the idealist explanation offered by a Platonic concept of innate spirit:

> Or if he rests from scientific tread,
> 'Tis only to sit back and sway his head
> Through ninety-odd degrees of arc, it seems,
> Between two metaphysical extremes.
> He sits back on his fundamental butt
>
> . . . .
>
> And back and forth he sways from cheek to cheek,
> At one extreme agreeing with one Greek,
> At the other agreeing with another Greek. . . . (p. 269)

Yvor Winters condemned "The Bear" because he saw the poem as an assertion that "impulsive man would be a wiser and a nobler creature" than "reasoning man" (*Function of Criticism*, p. 166). Mr. Winters misread the poem. Frost's analogy implies only similarity between man and the captive bear and only contrast between man and the uncaged bear. Nowhere does the poet suggest the superiority of "natural man"; for Frost, man's heightened consciousness and his consequent separation from nature obviate the possibility of his ever acting totally from instinct. Completely denying the possibility of "uncaged" man, Frost is concerned only with man's efforts to resolve the conflicts caused by his inescapable "caged" situation.

Frost also uses animal imagery to portray his view of the world in which man lives. While for the most part the poems of *A Boy's Will* present a benevolent natural order, the later poetry depicts not only the beauty but also the horror of nature. Frost's recognition of the more pleasant aspects of wildlife is evident in "Looking for a Sunset Bird in Winter" (p. 232), "The Oven Bird" (p. 119), and "Dust of Snow" (p. 221); in all of these, wildlife can have positive, if unintended, value for man. But the mature poet is also aware of the grim reality of the struggle for survival in nature, as seen in "Design" (p. 302), which presents natural savagery on a minute scale that is nevertheless horrible. A similar awareness appears in Frost's setting the "sullen" spider's anticipation of prey in "Range-Finding" (p. 126) against a backdrop of human warfare. And in "Good-by and Keep Cold" (p. 228) the speaker half-humorously, half-seriously reflects that his orchard might be eaten by rabbit, mouse, deer, and grouse; underlying the reflection is the awareness that, though the animals might be the rightful diners, the speaker needs the orchard himself. Characteristic of the later poetry, this recognition of economic necessity (or any other harsh reality) displaces the awed reverence, though not the appreciation of nature, that is common to *A Boy's Will*. In the later poetry Frost's use of animal imagery to depict both the beauty and the savagery of nature always functions on the human level.

While he is cognizant of nature as man's environment, in his mature poetry Frost is also keenly aware that man is fundamentally separated from the natural realm. Marion Montgomery has defined the conflict that forms the basis of many of Frost's best poems: "Man is never completely certain that the earth, the natural world, returns his love" (p. 340). Frost's belief in the separation of man from nature is presented in several poems, in major and minor statements. In "On a Bird Singing in Its Sleep" the poet states that protective instinct keeps the bird safe and enables it "To be a bird while we are men on earth" (p. 303). "A Winter Eden" implies a contrast between romping rabbits and human beings, for whom "An hour of winter day might seem too short/To make it worth life's while to wake and sport" (p. 254). Frost's most apparently affirmative statement about the relationship between man and nature is "Two Look at Two," in which a human couple encounter a pair of deer in the woods. Although there is a momentary union between the two pairs as each stands watching the other, the poet emphasizes the gulf between them by separating them with a wall. And though the last two lines of the poem would, at first reading, seem to stress resemblances and communion, the words *as if* greatly qualify any hint of affirmation:

> As if the earth in one unlooked-for favor
> Had made them certain earth returned their love. (p. 230)

"The Most of It" also dramatizes man's desire to discover heartening correspondences between the natural world and his love for it. The poem portrays a man who, while he "thought he kept the universe alone," seeks to find in nature some "counter-love, original response." Watching a mysterious movement through a body of water, the man discovers that the hoped-for response, "Instead of proving human when it neared" (p. 338), is only a large buck, which is "the most" that nature offers to man. Between man and nature, the separation is fundamental.

Nevertheless, Frost believes that the human capacity for transcending this essential isolation endows man with a unique nobility. This idea of human superiority appears in several of the poems, which employ animal imagery for the needed contrast. In "Something for Hope," after noting the tribulations of farmers, the poet states that *farmer* is another word for hope:

> Hope may not nourish a cow or horse,
> But *spes alit agricolam* 'tis said. (p. 376)

These concluding lines emphasize Frost's belief that man's ability to have faith in the yet unknown raises him above other creatures. One of the most famous examples of the superiority of human beings to animals is "After Apple-Picking," in which the speaker, exhausted from a day spent harvesting fruit, says:

> One can see what will trouble
> This sleep of mine, whatever sleep it is.
> Were he not gone,
> The woodchuck could say whether it's like his
> Long sleep, as I describe its coming on,
> Or just some human sleep. (p. 69)

In their thorough analysis of the poem, Cleanth Brooks and Robert Penn Warren (*Understanding Poetry*) have explored the implications of the speaker's speculations about sleep: "The woodchuck's sleep will be dreamless and untroubled. The woodchuck is simply a part of the nature from which man is set apart. The woodchuck toils not, neither does he dream. Man does work and does dream. He is 'troubled,' but the trouble is exactly what makes him human and superior to the woodchuck. The word *just*, in the phrase 'just some human sleep,' gives a faintly ironical understatement to the notion of man's superiority, but this is merely whimsical, a way, not of denying the fact of man's superiority, but of avoiding the embarrassment of making a grandiose claim" (p. 368).

In proclaiming human superiority, Frost even resorts to adopting the guise of animals, a technique found in one of his "beast-fable" poems, "A Drumlin Woodchuck." Assuming the voice of a clever woodchuck, the poet explains that he has been so "instinctively thorough/About my crevice and burrow" because he is so "small/As measured against the All" (p. 282). Here the poet-woodchuck recognizes that in spite of the finiteness of his being he must make a thorough and ultimate effort, for his only greatness lies not in the permanence but in the vigor of his endeavor. Frost's most explicit statement about the superiority of men to animals is found in "The White-Tailed Hornet," in which a hornet, after mistakenly attacking nailheads and huckleberries, finally discovers his rightful prey, a fly, but is unable to capture it. Witnessing the hornet's bungling efforts, the speaker says:

Won't this whole instinct matter bear revision?
Won't almost any theory bear revision?
To err is human, not to, animal.
Or so we pay the compliment to instinct,
Only too liberal of our compliment
That really takes away instead of gives.
Our worship, humor, conscientiousness
Went long since to the dogs under the table.
And served us right for having instituted
Downward comparisons. As long on earth
As our comparisons were stoutly upward
With gods and angels, we were men at least,
But little lower than the gods and angels.
But once comparisons were yielded downward,
Once we began to see our images
Reflected in the mud and even dust,
'Twas disillusion upon disillusion.
We were lost piecemeal to the animals,
Like people thrown out to delay the wolves.
Nothing but fallibility was left us,
And this day's work made even that seem doubtful. (p. 279)

What Frost is here decrying is the tendency of modern intellectual habit to concentrate on man's almost animal characteristics while ignoring those other capabilities which the poet sees as almost divine. Deprived of most of the merely instinctual motives for behavior, man is capable of living a supranatural life, for he has developed or has been endowed with the capacity to live his life not only physically, but also emotionally, intellectually, and spiritually. For Frost, therein lies man's distinction and his greatness.

But though this theme runs throughout the mature poetry, the limit of aspiration is always a human boundary; there is never any assurance that a creative design underlies the processes of nature. In "Innate Helium" (p. 541), which employs the aerodynamics of birds as a simile for religious faith, Frost refuses to commit himself about the efficacy of human spiritual striving. And, characteristic of *North of Boston* and the books that followed, even in the most optimistic pieces (such as "Two Look at Two" and "West-Running Brook") any suggestion of teleological purpose is speculative and qualified. In contrast, the poet of *A Boy's Will* had assigned to animals a major role and had received from them and their habitat an affirmation that was, by Frost's later standards, too facile and too absolute.

In conclusion, much of the poetry of *A Boy's Will* seems to belong to the nineteenth century, somehow reminiscent of the paintings of such artists as Cole, Durand, and Church; the bulk of this early poetry seems quite properly the product of one born in 1874. But the boy born when Ulysses Grant was president was also the man who read at the inauguration of John Kennedy. And when Frost came to formulate his own worldview from the complex materials of the twentieth century, he relegated animals to a minor role, using them frequently, but only as a means of capturing the intense variety of *human* experience.

"The Subverted Flower":
An Exercise in Triangulation

STEARNS MORSE

I doubt if some of us teachers will ever be completely absolved, despite our admirable intentions, for the mayhem we have committed on poetry. Robert Frost—the teacher, not the poet, told me that he once asked a class to list the things you could do to a poem. They dutifully responded; he dutifully wrote their answers on the blackboard; then as dutifully erased the items as they expressed their disaffection until only one answer was left: "read it." But of course if this injunction were to be rigidly adhered to there would be little left for us to do.

Some of us, too, have committed the perhaps more venial sin of dismissing Frost as merely a provincial, bucolic, popular and so a "simple" poet, though most of us, I fancy, have by now discovered that his simplicity was deceptive: I suspect "Directive" turned the trick for many. But "The Subverted Flower" could have done it just as well. For it is not an "easy" poem; moreover, superficially, it is quite unFrostian. UnFrostian because, though he has written movingly about love, both directly ("Earth's the right place for love") and subtly, this is the only poem—"The Discovery of the Madeiras" is perhaps another; at least it's the only one I can think of at the moment—in which he has been so explicit about love's sexual root.

Evenso it is not an easy poem, as I've said; it has been a troubling one for many. So I'm going to take a further look at it; attempt what I've seldom done before, fiddle with an explication. Or rather, look at it from three different angles. First to look at it more or less objectively, at the poem itself; approach it from what Sidney Cox has to say about it in *The Swinger of Birches*. "In 'The Subverted Flower,'" he begins, "a nice boy and a fine but educationally frightened girl are standing out where goldenrod and brake are

170

waist-high, but within calling distance of her mother's walled garden. He has just made a loving gesture toward her, impelled by a wildness akin, he feels, to the lovely wildness of the flower in his hand.

> She drew back; he was calm:
> 'It is this that had the power.'
> And he lashed his open palm
> With the tender-headed flower.

The actual flower becomes the emblem of his wild attraction."

I paraphrase and abbreviate Sidney Cox's explication: the wonder the boy feels, expressed in his smile, turns to cynicism—"another sort of smile"; he sinks to creature and his animal passion brings "her cynical miseducation into focus" as her mother calls and he becomes animal to her and, because to her, to himself; and then when her mother gets there, the denied wildness in her tears loose:

> Her mother wiped the foam
> From her chin, picked up her comb,
> And drew her backward home. (p. 341)

There are one or two things here that I'd like to speak to, but I turn now to another interpretation, equally legitimate, the poem in the context of Frost's life. Lawrance Thompson tells us, on Frost's authority, that the first draft of the poem could have been published in *A Boy's Will*; that he hesitated to publish because of his fear that it might be deemed too daring and too autobiographical; that, obviously written in his later manner, it first appeared in *A Witness Tree* in 1942, four year after Elinor Frost's death; and that it stems from a crisis in the relationship of Robert Frost and Elinor White, whose shyness and reticence thwarted his passionate and importunate lovemaking until the poetry of Shelley (ironically, it seems to me, in view of Frost's aspersions on Shelley's "Platonism") came to his aid. Thompson sums up the poem thus: "Metaphorically, the poem extends the meaning of the title until it includes or represents the unnatural attitude of the girl toward physical passion."

Sidney Cox's seemingly objective comment, I think, is really colored by subjectivity—not that I'd object to it for that reason; he was not only an intimate friend of the poet but in effect a "disciple" (which made Frost uneasy), with the loyalty that word implies. So there lurks, even if unconsciously, the image of the young Robert as a nice boy and of Elinor White, whom Cox also knew (as an older woman) as a fine but educationally frightened girl. I impishly cavil at these phrases: Hamlet a "nice boy," Ophelia an educationally frightened damsel? But I leave off carping. Lawrance Thompson was an equally warm friend but viewed Frost from a novelist's point of view, or rather, as he told me, from the point of view of one who had for years lectured on the novel. But, by no means shunning the light a biographical interpretation sheds on the poem and as one counting himself a no less devoted friend than these two, I'd like to tackle it from a less personal stance.

And in so doing, to adopt and extend the striking figure Frost once used to liken a young poet to a waterspout, taking into his sensorium from the great sea of the poetry of the past a welter of memories and impressions, and blending with these what he breathes in from his surrounding atmosphere; the sea, in my figure, being not merely the literary but all the cultural and racial experience of his heritage. For in the poem the boy's passion is biological and the girl's fright comes from something deeper than education or "miseducation."

"Culture," of course, is an amorphous mass of contradictory elements. But to concentrate on the sexuality which is the nucleus of the poem let me consider it first from the negative aspect: that hatred and fear of the body, of the "animal" in us, that plays such a large part in the centuries if not millenia of the Judeo-Christian tradition: that Puritan repression of the joy of life illustrated in our literature, to take only two examples, by *The Scarlet Letter* and *The Hamlet*, in which the only "love" is that of the poor idiot Ike H-mope for the cow. And to consider especially the repressive effect of our western culture on the sexuality of women in its various manifestations of modesty, inhibition, rigidity, repulsion, fear of rape, one may cite any number of examples from life and literature: James Joyce's wife, according to his letters recently published; Virginia Woolf; Sue Bridehead in *Jude the Obscure*; Miriam in *Sons and Lovers*. And these examples suggest that nature as well as nurture is at work.

Nor is the repressive effect confined to the female sex—by no

means! In the very poem I am belaboring Sidney Cox's "nice" boy
is sharply put off by the girl's revulsion:

> She looked and saw the shame:
> A hand hung like a paw,
> An arm worked like a saw
> As if to be persuasive,
> An ingratiating laugh
> That cut the snout in half,
> An eye became evasive.

And in *Sons and Lovers* Lawrence portrays the "virginity" of Paul
Morel, a "nice" idealistic boy, one of "the sons of mothers whose
husbands had blundered rather brutally through their feminine sanc-
tities." (This is one of the points, as I have noted elsewhere, at which
Lawrence and Frost, so seemingly antithetical, come together.)
Finally, to show how deep and pervasive is the effect of our taboos,
I may mention the curious fact that William James in his two volume
Principles of Psychology devoted only a page or two explicitly, if I
remember correctly, to the sexual function. Such, however, is the
whirligig of time that with Freud and the twentieth century we
seem to have come to the point of thinking about nothing else or
rather have seemed to dwell on the seamy side of sex under the
pretense or the illusion that we are celebrating its joy. (I resist the
temptation to pursue this paradox further since it is tangential to our
immediate concern.)

Furthermore the "acceleration of history" I have alluded to reminds me that it is time to look at the obverse of the seamy side, the
positive attitude toward sex rather than the negative. Henry Adams,
for example, as New England and "Puritan" as anybody, made up
for the reticence of his friend, in "The Virgin and the Dynamo";
finding in the mediaeval worship of the Virgin the pagan worship
of sex as a force of nature: the spires of Chartres, in effect, becoming phallic symbols; and in the worship of the dynamo the
worship rather of brute power.

I am not enough of a mediaevalist to say to what extent Adams
romanticized the Middle Ages, but I suspect he was right. At any
rate sex in Chaucer is nothing if not robust, full-blooded, whole-
some: one has only to cite the Wife of Bath and the frank love-

making of Troilus and Creseyde (despite her faithlessness). Nor
can we, to do justice to the Judeo-Christian tradition, forget "The
Song of Solomon," the love of Ruth and Naomi, of David and Jonathan, the compassion of Jesus for the woman taken in adultery—for,
what I am coming at, love takes many forms but is scarcely vital
if the senses are ignored. Nor, to do justice to our Anglo-Saxon
tradition, should we forget Milton's passion, his sensuous hymn to
wedded love, "natural" love as opposed to harlotry or the artificial
love of courts; the poetry of Keats and the Fleshly School of Poets;
Swinburne even; or Walt Whitman in America.

I quite agree with Robert Frost's remarks to Sidney Cox in 1911
that Shakespeare can teach us more about love than all the lecturers:
"even the bawdy passages would help us more." And this was because Shakespeare comprehended its power and passion, its subtleties, ambiguities, perplexities but was also aware of the seamy
side of sex: rape, lust—Sonnet 129— in short the "animal" in man:
"goats and monkeys." But this is Othello in his madness. For a
clearer view of animals we go to Shakespeare's youth, to "Venus
and Adonis": the stallion and his jennet; the "fleet-foot roe," "the
timorous flying hare"; and for sheer empathy with the subhuman
world the snail,

>   whose tender horn being hit,
> Shrinks backward in his shelly cave with pain.

So that we quite accept his later view—or Hamlet's—of man as the
paragon of animals. Still, we mustn't forget the angry boar—the
"wildness."

I come back to Frost's poem and the "wildness," our primitive and
animal nature and the striking images of this in the poem: "his
ragged muzzle"; "like a tiger at a bone"; "the dog or what it was,/
Obeying bestial laws"; "She heard him bark outright." But if we
are to think that in these images Frost is arraigning the bestiality in
man, a second thought catches us up short: what he is really saying
in effect is what René Dubos, the eminent biologist, says in *Beast or
Angel?*: "the use of the word bestiality to describe certain aspects
of human behavior is grossly unfair to the beasts"—no beast has

exploited the earth as man has; or so blindly engaged in mass slaughter; what by implication at least the ethologists are also trying to tell us.

So pervasive in the poem is this sense of our animal nature that I've had to re-read it to be sure that the word *wildness* was not there: for we can feel the "nice" boy's fine, even delicate face—whether that of the young Frost or another—twist in passion, the later agony; and in the girl's "too meager" heart is the constriction of aversion, terror. (Too meager heart: the adjective springs from a masculine arrogance: is it an echo of the resentment of the young Robert Frost at Elinor White's reticence and vacillation? Possibly. But I think we must be on guard against prying into inscrutable inviolable privacies, against taking the "autobiography" in this poem too literally. We have to remember that Frost was a poet with a strong dramatic sense; it is not too much to say that his lectures were an act. What is "autobiographical," what fictive, in the poem is impossible to say. But I will go so far as to surmise that the last few lines are drama rather than history; at any rate it strikes me that here the note is forced: the "bitter words" and the "foam": dramatic, granted; but they leave me, at least, with the ambiguity of the girl's emotion unresolved. But I'm not going to worry about it, I can let it go. And this is to quibble.)

For I can sense, far behind this essentially commonplace and trivial episode, the bewilderment of Cro-Magnon man at his blind anger and blood-lust, at the frightening, exhilarating surge of his mysterious sexuality; so that, leaping a million years later, we can understand, realize, Plato's charioteer, controlling with difficulty his superbly beautiful and his surly unruly violent horses. Yet, such is the power of love, our charioteer, miraculously, controls the horses so that in the end "the soul of the lover follows his beloved with reverence and awe." To put this sublime rhetoric into prose is simply to say how really deep and unconscious is our kinship with the beasts.

It would be sentimental, of course, to project our sensibilities into the subhuman world. Yet even the "affection" of our dog should tell us there is more to love than a behavioristic element, certainly in human love: the magnificence of Shakespeare—and especially in the sonnets where he speaks directly—is that he demonstrates both the primacy of sex and its emotional overtones.

Is it merely accidental that in the collocation of three poems in Frost's book the continuity of organic life is implicit? In "The Most of It," where the lonely man who wants not only life's "own love back in copy speech" but "counter-love, original response"; and gets it from the great buck, which, in those powerfully kinesthetic lines appeared,

> Pushing the crumpled water up ahead,
> And landed pouring like a waterfall,
> And stumbled through the rocks with horny tread,
> And forced the underbrush; (p. 338)

and then the birds

> From having heard the daylong voice of Eve
> Had added to their own an oversound,
> Her tone of meaning but without the words. (p. 338)

And finally the power of the flower—even if temporally subverted. The power of poetry, too, the power of the poem: which has called up, for me, these various associations; thus finding likenesses in unlikely places; leading me "to flash off into wild connections" so that I follow the chain of being in Frost's poems from that butterfly he saw in his early youth

> With all thy dazzling other ones,
> In airy dalliance,
> Precipitate in love,
> Tossed, tangled, whirled and whirled above,
> Like a limp rose-wreath in a fairy dance

through the comic woodchuck and the restless bear to that still mountain woodland where "Two Look at Two."

The "Estranged Point of View":
The Thematics of Imagination in Frost's Poetry

PATRICIA WALLACE

For years past she had looked from this estranged point of view at human institutions, and whatever priests or legislators had established; criticizing all with hardly more reverence than the Indian would feel for the clerical band, the judicial robe, the pillory, the gallows, the fireside, or the church. The tendency of her fate and fortune had been to set her free.[1]

I N Frost's poetry characters possessed of imaginative power are often more cursed than blessed. Like Hawthorne's Hester Prynne, their imagination puts them outside of one order implied by the poem and often destroys their relationship to the social fabric.[2] Consequently, many of Frost's most important poetic figures are outsiders. "Outside" in Frost's poems means a number of things, but most importantly marks the power of a question, reveals a hole in the whole circumscribed by "insiders," by figures of restrictive order, defined truth and rigid assertion. The imaginative power defined by Frost's poems works against restrictive orders; in an important way this imagination makes in breaking/breaks in making. In this respect Frost's poetry may be exemplary, in pointing out the tendency of all poetry to both order and disorder. While the language of poetry suggests an order made by the interplay of words, the language of poetry also challenges fixed order, to suggest what Roland Barthes calls "innumerable uncertain and possible connections."[3] Poetic order remains open, the text performs its own questioning. In Frost's poems the agents of that performance are most consistently outsiders, the possessors of an "estranged point of view." Many of these outsiders are women.

Frost's letters ascribe the unpredictable, impulsive, asocial and sometimes sexual versions of the self to the "bad bad man"[4] or to

177

mischief. Frost also connects that version of the self with creativity. The text of Frost's life, as presented in the letters and in Thompson's biography, seems restrictive, a text that will not accommodate a loss of restraints. But Frost's poetic texts give room to a play of forces restrained in the letters, and in this essay I locate that play in Frost's "transformation" of the bad bad man into the poetic figure of a woman. Women are perhaps natural outsiders in their very status as women, a status not fully a part of the social order. Certainly in Frost's poems women are often figures who act out asocial, sexual and sometimes violent behavior, and link that behavior with the imagination through imaginative disruption.

Imaginative power remains ambiguous in Frost's work, often located in the figures of outsiders who are incapacitated, fraudulent or diminished. This ambiguity suggests Frost's own fear of such power, a fear "not behind his poetic imagination but in it" as James Cox says of other fears in other contexts.[5] Locating the imagination in such figures curbs the power of poetry to challenge order. The potential threat of imaginative disruption ceases to be threat. In a shift of Emerson's phrase, such an imagination becomes the dwarf of itself. Frost's figures—especially some of the women—often take on power in the text and defy the restraints placed upon them by the text. These figures keep open the imaginative orders of the poetry. Critics have tended to see Frost's women as classic cases of hysteria or depression.[6] Their estranged point of view may, however, mark Frost's skepticism not only toward conventional values, as George Nitchie and James Cox have shown, but his skepticism toward a singular imaginative order as well.[7] The figure of the woman/outsider works to displace and disrupt the very order which the poetic text attempts to create.

How does Frost's poetry persuade us to see women as "allegorical" figures for the imagination? When we try to see Frost's outsiders as devices which allow the writing of the poem to qualify itself, they take on a power which realism refuses them, since Frost's women often do seem neurotic, on the verge of hysteria or trapped by depression, though their condition is often defined by an *insider's* norm, a norm the poem questions. As psychological studies these characters seem impotent, disabled by their condition of being.

That is, the reader places them outside the realms of power. But as figures displaying a theory of the imagination they open up the field of vision—redefine it. Women like "The Hill Wife" or "A Servant to Servants" or the woman in "The Fear" all see and hear what others cannot. As with the women to whom Frost gives the title "witch" ("The Witch of Coös" and "The Pauper Witch of Grafton"), the poetry places these women in contact with a darkness or a wildness which other characters avoid, but which the text of the poem must admit. As Frost's bird ("On a Bird Singing in Its Sleep") sings "out of sleep and dream" (p. 303), Frost's women often speak a language which brings into a poetic shape the realm of sleep and dreams. Sometimes these figures actively assert magical powers, of a magic itself often ambivalent. Like the two witches, Frost's outsiders seem to suspend the "rules" of normal life, as magic suspends such rules. They involve themselves in *craft*: they are pointed out as story tellers, or singers. Their craft often gives them a mastery over the disruption they embody, for these figures resemble poets as they work to bring disorder into figuration or narrative or song.

Sometimes women/outsiders are paired with figures of constrictive order, like the farmer-husbands James Cox sees acting out "how much Frost realizes, for all his willingness to exploit the poetic possibilities or aphorism, how blind and hard a proverb-quoter can be."[8] Often the proverb-quoter in Frost's poems suffers precisely from failed imagination. Like the neighbor in "Mending Wall" he cannot see behind his saying; he has restricted his vision and his language. The characters who work against proverb-quoters (sometimes wives of such farmer-husbands) expand the possibilities, sometimes to a frightening degree, of both vision and words. They function both to disrupt the repressive order of the proverb-quoter (the "insider") and to revise order itself—to include their estrangement.

The structure of the imagination implied by Frost's poem sets boundaries and trespasses them. This imagination is elation and threat, curse and blessing. As a blessing, the imagination disrupts restrictive order to make a richer order, one encompassing infinite suggestion as wonder. As a curse, imaginative power suggests the unchecked realm of nightmare (specifically invoked by certain of these poems), and the order issuing from its acts is sometimes terrible. In both cases the text remakes itself to suggest continual remaking. In "The Hill Wife," "The Witch of Coös" and "The Pauper Witch of Grafton" women are agents of disruption who work to displace one form of order of the poetic text and signal the violence of imaginative power. In "Paul's Wife" is the figure of a man who contains a woman within him. The marriage of Paul and his mysterious wife provides a union to bring the power of imagination to the side of a richer, more marvellous order. "Paul's Wife" celebrates what appears as threat in other poems. In a way, the poem reverses the estranged point of view marked by "The Hill Wife" and the "Witch" poems and dismantles the effective opposition of the terms inside/outside. So I will begin my own argument with a distinction I intend to qualify.

Like Wordsworth's Lucy Grey the Hill Wife takes flight, a flight which signals breaking out of enclosures. In a sense the wife disappears because she has already ceased to inhabit the space defined by the boundaries of family, farm and bedroom. She exists as outsider from the poem's start—outside town but outside the lonely farm as well.

"The Hill Wife" suggests the move to *figure* in the opening subtitle (repeated in the poem's third section): "Her Word." The subtitle not only assigns the narrative of the section to the wife but also fixes attention to the fact that what will represent the Hill Wife here is her *word* rather than her self. In the opening, her word is the poem's word as well. If we think of *her* as *word* the Hill Wife acts out a power in the text, the capacity of words to remake the order of a numbered stanzaic sequence, increasingly open the binding pressures of rhyme, and shift and break the line length. The poem's conclusion tells of the husband's "lesson": "Sudden and swift and light as that/The ties gave" (p. 129). The wife's disappearance works against the ties of family (the husband asks for her "at her mother's house," for his is the impulse of family) and farm. But the Hill Wife's disappearance from the poem in the final stanza also works against the ties of poetic order. The poem itself cannot seem to hold her; she moves into the spaces between the lines.

The poem assigns to the poet the stanzas which alternate with

"Her Word." His words move increasingly closer to the Hill Wife: in "House Fear" he addresses the couple, but in "The Oft Repeated Dream" and "The Impulse" the poet interprets the wife. "The Oft Repeated Dream" is her dream, a dream of the threat against enclosure, and the poet locates his metaphors in the wife. "The Impulse" of the final section is also the wife's, and the title itself suggests something driven by force, something powerful. What the wife does forces the reader to apprehend the word *impulse*. She performs several acts in the stanza: she follows her husband, then tosses log chips in a gesture that opposes the linearity ("furrowed") of her husband. She sings a secret song (an echo of her questions about the birds in the poem's opening), and she *breaks* a tree bough. Then she disappears. Her disappearance divides her from her husband as their activity is divided (she tosses, she breaks) and also as their language is divided. He calls, and she does not answer or speak in return. But his call is reported—the husband's words are never given directly. In a sense the wife does not speak the same language as her husband, but the language she represents (her/word) is the poem's language.

The Hill Wife "has no saying dark enough" for the dream of the pine against the window. Yet her presence in the poem forces us to consider a *saying* dark enough, forces us to go behind the surface of the language. The poet tells us in "House Fear" his own dark saying. Something—"whatever"—lurks in the house, needs time for flight, urges the opening of doors. The metaphor of *dwelling place* (*house fear*) suggests the text itself, the place which the poet inhabits. The image of the birds in the opening stanza supports such a reading of house; the birds occupy themselves with "built or driven nests" calling attention to an act of construction which may involve impulsion. The poet acts to construct the house—the frame or syntactic skeleton of the poem—which contains a ghost within, something which would press against enclosures. The poem "contains" the Hill Wife, who grows in the powerful impulse to disturb the surface of the poem, who becomes more and more suggestive, until she takes flight. Psychologically she may exhibit a disturbed sensibility which reads a trespasser's smile as threat and imagines him lurking in the woods. But within the text her word brings to bear the pressure of trespass and disturbing vision embedded in the construction of the poem. The text itself supports the figure of the Hill Wife too much to allow us the "explanation" of her psychology. The pressure of her word works against one imaginative order signaled by stanzas and title, pulls the poet's narrative sections closer to the word of the wife, and suggests the remaking of the poem's own boundaries. The poem's final word is "grave"; the concluding word of the opening stanza ("Her Word") is "nest." This shift in metaphors tells us that a dwelling place may be nest or grave, may "contain" life and death, presence and absence, creation and dismantling. The Hill Wife acts out the shift of the metaphors, acts out the imaginative urgency which reorders.

"The Witch of Coös" is also marked by a power pointed out as imaginative. The witch is an entertainer, a story teller, a magician, a conjurer, a "witch." If her powers are suspicious, the imagination too is suspect in Frost's work. Like the Hill Wife, the Witch of Coös sees what others do not, and the poem places her in the context of sleep and dream, with knowledge of dark sayings. Even more emphatically than the Hill Wife, the witch provides an estranged point of view. She occupies both the literal and the symbolic position of outsider. Her isolated farmhouse stands apart from the social order (the town), and her own language makes a distinction between herself and "folks." Furthermore the structure of the poem places the witch *outside* the reader's and the narrator's circle as well. The frame of listener-commentator places the witch for us; she and her son are "two old believers," remnants or relics of another age of belief than our own. In fact, the witch's situation depends upon belief: what the witch believes signals another kind of order than narrator or reader bring to the poem. Reading "The Witch of Coös" opens the definition of truth to accommodate the unverifiable, and in a sense the witch works against the restrictions of the reader's norms as much as she questions the town. The witch also works against the effort of the text to frame her and thereby curb her suggestiveness.

The question of the poem is the question of the witch's power. To the degree that the text undermines her power, the witch is restrained. To the degree that the text assigns her power, the witch begins to threaten the text itself. As a figure of imaginative power the witch often seems a shabby, neurotic curiosity. Contrasted with a poetic figure like Shelley's "Witch of Atlas," whose powers of harmony are celebrated, Frost's witch lacks mystery, strength and stature.[9] We learn something about Frost's attitude toward the imagination when we consider the stature of his witch. Shelley could celebrate the beauty of the Witch of Atlas, who joins everything together; but Frost, whose skepticism extends to the imagination and whose anxiety toward imaginative power is predicated on disruptions, offers a curious, violent, disruptive figure.

The language of Frost's poem is aggressively colloquial, combining the informality of colloquial language with the presentation of the fantastic, a characteristic of Frost's most "fanciful" or overtly magical poems. The informal language mediates the Witch of Coös by placing her within the realm of "common" occurrence and by indicating the uncertainty (via the uncertainty of colloquial language) of her claims.[10] Yet the informal language which restrains the figure of the witch also renders her powerful. When Frost associates fact and fancy in the democracy of colloquial speech, language and fancy dispute a single, ascertainable truth. Everything becomes problematic, including the value of "folks'" truth, the given order which excludes the witch. As an outsider the witch takes on the power of the estranged point of view, the power of skepticism founded in the informality of her language.

The poem has a kind of double story line. The witch tells the story of the "bones." Her story keeps us uncertain of her power over the bones. Did she in fact "summon" them, or did the bones take hold in a moment of sleep, when her consciousness became unbridled? Although the bones were buried in the cellar, and are now closed up within the attic, they still seem an other that the witch cannot quell. She can contain the bones, she can put them into the "spell" of a story, she can explain them away, but they continue to trouble her; they continue to threaten the limits she sets for them, as they acted to rise from cellar to attic. ("Brushing their chalky skull with chalky fingers,/With sounds like the dry rattling of a shutter," p. 206).

The other story teller offered by the poem is the poet himself.

He frames the story of the witch, he controls her suggestiveness, he questions her power. But the witch seems a potential disruption the poetic text cannot quell, just as she cannot still the bones. She is the "skeleton" of the poem's structure, the disturbing argument which attempts to bring the generative chaos of the cellar—the underground, or buried meanings of the text—into play. Like the Hill Wife, the witch reads the darkness; she *sees* nothing (no thing). On one level the poet suggests the comedy of the witch's vision, even the comedy of her own equally hyperbolic and matter-of-fact mode of narration. But Clark Griffith is right to say that in Frost's poetry comedy or wit is "an important aspect of terror."[11] "The Witch of Coös" is a *terribly* funny poem, a comically terrible poem. The witch disrupts pure comedy as her figure suggests a power capable of being terrible. This power takes the names of sexuality and violence, but those names stand for a power of transgression, an imaginative power to trespass boundaries.

What boundaries does the witch trespass? The story she tells disputes the line between fact and fancy (real/unreal)—indeed, in the witch's discourse the two are not distinguishable. The "confession" issuing from her story disputes the line between created fiction and autobiography. The details of her confession reveal a double transgression of "moral" norms—an act of adultery and an act of murder. All these transgressions work to disrupt orders implied by the poem. The narrator attempts to "verify a name" in the poem's conclusion, carrying on the impulse of the text toward verification. The witch complicates veracity ("tell the truth for once"), suggesting to us that truth must accommodate the unverifiable. As the witch breaks apart her crafted narration (she and her son have often told a false version of the story—their responses fill out the rhythm of a line) and "confesses," we feel as if she had seized the power of the narrative from the poet's hand. The "distance" or frame between witch and the poet becomes problematic. Listening to Frost read "The Witch of Coös" aloud, on the Library of Congress recording, we can experience the witch's confession as the conclusion of the poem: In the recording Frost omits the return to the narrative frame. The final and controlling voice of the recorded poem belongs to the witch.

The witch's confession disrupts the reader's comic, "safe" response to her. We suddenly wonder why we are laughing. Reuben Brower writes of a "moral horror"[12] in the witch's final statements, and certainly the reader feels a shock. The witch trespasses moral norms associated with most readers as well as with the implied world of "folks" in the poem. The reader sees her in the cellar, digging a grave, and her connection with the dark has become very complicated. One feels her power to disintegrate not only a moral code but also a man. She says of the bones: "They were once a man's," and in fact contact with the witch breaks up a unified human subject. Stevens says in "Poetry Is A Destructive Force" that "It can kill a man";[13] when the witch says "We were about it one night in the cellar" we feel her potential destructive force far more than in her son's earlier list of tricks such as moving tables in the dark. The poem assigns the power for this figure to sexuality and violence, to an intimate knowledge of the dark. Over and over again these forces are for Frost attributes of an imagination which oversteps its own limits.

The poem, as opposed to Frost's recording, does not permit the witch of the confession an unchecked hold on the narrative. The frame of the listener-narrator reasserts a claim on the text and returns to us an image of the witch searching her button box for a finger bone. That image puts the witch at a remove from her mystery as it brings her closer to us, domesticates her, and makes her claim to power once again comic. The poem does not allow the witch to remain in the cellar but acts to restrain her ("up attic") as she restrained the bones. Of course the witch's own story tells us that the nailing up of an insistent figure can never be fully effective. The witch hears the bones brush their chalky fingers, and the reader "hears" the confession of the witch *through* the narrator's conclusion. Her use of "truth" qualifies the narrator's "verify," and her use of a "story" qualifies the poem as story. As she disrupts one kind of order in the poem, the figure of the witch also reveals grave connections between a story and "buried" things, between a narrative and its claim to truth. The experience of Frost's text puts us in touch with an imagination that trespasses boundaries. We react to the violence of the witch's confession without admiration, but we ourselves have been affected by the ways in which she alters the poem. "The Witch of Coös" suggests that the boundaries between real and unreal, fact and magic, up and down, insider and outsider all contain gaps; "something" works to unmake the walls between such things. In part the "something" of "the Witch of Coös" is the power of being an outsider who can question just such neat distinctions. No wonder then that the witch is a story teller. The deceptively casual and colloquial story telling language of Frost's poem becomes equally capable of rendering ambiguity. No wonder as well that Frost is reported to have warned of his "Witch of Coös": "There's a difference between a trance-medium and a witch. Saul's Witch of Endor was a trance-medium, but this is a witch. Do not approach this witch with condescension."[14] Is the suggestion perhaps of an "origin" rather than a medium?

One certainly does not approach the "Pauper Witch of Grafton" with condescension. This witch is sister to Coös (Frost pairs them as "Two Witches"). Like Coös, this witch is literally an outsider, claimed by neither of two towns for its doles. She is also a relic of another age—one in which she had value—and a relic of her former, youthful self. Both suggest incompleteness. As a relic she appears a true pauper, for her threats ("Double trouble's/Always the witch's motto anyway," p. 207) are poor as well. All the power she asserts seems power lost, and the design of the poem continuously suspends belief even in her assertions. Like the Witch of Coös this witch confronts the reader with the question of power.

The Pauper Witch tells stories too: the story of the transformation of Mallice Huse, the story of the conversion of Arthur Amy. (She seems to have an acute sense of the topics of traditional stories.) She claims magical powers as well, powers to suspend the "rules." She can, she claims, change man into horse and set him bolting about the town. And she not only tells magical stories, but, like the Witch of Coös in her descriptions of the bones, this witch also aspires to the poetics of story telling. Following the structure of the sister poem, "The Pauper Witch" moves from story to confession, mixing fiction and autobiography; the move is made earlier in the narrative, which also contains a revelation. As the Pauper Witch "confesses," her language takes on a lyric nostalgia, and the witch becomes more clearly an imagemaker. She speaks the poem of her own youth; and in that moment (the moment before the snowberry melts), she too seems to threaten the narrative which she herself constructs.

All that characterizes the witch as story teller also places her "outside." Neither town will claim her since record books and law courts provide no evidence. The witch kicks the unproblematic notion of facts and record books out of its niche: she is the principal in the text both to dispute such facts and to name as illusory the given order of the law courts and the towns. Her *evidence* is human memory, and in the poem she suggests memory (in all its unverifiable power) as a substitute for evidence. This substitution works itself out through her two stories. The story of Huse's transformation models itself on evidence. Folks didn't believe her transformation because the evidence was questionable. Most of the story is given over to a complicated "proof" the witch offers, proof of Huse's being a "cribber." The proof itself is very funny, but the story of Huse lacks power as story and seems to remain on the level of anecdote. Only when she turns to Arthur Amy do we begin to feel the suggestiveness of Mallice Huse, for in the conversion story, memory replaces evidence.

The witch tells the story of Huse matter of factly. The story itself is outrageous, but the language suggests nothing extraordinary. That nice distinction between fact and fancy once again blurs. But the story—and the confession—of Arthur Amy moves away from matter-of-fact discourse, works to suggest innumerable and possible connections. The witch's powerful sexuality emerges from the Arthur Amy story; for once a "smarty someone" who disputed her power, Arthur Amy converted when he married the witch: she tells us "something happened/to turn him round." Well, part of what happened was marriage; the intimate contact with the witch's sexuality pulls Arthur Amy *outside* as well, causes him to become a believer on the other side. (Now we recall the suggestiveness of the witch's description of herself riding Huse, until she'd worn him to skin and bones.)

In a very powerful passage, the witch narrates her second story to a conclusion. In this narration is all the intensity of a nostalgic moment, the moment before the snowberry melts (the image itself suggests dissolving, for the snowberries are "wet"), the moment of youth, the moment of sexual union ("only bewitched so I would last him longer"). In "The Pauper Witch" this moment is full of energy and full of threat—the threat lies in dissolution, the moment comes apart even as it is created. (I am suggesting, of course, that this is the nature of imaginative performance in Frost's poems):

> Well, I showed Arthur Amy signs enough
> Off from the house as far as we could keep
> And from barn smells you can't wash out of plowed ground
> With all the rain and snow of seven years;
> And I don't mean just skulls of Rogers' Rangers
> On Moosilauke, but woman signs to man,
> Only bewitched so I would last him longer.
> Up where the trees grow short, the mosses tall,
> I made him gather me wet snowberries
> On slippery rocks beside a waterfall.
> I made him do it for me in the dark.
> And he liked everything I made him do. (p. 210)

The energy of the passage is sexual energy, "woman signs to man." This sexual power gives vitality to the figure of the witch but conceals within itself the power to kill a man. The witch's signs are double, not only woman signs but also the signs which are the skulls of Roger's Rangers. The double sign brings together life and death, creation and dissolution, and the particular imagery and the syntax of the passage support this knotting. The skulls seem both an image for testicles and a memento mori. The order of syntax is made to yield a double subject in the line "I made him do it for me in the dark." Given the sexuality of the passage, we can understand why Randall Jarrell writes of the passion in the line.[15] When we obey the sign of woman to man, we envision that place far from the house where Arthur Amy and the Witch "do it" in the dark. When we respond to the sign of the skull, we read the subject as the act of gathering snowberries on slippery rocks, precarious enough in daylight let alone the dark. So Elaine Barry tells us that Amy "went the way of most husbands of witches" presumably adding his skull to those of Roger's Rangers.[16] Ironically, then, Arthur Amy disappears at the moment of *gathering*, just as in the passage as a whole everything comes together only to split apart, to dissolve.

This moment appears in the text only to be curbed by the poem's conclusion ("You can come down from everything to nothing"). Like the confession of the Witch of Coös, the passage involves memory and a highly ambiguous syntax and imagery. Both passages swell with meaning almost to the point of meaninglessness: they both insist upon a certain indeterminacy whose insistence is quelled by the poem's conclusions. That indeterminacy characterizes the language of the texts and their central characters.

Both witches are potentially dangerous to order. They dispute clear distinctions, even clear distinctions about their own nature. As relics they resemble Roger's Rangers, whose "meaning" in the narrative is emblem, with the power of the memento mori. The historical meaning of Roger's Rangers is lost for most readers. The relic has the power of incompleteness, and so these poems push the reader to enact verification and so to discover how inadequate and impossible is such verification, thus making a point for the poem's own argument. The reader's own act of "filling in" always remains a contingent and questionable act. Frost's witches take their power from the way they permit the text to question itself, a self-questioning they force the reader to enact as well. They mark a certain incompleteness in the text, just as they mark a "hole" in the whole defined by town or folks or law courts. They are insistent, suggestive figures whose meaning is indeterminate. They signal the poem's strategy of making an order through words and syntax, and opening that order to question through ambiguity. The Pauper Witch substitutes the principle of memory for evidence and works to convince us of that substitution. But the nature of her memory is a double sign. So she closes her poem with one of Frost's own favorite phrases, "as if." The phrase is the contingent pivot on which the poem balances, the "maybe" which qualifies any conclusion, a "maybe" built into the estranged point of view, which sees all things with a questioning eye.

The Hill Wife and Frost's witches are figures who allow Frost to write about the alien, disruptive parts of the self crucial to the poetic act. They also allow Frost to narrate an imaginative power which evidences itself in transgression and destruction. So Frost poetically masters the risk of the imagination which he also fears.

But when Frost writes about a man who contains a woman inside him—"Paul's Wife"—he gives us an imaginative power creative of a richer, more marvellous order. Although Paul's imagination in a sense destroys his relation to the social fabric (places him outside), the social fabric simply isn't worth having. No one who reads the poem would choose the world of Murphy and the lumber camp over Paul's. Paul and his wife work in the poem as *ordering* principles, opposed to the disorder embodied in the "yell" of Murphy and his brutes, whose drunkness parodies imaginative power.

Like the female figures, Paul too is marked by a power pointed out as imaginative. Clearly related to Paul Bunyon, Frost's Paul performs wonders, gives the lie to the laws of gravity or human strength: he's reported to have jumped to land with both feet on the ceiling. His spectacular feats set Paul apart, but the principal distinction between Paul and the lumber camp lies in the principle named "wife." The basic story line of the poem tells us that Paul disappears every time someone asks him about his wife. Naturally such disappearance causes all sorts of speculation in the lumber camp, attempts at explaining Paul's extraordinary behavior. All this attempted explanation is handled by a narrator. One of Frost's typical threshold figures (those who stand between two distinct spaces), the narrator mediates between Paul and the lumber camp, sympathetic to Paul yet mystified, his tone more often than not that of the camp and its questions. Once again the narrator works as a frame, a device in the text to *place* Paul, to control the reader's access to Paul, and to "translate" Paul's muteness to the world.

This narrator also poses himself between fact and "yarn"; in "Paul's Wife" as in the "Two Witches" the norm of the poem includes the fantastic, although some of the norm is predicated upon the tall tale, where disbelief is the expected response. The most magical occurrence in the story of Paul's wife is the creation of his wife, and the meaning of that act. The world of the lumber camp distrusts this magic, which demands belief. In part, the poem suggests their distrust stems from the way Paul and his wife question the values of the lumber camp, suggest alternative values.

We know that Paul has magical status in the poem, but how does his wife acquire such status? She first enters the poem (as the word *wife*) in an utterance become magical. Everytime someone says "How is the wife?" Paul disappears. Everytime the "wife" surfaces in the text, something is reordered. The story of Paul's Wife tells us that Paul creates her; in a sense she is born both from a hollow log and as Paul's emanation. From the narrator's description of the wife, we learn she is beautiful and powerful, but the explanations of the lumber camp question both beauty and power. These "insiders" cannot imagine Paul's wife as anything but something stunted or impure. They fear the mischief of "wife," the principle in Paul she seems to name, because they fear mystery. For them, mystery suggests wildness as threat, the threat of the Indian; and instead of a vitalizing, dark-spirited Pocahontas of American literature they can apprehend only a diminished thing, "some half-breed squaw."[17] The poem says some imagine Paul "married a wife not his equal./Paul was ashamed of her. To match a hero/She would have had to be a heroine" (p. 192). A heroine is a concept beyond the discourse of these men. In their explanations, they diminish not only Paul's wife as wife but also her symbolic status as a principle within Paul. The other story about Paul's wife—the story of her creation—disputes such placement and gives over to the imagination a radiance and a beauty denied it elsewhere.

Paul's creation of his wife is a true creation story. The language of the poem suggests creativity of all kinds: imaginative, sexual, mythical and literal. The story reinforces the sense of Paul as an imaginative figure (and so links "wife" as an associated principal). Everyone else sees the black streak of grease on the log as a deformity, or a "normally" explainable hollow. The hollow in the log *belongs* to Paul because he is the figure in the poem who sees nothing. He sees the hollow as a space for the imagination to fill, and so he puts his powers into that space—suggesting that his imaginative act is a sexual act as well.

Paul is "open" to the hollow as original ("some new kind of hollow") originating at this moment. His openness reclaims the suggestions of *hollow* just as the strategy of the text asks the reader to be "open" to the various meanings of *wife*. His openness leads him to *wonder*, and in fact Paul is an imaginative figure because he is capable of wonder; he allows mystery to approach him (as in a less affirmative way the witch "allows" the bones to rise from the cellar).

Paul takes the "pith" inside the log to the water; and with the agency of water and breath (he blows it in his hands), the pith floats into the water, disappears, and slowly rises as a girl. This passage in the text is a very highly charged and beautiful moment, not only because Paul is powerful but also because the girl who rises from the water resembles Venus (and Eve); and her hair being "heavy on her like a helmet," she suggests Diana as well. She is powerful, as a relic is powerful, because she is incomplete, mysterious. She demonstrates that power in the commanding gesture of *looking back* (in Frost's poetry, this backward glance is always potentially frightening), and she looks back at Paul, who then himself looks back. In all of her features the girl reorders a complacent present, and the form of the disruption is classic: "Falling in love across a twilight mill-pond." The imagery of the passage brings into order this disruptive force by suggesting the orders of mythology, the principles of creation. The wife emerges in the text to efface one order (the lumber camp) and to make another.

The poem reminds us of the world of the camp immediately following Paul's "creation." The language returns to the tall tale, comic imaginative power, and the narrator says Murphy, concealed behind a shed, is our witness, our authority, for this version of Paul's wife. Murphy constructs the "as if" of the story; he makes the story dependent upon an ordinary human witness and provides an analogue for the reader who must also witness. "There was a moment of suspense in birth" the poem tells us *after* the girl has surfaced—that moment of suspense asks Murphy (and the reader) to leave the "truth" of the lumber camp and extend the boundaries.

The rest of the story of Paul and his Wife is Murphy's story as well: the story of what happens when Murphy is exposed to imaginative vision. His response presses him to a reunion with the "insiders"—"some other fellows" from the lumber camp, with whom he can get drunk before setting out to track Paul and his wife. Drunkenness is Murphy's substitute for imaginative vision; it releases him from his "normal" self, but the release has no nobility. So although Murphy and his crew move outside as they search out Paul and his "creature," they never really open themselves to that movement, any more than they know how to respond to Paul and his wife once they find them. The language of the poem first names them "Paul and his creature." Only as the text moves from Murphy to Paul does the "creature" take the name of "the girl herself."

Murphy locates Paul and his wife in a niche halfway up a cliff. This niche is another hollow, a space filled with the radiance of Paul and the girl. Within that space light and dark play as inseparably as a man and his shadow or, in this case, a man and his wife. Such play makes the niche into a world, illumines space, and suggests powerful ordering (they sit together, they harmonize). Once again, as the girl herself surfaces in the text, the language moves from tall tale into infinite suggestion, a rich play of images. Once again, the moment of the passage does not last. Murphy and his crew cannot perform Euclid's feat and look on beauty bare; they cannot witness the play of Paul and his wife without response, and their response is disruptive, destructive: "All those great ruffians put their throats together,/ And let out a loud yell, and threw a bottle."

As the text narrates Murphy's response, it pushes us to reading "Paul's Wife" as *figure*. The "yell" suggests a disordered cacophony of language, a cacophony that denies (or kills) the suggestiveness of poetic language, as well as the articulation of language itself. Murphy's crew must make a violent, physical gesture (throwing the bottle) because language fails them: they have no speech. As soon as the "shout" reaches Paul's wife she disappears. The poem gives the image of her light put out (we think perhaps of Desdemona) "like a firefly," the very image diminishing her in its two parts. Like Paul, his wife must disappear as she is addressed by the lumber camp, which has no language for her.

Murphy and his crew are frightening figures for a critic to discuss, for their tribute only puts out the magic of what they see (or read). They have no *terms*, no order, which will encompass vision. In "Paul's Wife," the real disruptive force is not imaginative power, but the lack of it, not the world of Paul and his wife (which suggests all sorts of rich orderings) but the world of the camp.

The conclusion of the poem returns us to the balancing tone of the narrator, who once again brings forward the language of the camp: explanations, judgment, owning: language which cannot describe the relationship between Paul and his wife, a relationship like light and shadow, two aspects of a single thing. The poem provides us metaphors to dispute the terms of the camp, but it never does *name* the "she" of Paul, for she is that in Paul which counters names.

The last lines of the poem gives us the dilemma, "A man like Paul/ Wouldn't be spoken to about a wife/In any way the world knew how to speak." The world's speech offers only the dichotomy of the tall tale or the fact. "Paul's Wife" shows us how words break down such distinctions, how *wife* itself suggests the magic of utterance. The moments in which Paul and his wife command the text challenge the world's speech, or the world of the camp or the poem's frames, a challenge both powerful and fragile, as is Paul's wife. They challenge a reader's response as well, call upon us to devise our own imaginative reply. Fireflies in the landscape of the text, these moments illuminate what we read in the radiance of their disappearance.

In "Paul's Wife" the imagination which revealed itself as disruption, as allied with dark saying and violence, now reveals itself as an ordering principle allied with illumination. The boundaries which place Paul and his wife outside have no real meaning: all the power of meaning abides in Paul and the woman within. In "Paul's Wife" Frost masters (by giving a poetic shape) an imaginative power to celebrate: the poem affirms the orders suggested by Paul's story, welcomes the displacement of the camp's disorder. "Paul's Wife" effectively positions the lumber camp in the estranged point of view. When Frost places the figure of a woman within (and without) a figure of a man he *marries* the distinctions between outsider/insider, order/disorder, and writes about the figure of a woman as if he did not fear her, or the imaginative power she represents.

Notes to The *"Estranged Point of View"; The Thematics of Imagination in Frost's Poetry* by PATRICIA WALLACE

1. Nathaniel Hawthorne, *The Scarlet Letter*, ed. Larzer Ziff (New York: Bobbs Merrill Company, 1962), p. 189.
2. Harold Bloom describes the Romantic imagination as destructive of the social self, "Internalization of the Quest Romance," *Romanticism and Consciousness* (New York: W. W. Norton and Co., 1970), p. 6.
3. *Writing Degree Zero and Elements of Semiology*, trans. Annette Lavers and Colin Smith (Boston: Beacon Press, 1970), p. 47.
4. *Selected Letters of Robert Frost*, ed. Lawrance Thompson (New York: Holt

Rinehart and Winston, 1964), p. 482. For other letters supporting the idea of the bad man or mischief, and the link with creativity, see pp. 344, 435, 451, 456.

5. "The Triumph of Lawrance Thompson," *Virginia Quarterly Review*, 47 (Winter 1971), 127.

6. For example, Elaine Barry, *Robert Frost* (New York: Ungar, 1973), p. 63; James Cox, "Robert Frost and the Edge of the Clearing," *Virginia Quarterly Review*, 35 (Winter 1959), 73–88; John Lynen, *The Pastoral Art of Robert Frost* (New Haven: Yale University Press, 1960), pp. 116–17.

7. James Cox, "Robert Frost and the End of the New England Line," *Frost: Centennial Essays* (Jackson: University Press of Mississippi, 1974), pp. 545–61; George Nitchie, "Frost as Underground Man," *Southern Review*, 2 (October 1966), 817–21.

8. Cox, "Robert Frost and the Edge of the Clearing," p. 77.

9. Of Shelley's witch: "The magic circle of her voice and eyes/All savage natures did imparadise" ("The Witch of Atlas,"), *The Complete Poetical Works of Shelley*, ed. George E. Woodberry (Cambridge: The Riverside Press, 1901), VII, 274.

10. See Cox, "End of the New England Line" for a discussion of the skeptical nature of colloquial language.

11. "Frost and The American Use of Nature," *American Quarterly*, 20 (Spring 1968), 37.

12. *The Poetry of Robert Frost: Constellations of Intention* (New York: Oxford University Press, 1963), p. 167.

13. *The Collected Poems of Wallace Stevens* (New York: Alfred A. Knopf, 1954), pp. 192–93.

14. Quoted in Marion Montgomery, "Robert Frost and His Use of Barriers," *South Atlantic Quarterly*, 57 (Summer 1958), 343.

15. *Poetry and the Age* (New York: Knopf, Vintage Books, 1953), p. 56.

16. *Robert Frost*, p. 70.

17. The metaphor of Pocahontas is Sherman Paul's unpublished observation about the female figures in William Carlos Williams' poetry.

Robert Frost's "Sentence Sounds":
Wildness Opposing the Sonnet Form

KAREN LANE ROOD

From the beginning of his poetic career Robert Frost stressed the necessity of capturing natural speech tones. Calling these tones "sounds of sense" or "sentence sounds," he pointed out their importance in adding drama to poetry: "Sentences are not different enough to hold the attention unless they are dramatic. No ingenuity of varying structure will do. All that can save them is the speaking tone of voice somehow entangled in the words and fastened to the page for the ear of the imagination. That is all that can save poetry from sing-song" (*SP*, 13–4). As early as 1913, he wrote to John T. Bartlett, "I alone of English writers have consciously set myself to make music out of what I may call the sound of sense" (*SL*, p. 79).[1]

But if Frost's poetry is based upon sentence sounds, as he says it is, why does he not write free verse? William Mulder identifies "a kind of tug-of-war" between form and sentence sounds in which "the best poetry results from the nicest compromise between them."[2] Ford Madox Hueffer wonders why Frost should bother "to put his work into lines at all." Though "not in the least suggesting Mr. Frost should write vers libre, I am only saying that it seems queer that he does not."[3] Why does Frost bother to work with the kind of opposition which Mulder identifies? This confrontation of form and sentence sounds is a basic part of all Frost's poetry, and it appears to be a direct reflection of Frost's world view. For if Frost admires freedom or wildness in the rhythms of poetry because wildness mirrors the confusion of his world, he also stresses the need to impose some kind of order upon it. As he says in a letter to R. P. T. Coffin, "A real artist delights in roughness for what he can do to it" (*SL*, p. 465). Despite his love for the freedom he finds in natural speech rhythms, he must assert again and again that "There is at least so much good in the world that it admits of form and the

196

making of form. And not only admits of it, but calls for it. . . . The background in hugeness and confusion shading away from where we stand into black and utter chaos; and against the background any small man-made figure of order and concentration. . . . To me any little form I assert upon it is velvet, as the saying is, and to be considered for how much more it is than nothing" (*SP*, 106–7). Since any form the poet can create is only a "momentary stay against confusion," the equilibrium can quickly shift in the direction of chaos and fear. But must a poem always contain a perfect balance between form and sentence sounds? Sometimes Frost allows sentence sounds to override rhyme and meter to demonstrate the dangers of not creating enough form, and at other times he seems by creating too much form to demonstrate the problems involved in trying to ignore the world's confusion. A poem is not a failure simply because Frost does not achieve a balance between order and confusion. When the balance is reached, the poem is affirmative because it provides a "momentary stay against confusion." Imbalance makes a poem fearful.

In experimenting with the shifting equilibrium between the freedom of spoken language and the restrictions of poetic form, Frost illustrates various attitudes toward the creation of form. Thus, some of his speakers are closer to Frost's own point of view than others. If the points of view of his speakers demonstrate different and more or less successful approaches to the world's confusion, it seems logical that the form of a poem must reflect the speaker's success or failure at establishing the necessary balance between form and confusion. One way to study the interactions of form and sentence sounds in Frost's poetry is to examine the ways in which he varies an *established* form like the Italian sonnet. Indeed, despite their deviations from convention, all twelve of Frost's Italian sonnets have clearly recognizable formal characteristics. Two of the variations are quite common. All but one of his Italian sonnets end with couplets, and occasionally he uses a second set of rhymes in the octave.

But one pattern of variation seems unusual. The conventional Italian sonnet often has four or five rhymes, but the number of rhymes in Frost's Italian sonnets ranges from three to seven.[4] In each poem, Frost seems to vary the number of rhymes to indicate the ability of his speaker to deal with confusion through the creation of form. Those sonnets with more than the usual number of rhymes seem to illustrate the danger of allowing too much confusion to enter the poem, while those with fewer rhymes show the problems of imposing too much form. A discussion of some of these sonnets will show how Frost deals with opposition between formal order and the confusion of sentence sounds.

"The Investment" seems to be a conscious effort to show the danger of not understanding the value of the proper use of form. Comparison with "West-Running Brook" illustrates the failure to create a sufficient "backward motion toward the source" which Frost celebrates in the book's title poem. The two major ways in which this sonnet violates conventional Italian form contribute a sense of failure to create a counter motion to the confusing flow of the universe. Not only is the speaker unable to maintain the same two rhymes in both quatrains of the octave, but in the sestet, he uses the same rhyme pattern with a third set of rhymes, instead of varying the pattern, as is common in the Italian sonnet. This repetition of the rhyme pattern, using a different set of rhymes each time, gives the poem a flowing sensation which echoes "The universal cataract of death/That spends to nothingness" in "West-Running Brook."

In "The Investment" implicit criticism of the speaker for not understanding the value of the form which he is using is supported by Frost's choice of subject. A young couple who know how consciously-created form may be used to stay confusion are contrasted to a speaker scornful of what he considers their useless actions. Even the title hints that Frost is on the side of the man and wife, implying that their actions have some value. Even if what they do is only a "momentary stay against confusion," they can continue to create form in other ways once they realize its value. Another clue to Frost's approval of them and to his criticism of the speaker is "staying," which the speaker uses ironically:

> Over back where they speak of life as staying
> ("You couldn't call it living, for it ain't"),
> There was an old, old house renewed with paint,
> And in it a piano loudly playing. (p. 263)

Both the poet and the poet figure seem agreed upon the hardship of rural life, but the ironic way in which the poet figure treats the concept of "staying," which is an important part of Frost's poetic theory, immediately suggests the division between the poet and his speaker. What is more, if Wordsworth can compare the sonnet to a "convent's narrow room," Frost may have intended the "old, old house renewed with paint" as an analogy for his modern use of the traditional sonnet form.

But the speaker fails to comprehend what the young couple have done, and he concentrates on the unpleasant realities of their life:

> Out in the plowed ground in the cold a digger,
> Among unearthed potatoes standing still,
> Was counting winter dinners, one a hill,
> With half an ear to the piano's vigor.

The speaker does not think the digger, who is facing the possibility of starvation, can get much comfort from the music. But the digger is listening and is creating form himself. In this quatrain is still an emphasis on staying confusion: the digger is "standing still" among the potatoes, piling them up to plan his starving family's winter meals. The speaker is unsure about the worth of such a limited stay. He thinks the situation is hopeless, and he sees no sense in trying to deal with it through minor actions:

> All that piano and new paint back there,
> Was it some money suddenly come into?
> Or some extravagance young love had been to?
> Or old love on an impulse not to care—
>
> Not to sink under being man and wife,
> But to get some color and music out of life?

The poet figure would like to attribute the paint and the music to chance, or to extravagance, or to impulse, and his lack of knowledge about form is illustrated in his inability to maintain control over the form of his poem.

He has observed the situation and, without understanding it, has decided to write a sonnet about it. But since he does not know enough about what he has seen or about form in general, he does not know how to balance form and confusion. Superficially at least, he is able to control the sentence sounds. That is, he is able to make all the pauses in the natural speech rhythms occur at the ends of lines. In fact, every line in the poem is end-stopped, emphasizing the rhyme. The only pause occurs within line seven, and this pause seems quite weak.

Yet though he can make all the natural pauses coincide with line endings, the strong rhymes do not stay his confusion. Failure to understand the value of form leads to incorrect use of the Italian sonnet. A lack of knowledge is apparent in the inability to use the same two rhymes throughout the octave. Nor does the sestet lead to resolution. The poet figure has created his own confusion. While he has been trying to stem the flowing sensation of the increased freedom of sentence sounds, his lack of control over his own rhyme-making ability creates a sense of rushing toward confusion. Even the concluding couplet only states another question. Thus, the poem ends with an increased sense of the world's chaos.

In contrast, the balance between form and confusion, as it is communicated through the interaction of rhyme and sentence sounds, appears perfect in "Meeting and Passing." In the octave where the rhyme scheme follows conventional form, the sentence sounds dominate. But in the sestet where the rhyme scheme deviates from tradition, rhyme dominates sentence sounds.

In the octave, the sentence sounds dominate by carrying the reader through the ends of lines, only to stop short in the middles of others. For example, no stops occur until line four where two stops appear in the middle of the line. The only other stop in the octave is in the middle of line eight. The control of the sentence sounds suggests both the confusion of nature and man's alienation from it. The emphasis in the octave is upon the two kinds of isolation which the speaker has identified. The first section shows his awareness of the otherness of nature:

> As I went down the hill along the wall
> There was a gate I had leaned at for the view
> And had just turned from when I first saw you
> As you came up the hill. (p. 118)

He looks at nature, but he is separated from it by a wall. He leans on the gate, but he does not go through it, as if he is aware of a permanent isolation from nature that going through the gate will not relieve. Thus, he turns from looking through the gate and glances down the road. He sees *her* coming up the road:

> We met. But all
> We did that day was mingle great and small
> Footprints in summer dust as if we drew
> The figure of our being less than two
> But more than one as yet.

The speaker realizes his separateness from the woman, but their temporary separation and eventual union are best illustrated by the footprints they leave in the dust—together, but pointing in opposite directions, or "meeting and passing." Indeed, underlying the flow of the sentence sounds, but subservient to them, has been the regular rhyme scheme which seems to promise future togetherness, the conscious creation of form through love.

The turn of the sonnet reiterates the basic tension of the poem. Her action is both a promise of union—"being less than two"—and a restatement of their separation—being "more than one":

> Your parasol
> Pointed the decimal off with one deep thrust.

But in the sestet, the rhyme begins to dominate the sentence sounds as the lines become end-stopped and the positive side of the tension is emphasized. In describing their conversation, the speaker seems sure their separation will be ended:

> And all the time we talked you seemed to see
> Something down there to smile at in the dust.
> (Oh, it was without prejudice to me!)

The conventional image suggested is that of a girl smiling and shy in the presence of her lover. But here apparently she, too, sees the footprints in the dust and understands their significance. What is more, the speaker's insistence that her feelings are "without prejudice" toward him indicates her pleasure at their promised union, not at their separation. Thus, even though their conversation is not given, some sort of communication has taken place, however trivial. The communication occurs through symbolic, almost unconscious actions. Neither of them may have realized that communication had taken place, but later the speaker is able to articulate it. Their communication is actually so deep that it colors the landscape through which they walk:

> Afterward I went past what you had passed
> Before we met, and you what I had passed.

They are still separated from nature, but now nature has a personal meaning which they have projected upon it: simply passing what the other has passed symbolizes their future union. Even in separation they are united. The rhyme of this concluding couplet—actually a repetition of the word—suggests control and sureness, and the resolution is strengthened by the speaker's use of "we met" in the last line. In line four these two words make a complete sentence, emphasizing the lovers' separation. When the speaker repeats "we met," the words are a part of a longer sentence which affirms their future union.

Thus, "Meeting and Passing" maintains a careful balance between form and confusion, rhyme and sentence sounds, not found in "The Investment." Yet, although "Meeting and Passing" is undoubtedly a superior sonnet, the achievement of a balance does not necessarily make the poem better than a poem without balance. Frost the poet is consistently aware of the value of balancing form and confusion whether or not the balance appears in a poem.

The balance of form and sentence sounds in "Meeting and Passing" is repeated more precariously in "Range-Finding." This is the only one of Frost's Italian sonnets which does not end in a couplet, although it actually has one more couplet than "Meeting and Passing." The more tenuous balance is understandable, for this is not a love sonnet. Rather, the narrator is considering the minute particulars of nature on a battlefield, and any generalizations are clearly the subjective creation of the poet, not objective perceptions of an ordered universe. As John Lynen says about this poem, "The upland pasture contains two distinct worlds, the battlefield where the human struggle is played out and the realm of the bird, the butterfly, and the spider. Though man's world is superimposed upon theirs, he cannot ever penetrate it" (*Pastoral Art*, p. 155).

At first, the speaker tries to establish a correspondence between the worlds of man and nature:

> The battle rent a cobweb diamond-strung
> And cut a flower beside a groundbird's nest
> Before it stained a single human breast.
> The stricken flower bent double and so hung. (p. 126)

But it soon becomes apparent that man's actions have little effect on nature:

> And still the bird revisited her young.
> A butterfly its fall had dispossessed,
> A moment sought in air his flower of rest,
> Then lightly stooped to it and flutteringly clung.

Lynen says the view of nature in this poem "suggests that the natural world is better than man's. It is pure, simple, innocent." He notes that "the world of nature comes to serve as a commentary on the human world" (Ibid., pp. 156, 155). Indeed, the speaker might like to see nature in this way. For even if man and nature are separate, nature could represent a moral order, and man could look to it for moral justification of his actions.

Yet in the sestet, the speaker returns to consideration of the spider's web which he seems to have passed over quickly in the first line:

> On the bare upland pasture there had spread
> O'ernight 'twixt mullein stalks a wheel of thread
> And straining cables wet with silver dew.
> A sudden passing bullet shook it dry.
> The indwelling spider ran to greet the fly,
> But finding nothing, sullenly withdrew.

But now death appears in nature, too. The spider's search for its prey is no more moral than the gunner's search for his target, and the speaker is forced to acknowledge that nature has no moral precepts to teach. The natural world is no less chaotic than man's.

In both the octave and the sestet, the speaker allows the sentence sounds to dominate for the first three lines, where no pauses occur, before he asserts his control by end-stopping lines three through eight and eleven through fourteen. But in the sestet where conditions have become more fearful, the speaker uses a couplet in the first two lines. The sentence sounds dominate still, but the placement of the couplet presents a firmer counterpoint to them. In the last four lines, the speaker returns to the rhyme pattern used in the octave, in what seems to be an attempt to reestablish the balance of the poem's first section. Use of this device in "The Investment" makes the form seem too weak to stay confusion. In "Range-Finding," however, this repetition of the rhyme pattern from the octave does seem to provide the form needed to counter the confusion and fear suggested by the sentence sounds. This poem does not provide the resolution found in a pleasanter sonnet like "Meeting and Passing," but the balance seems precariously maintained, close to the point of lapsing into confusion.

The tendency toward chaos in "Why Wait for Science" is more firmly controlled, possibly explaining why this sonnet is less interesting than "Range-Finding," "Meeting and Passing," or "Design." But Frost told R. L. Cook[5] that the form of "Why Wait for Science" pleased him. Why? Even though the rhyme scheme of the sestet makes the form seem tighter and more controlled than that of "Range-Finding," the speaker allows the sentence sounds to dominate in the octave. He accuses science of sarcasm, but he seems equally guilty of it himself:

> Sarcastic Science, she would like to know,
> In her complacent ministry of fear,
> How we propose to get away from here
> When she has made things so we have to go
> Or be wiped out. (p. 395)

While he directs his attention to "Sarcastic Science" in the first two lines, the poet figure is able to emphasize the rhyme with end-stopped lines; but after line three where he turns to the real problem, what to do if the earth is destroyed, the sentence sounds override the rhyme until the end of the octave. The only stops until the end of line eight are the period in the middle of line five and the commas in line seven. Neither of these stops serves to emphasize the rhyme at all; and although line eight is end-stopped, even this stop is very tentative—achieved through the use of a question mark:

> Will she be asked to show
> Us how by rocket we may hope to steer
> To some star off there, say, a half light-year
> Through temperature of absolute zeró?

The problem is serious indeed. But in the sestet, the speaker is able to reassert the rhyme and respond to the question ironically:

> Why wait for Science to supply the how
> When any amateur can tell it now?
> The way to go away should be the same
> As fifty million years ago we came—
> If anyone remembers how that was.
> I have a theory, but it hardly does.

The use of two extra sets of couplets helps to assert the form against the sentence sounds, especially in the sestet's first four lines where the sound of sense is only partially under control with two of four lines end-stopped. By the last two lines, each of which is a complete sentence, the form is firmly in control. The last line appears to be a reference to Frost's belief that the conscious creation of form is the most effective way to deal with the chaos of a frightening world but that since any form serves that purpose for only a moment new forms must be created constantly.

Thus, if the rhyme and sentence sounds of this poem are studied alone, "Why Wait for Science" creates the same perfect but momentary balance between form and confusion that appears in "Meeting and Passing." But what tips the balance of "Why Wait for Science" toward too much form is the use of irony—or ridicule. The speaker in this poem can be identified with Frost—there is no distance between the two as in "The Investment" where irony is employed. Since no irony is directed toward the speaker, his position seems absolute. The poem apparently ridicules all those who do not know his precarious answer. Irony does not always work this way in a Frost poem. If the irony in "Why Wait for Science" were directed toward man's desperate position in the universe, the poem would be a heroic assertion of form in the face of impossible odds. But the target of the irony is too easy, and the basic problem is not confronted; it is easier to attack science than to face the possibility of chaotic nothingness. The overconfident use of irony shows that the speaker has never relinquished control over the poem, even when the sentence sounds have seemed to dominate. His smug irony overrides the freedom of the sentence sounds, and the balance tends toward too much form. As the discussion of "Design" will suggest, ironic humor does have a place in the defense against fear. But the poet's target must be worthy of the irony expended upon it if the reader is to recognize the heroism.

Frost once said in an interview, "If people are looking for something to be brave about, there's their chance in poetry. . . . It's one of the ways of being brave."[6] The idea of poetry as bravery is never more apparent in Frost's poetry than it is in "Design." Too much form is used creatively and uniquely in an impossible attempt to create order from a situation entirely beyond the speaker's understanding. Both the tightened rhyme scheme and the defensive irony are appropriate because the speaker is facing a situation which requires all the form he can create, and more. At least in the octave, the speaker can maintain the conventional rhyme scheme, and his tone is almost conversational—with overtones of ironic humor. He seems able to submerge his ambivalence about the situation in the ironic images and to contain it within the regular rhyme scheme. In the first quatrain, the humor seems to hold:

> I found a dimpled spider, fat and white,
> On a white heal-all, holding up a moth
> Like a white piece of rigid satin cloth—
> Assorted characters of death and blight.

A white spider which looks like a fat, dimpled baby carries a dead moth across a presumably innocuous flower. For those of Frost's readers unfamiliar with the usual color of the heal-all, the situation seems harmless enough. But the third line indicates that the situation is serious. A dimpled spider is merely bizarre; a moth like "rigid satin cloth" is more ominous. True, wedding dresses are often made of white satin, but the satin in this poem is rigid. Satin is a soft fabric that flows with any movement. It can remain rigid only if it serves as something like a shroud. The death of the moth begins to take on a broader significance. But the speaker still tries to avoid confrontation with it. "Assorted characters of death and blight" might be almost as innocuous as a bag of mixed jelly beans. Still, the very lightness of the humor strengthens the apprehensive tone. Too much humor, like too much form, only increases confusion and fear.

Even by the time the reader gets to the second quatrain, he realizes that the ironic humor cannot balance the speaker's fears. The speaker must reveal more. Still his continued use of metaphor suggests he has not given in yet. Spider, moth, and flower are

> Mixed ready to begin the morning right,
> Like the ingredients of a witches' broth—
> A snow-drop spider, a flower like a froth,
> And dead wings carried like a paper kite.

Line five, as another attempt at light humor, is even less successful than line four. For the speaker seems to have made an unconscious pun on *rite*, and suddenly the reader is involved in the images of a witches' sabbath. The poet figure ironically calls the spider a snow-drop, but the humor is negated in the same line when he compares the flower to "froth," suggesting hydrophobia or madness. And finally, his last comparison of the moth to a paper kite fails to stay his terror. Evil in the guise of innocent child's play is no longer the least humorous.

In the conventional Italian sonnet the octave and the sestet have different rhymes, but here the *a*-rhyme from the octave is carried into the sestet. Indeed, the first lines of both end with *white*, emphasizing the speaker's obsession with the word. Until this point the sonnet has followed the traditional development which Hazard Adams describes as "the octave setting the scene and leading up to the climax in the sestet. . . ."[7] But here the speaker does not want to reach the climax, to unmask his fears to either himself or his readers. Thus, he drags into the sestet a rhyme which has helped to stay his confusion in the octave. Adding only one new rhyme tightens the form. Instead of the usual four or five rhymes, he has three. He is able also to increase the number of couplets from the usual three to six.

None of this added form prevents the speaker's terror, however. As Reuben Brower says, "The sestet brings the expected change in tone, now no longer easily observing and half-singing though in mockery, but self-questioning and increasingly serious" (p. 106). Finally, the speaker must ask the questions he has successfully avoided in the octave:

> What had that flower to do with being white,
> The wayside blue and innocent heal-all?
> What brought the kindred spider to that height,
> Then steered the white moth thither in the night?
> What but design of darkness to appall?—

And his only defense is the slight equivocation:

> If design govern in a thing so small.

Here is a case of too much form which only increases fear by what it leaves out.

Indeed, tight control of the sentence sounds is achieved because all the lines are end-stopped to emphasize the rhyme. By preventing the free flow of everyday speech rhythms, Frost increases the sense of overformalization. But the dashes at the ends of lines three, six, and thirteen suggest that the speaker has forced himself to pause and not to articulate the terror and confusion with which he is incapable of dealing. No amount of rhyme in any pattern could enclose such fears. The extra couplets serve only to emphasize the impossibility of conclusiveness, or summary of the situation. Yet, the speaker does not try to reduce or abstract reality to something which can be dealt with more easily, and his attempt to face a frightening, chaotic world makes him heroic. His awareness of the value of form and his creation of it are the only means through which he can face reality. Even if these means are insufficient and the form is defeated before he completes it, his heroism remains.

In 1913, shortly after publication of his first book, *A Boy's Will*, Robert Frost wrote in a letter to John T. Bartlett, "To be perfectly frank with you I am one of the most notable craftsmen of my time" (*SL*, p. 79). Certainly Frost's use of the Italian sonnet suggests that this statement is not mere boasting. Because Frost is so very conscious a manipulator of poetic form, he can adapt a traditional form like the sonnet to suit the needs of a unique situation without obliterating the basic characteristics of that form. But Frost's talent lies equally in knowing what not to manipulate. A poem must have both form and confusion: "If it is a wild tune, it is a poem. Our problem then is, as modern abstractionists, to have the wildness pure; to be wild with nothing to be wild about. We bring up as aberrationists, giving way to undirected associations and kicking ourselves from one chance suggestion to another in all directions as of a hot afternoon in the life of a grasshopper. Theme alone can steady us down. Just as the first mystery was how a poem could have a tune in such a straightness as meter, so the second mystery is how a poem can have wildness and at the same time a subject that shall be fulfilled" (*SP*, p. 18). A reader of Frost's poetry can recognize the irony of his statement that the modern poet has "nothing to be wild about." Indeed, as he suggests in the next sentence, his greatest problem is "steadying down" the world's wildness in such a way as to have both confusion and form. While form is important, so is wildness, and the sonnets consistently praised are those in which the wildness of the sentence sounds is strong. "Why Wait for Science," where the balance is smugly maintained, is clearly inferior to "Design," where the world's wildness is obviously in control. "Meeting and Passing" and "Range-Finding," where the balance of form and confusion is maintained, show a strong sense of the chaos of the universe and a realization of the momentary nature of any stay against it. Thus, Frost's artistry is like the art of swinging birch trees:

> I'd like to go by climbing a birch tree,
> And climb black branches up a snow-white trunk
> *Toward* heaven, till the tree could bear no more,
> But dipped its top and set me down again.
> That would be good both going and coming back. (p. 122)

Knowing that no poem can stay confusion indefinitely, Frost asserts that a poem must defend against confusion and prepare its reader to face the world again. Wildness and form are opposites that must be combined in one poem.

Notes to *Robert Frost's "Sentence Sounds": Wildness Opposing the Sonnet Form* by KAREN LANE ROOD

1. The uniqueness of Frost's concern for capturing the rhythms of natural speech is emphasized when Robert S. Newdick can say in 1937 that Frost has "led by at least two literary generations the present hue and cry for the right metrical tran-

scription of the natural speech of men . . ." ("Robert Frost and the Sound of Sense," *American Literature*, 9, p. 296). And critics like Tom Vander Ven have recognized the importance of sentence sounds to Frost's poetic theory: "Robert Frost's Dramatic Principle of 'Oversound,' " *American Literature*, 45 (1973), 243.

2. "Freedom and Form: Robert Frost's Double Discipline," *South Atlantic Quarterly*, 54 (1955), 391.

3. "Mr. Robert Frost and 'North of Boston,' " *The Outlook* (27 June 1914), p. 280.

4. This tablulation may help the reader:

	NUMBER OF RHYMES	RHYME SCHEME
"The Flood"	7	abbacddceffegg
"A Soldier"	7	"
"The Investment"	7	"
"The Vantage Point"	6	abbaaccadeedff
"A Dream Pang"	5	abbaabba cdcdee
"Meeting and Passing"	5	"
"Any Size We Please"	5	"
"Range-Finding"	5	abbaabba ccdeed
"Why Wait for Science"	5	abbaabba ccddee
"The Broken Drought"	5	"
"Bursting Rapture"	4	abbaabbaccdcdd
"Design"	3	abbaabba acaacc

5. "Frost on Frost: The Making of Poems," *American Literature*, 28 (1956), 68.

6. Mary Handy, "Something Brave to Do," *Christian Science Monitor*, 21 December 1955; rpt. in *Interviews with Robert Frost*, ed. Edward Connery Lathem (New York: Holt, Rinehart and Winston, 1966), p. 151.

7. *The Contexts of Poetry* (Boston: Little, Brown, 1963), p. 53.

PLAY

Marion Montgomery's essay heads this section both because of its breadth and because of its explicit statement of an implication underlying the broad and varied definitions of play and irony found in the essays that follow. Professor Montgomery says "Frost is in large part a wily Odysseus" concerned with survival; and his subtitle is important: "One Who Shrewdly Pretends." The essay deals with Frost and Poe (and William Carlos Williams on Poe) as well as with the theme of homesickness so prevalent in American literature.

A major significance of the concern with concepts of play is that students of Frost are reading beneath the roles as crackerbarrel philosopher and national poet—with the intent of studying the man revealed in the art and the technique rather than the one who has become a source of gossip and rumor. Possibly they are investigating the Frost whom Frost himself really presented and really wanted studied and understood.

Marjorie Cook finds play a serious matter in Frost's approach, and she explores a depth still not sufficiently understood. She takes up particularly the critical matter of acceptance and, though she writes something of an apologia, finds no reason to apologize for the idea of a step backward taken for the purpose of a renewed offensive in man's struggle against the secret that sits sphinxlike and knows. She discovers in Frost a good deal of the practical sensibility and some of the resourceful slyness, itself playful against erratic odds, required in a universe that apparently builds man to be a deliberate antagonist to the paradoxes he recognizes. The fun's in how you say a thing in trying to tell the unknown truth and in how well you play the game when the rules are unclear. These essays are generally discerning a Frost who moved into a chaotic twentieth century able to face future shock with equanimity, despite

211

the numerous tragedies in his personal life and a sensitive awareness that on Virginia Woolf's famous date, as well as on numerous others thereafter, changes suddenly occurred.

Margaret Edwards uses a definition of Frost's concept of play to deal with his use of animals in a way that recalls the satirical beast fables. The reader may use his own knowledge of Frost's methods to judge how playful or how ironically severe Frost was being in his comments on man. Even the "upward comparison" of "The White-Tailed Hornet" deals with one of man's theories about nature. The animals discussed here may be compared with those discussed in Richard Reed's essay (in METHOD AND THEORY).

Walton Beacham concentrates on two—perhaps the main two—of the several Frosts—one who had his popular appeal and the other who hinted, often through technique—that a Frost as craftsman was working subtly at an art for the serious student of both culture and craft. The implication is that Frost had more kinds of fooling and schooling than his students have yet appreciated.

Stephen D. Warner's succinctly informal essay states a concept of play in the somewhat personal introduction. While seriously discussing another aspect of the poetic craftsman, Professor Warner recalls both Marion Montgomery's man who shrewdly pretends and, with or without intent, something of the distinctly American Yankee storyteller and humorist.

The essay by David Sanders closes the section with a new and original interpretation of "Directive" that at least by implication demands further investigation of the awareness a Frost desirous of immortality had of the Whitman (of "Crossing Brooklyn Ferry") whom Frost may have admired—and resented.

J. T.

Robert Frost: One Who Shrewdly Pretends

MARION MONTGOMERY

Wᴵᴸᴸᴵᴬᴹ Cᴬʀʟᴏˢ Wᴵᴸᴸᴵᴬᴹˢ (*In the American Grain*)
praises Edgar Allan Poe as the first American writer in whom place
is decisive. Poe is "a genius intimately shaped by his locality and
time." In him is "a *new locality* . . . ; it is America, the first great
burst through to expression of a re-awakened genius of place." And
again, "What he says, being thoroughly local in origin, has some
chance of being universal in application. . . . Made to fit a *place*
it will have that actual quality of things anti-metaphysical—" "The
language of his essays is a remarkable HISTORY of the locality he
springs from." Williams's use of *place* and *locality* are confusing to
say the least, given Poe's actual work, and his praise might seem
better suited to a poet like Robert Frost. But then one sees that he
is giving a special twist to the terms, the meaning of which in his
usage points, I think, to a fundamental if unexpected kinship between Poe and that New England poet of the local, Frost. It is a
kinship beneath the surface of Frost's local images and Poe's surface
which deliberately excludes the local. And it is precisely in the
metaphysical ground of each that we find it, in spite of Williams's
attempt to rescue Poe from the onus of a position, metaphysical or
other. For the burden of this praise of Poe is of Poe's independence—
his rejection of the traditions of language and, in the final analysis,
of place itself. Poe dares to be "original." He does so "in that he
turned his back and faced inland, to originality, with the identical
gesture of Boone."

Poe faces not inland but inward; he does not address himself to
that vague "America" realizing slowly westward, about which Frost
speaks, but to that vague modern country without national bound,
the self. In that cosmological poem he calls *Eurika* there is the concern with origin and end of *thing*, but most particularly a concern
with that thing of all things, the individual consciousness. And he
anticipates for it an ultimate annihilation. In his own words, "*In the*

Original Unity of the First Thing lies the Secondary Cause of All Things, with the Germ of their Inevitable Annihilation." His best poems and tales, his prose poems and criticism, engage the struggle to escape annihilation, to arrest a moment of consciousness as a stay against the confusion of a world outside consciousness. And since that attempt is finally focused "inland," and because he is in revolt against the traditions anchored in the mother tongue and mother-land—what Hawthorne called "our old home"—Poe's work carries on its surface no significant marks of place, of the local, such as is the traditional anchor of language.

Williams admits as much. "What he wanted was connected with no particular place; therefore it *must* be where he *was*." But where Poe was as writer was not Philadelphia or Boston or Virginia. If in him "American literature is anchored, in him alone, on solid ground," Williams's words are metaphorical, Poe's "solid ground" being the vague, rootless homesickness that is common to much American literature sprung out of a disappointment with this new Eden we call wistfully America. Frost is himself in this tradition, though he is much more cautious about his own homesickness and hides it from us skillfully through the concrete particular that speaks its New England locale.

One is not surprised to find Williams setting Poe above that other New Englander who, like Frost, uses the local; who, like Frost, is heavily dependent upon traditional forms. Williams says, "what Hawthorne *loses* by his willing closeness to the life of his locality in the vague humors; his lifelike copying of the New England melancholy; his reposeful closeness to the town pump—Poe *gains* by abhoring, flying to the ends of the earth for 'original' material—" What Williams's argument boils down to finally, after one gets through the mimicry of Poe's rhetoric and typography, is that Poe is our first great genius, the founding father of American literature, because he chooses originality over all else and has the courage to reject both the past and the particularity of the local so that he may assert the absolute independence of the Self. Such an independence proves grievous to us at this juncture of our history, its cost being isolation, alienation. The separation from both the past and the present local is of such a degree that he often feels he writes only for himself. Reading *Marginalia* is like reading the notebooks of Stephen Dedalus, in spite of the fact that Poe sent those paragraphs abroad into the proliferating periodicals to woo a popular audience, for which he hungered. That is one of the added ironies, which explains his constant quarrel with the reader, for whom he nurtures a generous contempt.

Now such a reading of Poe makes him appear diametrically opposed to Robert Frost. What poet of the new world has a closer, more careful concern for the particulars of the local, or more assiduously cultivates a closeness to the town pump? What sharper eye for a white feather in the tail of a frantic bird, a smouldering woodpile, cobwebs, hay stubble? Who knows hired men better, or the loneliness of isolated women? But if Poe has made his address to the dangers of the abyss, to the threat of the absurdity of existence, by divesting poem and tale of the local particular to lean upon tone and rhetoric to court horror—which he sometimes calls Beauty—we need not conclude prematurely that Frost's address to the secret of existence through his explicit images of the local sets him a pole apart. In so far as the ground—the metaphysical ground—of his work goes, he is hemispheres closer to Poe than to Hawthorne.

One is advised to remember that Frost is in large part a wily Odysseus, one who believes that in the interest of survival in strange seas it pays to be shifty and secretive. One may on some occasions admit to being acquainted with the night or speak of those desert places near home, closer even than snow-filled stubble. But for the most part, the strong are saying nothing about the suggestion in a vague homesickness that leads to uncomfortable conclusion about annihilation. Hints of spring are not evidence of immortality. The strong may say nothing, or they may tell a lie with metaphor, just for fun. And it is the poet who is best equipped to tell the lie, as Plato complained long ago. But the poet's danger comes when he *believes* the lie. When the strong talk, they do so in the subjunctive mood. The "extravagance" Frost allows himself as poet is to play the game called " 'it sometimes seems as if.' "[1] He adds, "politics is an extravagance ... about *grievances*," (which he enjoys at times, as in "New Hampshire"). But "poetry is an extravagance about *grief*." At his best, grief is his occasion, in "Home Burial," for instance, and in

"After Apple-Picking." But it is an *extravagance*; one must never forget the deliberateness of the excess. To do so may result in one's being pulled into the game of poetry over his head—lost in higher agonies of the self through illusions about metaphysical ultimates of a Platonic cast. That is, one must stay on guard by remembering that poetry is a game one plays, like restoring a wall or clearing a patch on the face of the natural world. The figure a poem makes is a momentary entertainment of the consciousness for its own protection, lest its self-universe be shaken to its foundations. Because that threat is a constant, one must be prepared to take one step backward if necessary. "The play's the thing," he says in the introduction to Robinson's *King Jasper*. "Play's the thing. All virtue in 'as if' . . . As if, as if!" (*SP*, 67).

There are poems other than these introduced by allusion in which Frost is threatened. "For Once, Then, Something" is one. Here he recovers through playfulness, a pattern repeated to the point that some of his best poems are weakened. He will retreat into the coy or sentimental, neither of which poses is to be taken too seriously, as the threat itself must not be taken too seriously lest the beauty of the game turn toward horror and despair or even hope for a transcendent. And in this ruse he is most unlike Poe, who courts despair. Frost's retreat is a sign of a deliberate recovery of equilibrium, the step backward taken. "What was that whiteness? / Truth? A pebble of quartz? For once, then, something?" So too ends *The Narrative of A. Gordon Pym*, with the image of the vague figure of man standing over the abyss. But Poe's novel ends with no question mark. Frost reduces the terror and awe that creep in about the edges of his playfulness by the juxtaposition of inordinates—quartz and truth—to maintain (to borrow from another New England poet) a quartz contentment. So too at the end of "After Apple-Picking" in the juxtaposition of a woodchuck's "sleep" to "just" some human sleep. The effect is to undermine, to reduce, the seriousness of that encounter that borders upon vision and reduce it to an illusion from which the speaker has recovered.

Allen Tate ("Robert Frost as Metaphysical Poet") complains of "Birches" that the trees "seem too frail to bear such a portentous allegory." And he objects as well to the concluding line: " 'Marse

Robert' might have spared us the sententious meiosis of the last line."[2] But Frost isn't simply playing devices of prosody out of Quintilian. He might have spared us, but to do so would have required his going beyond the game of poetry, beyond playacting in the role of the poet as wise man, even the crackerbarrel wise man. He would need to *become* the wise man, perhaps as Socrates was, whose wisdom lies in his knowing that he knows nothing. Socrates's is a movement of consciousness such as requires a surrender to something other than its own devices. But as long as we dance in a circle and suppose, so long as we play *as if*, we can distract ourselves in the dance and set aside the threat of the secret in the middle. Truth? Quartz? The "matter of fact" about ice storms, which is rather a delightful dance of fancy on ice than fact's matter?

Not that Frost hasn't pretty well decided about that secret. He speaks of it rather directly in the letter to *The Amherst Student.* "The background in hugeness and confusion shading away from where we stand into black and utter chaos . . ." (*SP*, p. 107). That is what remains when the dancer and the dance are separated out. Chaos is the antagonist of mind, and chaos will prove victorious if mind, through self-delusion, supposes that form resides in chaos or beyond chaos or anywhere except in the action of the mind where we stand. For Frost as for Poe, in Williams's words, place is "where he *was.*" There is more of Sartre in both poets than usually noted, though it is less grimly and humorlessly present in Frost.

We note Frost's opposition to "Many of the word's greatest—maybe all of them" who are "ranged on that romantic side" called Platonism, as Frost remarks in contrasting himself to Robinson.[3] Plato's Idea is transcendent and requires an action of the individual consciousness for which the consciousness may take no credit. There is, one discovers, something of the New England trader about Frost in this respect. ("The Road Not Taken" is still "told" by the words, Frost's deposit in the world. He is flirting with immortality in the poem as Shakespeare does in Sonnet 18. And he is good enough, one adds, that his account is still solvent.) His mean words about Robinson, a poorer poet and greater soul than Frost, are out of the same ambition in Frost to be seen as the one great American poet of his generation. One sees that hunger for acclaim in the sharp jealousy toward Edgar Lee Masters, who seemed to threaten Frost as the American poet after *Spoon River Anthology*. It is also in his public, playful encounter with Sandburg over the question of form in poetry—kitten play, but with his claws not quite sheathed. One prefers Frost's advancement of the Self as gamester in the poems, of course.

It is in the poems that Frost makes the best of his antiPlatonism, rather than in unfortunate remarks to Louis Untermeyer or in his occasional prose statements and prefaces. One doesn't need to be told separate from the poems that Frost takes mankind to be "thrust forward out of the suggestions of form in the rolling clouds of nature" or that what really signifies is "any small man-made figure of order and concentration" cast against "the background in hugeness and confusion shading away from where we stand into black and utter chaos" (*SP*, p. 107). And one knows, reading his poems "in the light of all the other poems ever written" as he suggests, that "So many of [the poems] have literary criticism in them—*in* them." He adds, typically, "And yet I wouldn't admit it. I try to hide it." How skillfully and effectively hidden is revealed by one's reading "Birches" or "After Apple-Picking" against Keats's "Ode to a Nightingale," through which reading one sees Frost's criticism of the dangers of Platonic illusion. The same may be done with "A Boundless Moment," a more playful reading of the Platonic inclination. And Wordsworth's wooing of "something deeply interfused in nature" in "Tintern Abbey" receives a rather more caustic commentary in Frost's "Mending Wall." Wordsworth is attracted to hedgerows that have become "little lines of sportive wood run wild," thus violating the poet's mind through illusion, as they violate hedgerows' responsibility to constrain nature. Something in nature doesn't love a wall. But it isn't elves: it is inrolling clouds of chaos, with which one may play the game of personification if he will, so long as he doesn't succumb to the belief that something in nature binds consciousness in a larger order than of its own devising. (It is at such points that one finds Frost aligned with Wallace Stevens, incidentally.)

Allen Tate, in his remarks on Frost as metaphysical poet, remarks of "Mending Wall" that "Good neighbors are good to have, but good fences do not make them good neighbors. Here we have Frost's perilous teetering upon the brink of sentimentality. Fences good or bad make nothing; but upon the rhetorical trick that attributes causation to them the poem depends." Mr. Tate finds the poem subject to the same weakness in its conclusion that I have suggested one finds in "For Once, Then, Something" and "After Apple-Picking." But I do not think sentimentality threatens "Mending Wall" as it does "Birches." There is rescue possible, which requires first a more extensive quotation from Mr. Tate. He continues: "I could wish that this fine poet had drawn upon his classical learning and had alluded to the first thing that the Romans did when they were making a settlement: they built a low wall that would enclose a forum and in the middle set an altar. The wall around the altar shut out the infinite . . . as if they might have foreseen the disorderly love of infinity that Walt Whitman would bring into the world."[4] I could wish the same, but I recognize that Frost's position opposes both a Walt Whitman and the Romans. For all his celebration as public poet and in spite of his classical training, Frost is not a poet of community, anymore than he is a poet who will allow consciousness to bleed freely into the world as Whitman does. "Mending Wall" precisely reflects Frost's position. The act of building walls does indeed preserve *one* (not the community) from both the encroachment of infinity and the dissipation of the self in infinity where all walls are down (as with Whitman). There stands the figure of chaos in the shape of a man, the neighbor hulking beyond the wall "like an old-stone savage armed." The poem, given such an antagonist, becomes finally a game like that of swinging birches—one which the narrator must play alone, since the "neighbor" will not go behind the scripture on walls. That neighbor might possibly agree to "elves" as the culprit, but that reduces the game to a rather primitive level not worth the wit expended. The suggestion isn't even made aloud. For there has been no response to the suggestion that "My apple trees will never get across/And eat the cones under his pines." A response is possible: pines invade and take over ordered trees—apple orchards. Even that domesticated cow can be affected by disorder in fallen fermented apples, go wild, as the neighbor well might know. But he moves in darkness himself, a darkness of the mind that doesn't

...now the game of the mind with chaos, which game depends upon the mind's cleverness with walls, one of which walls is the language itself. The *why* of walls is left the sole interest of the narrator, who plays with words against himself. The interruption of the game by the repeated "saying" from a New England almanac that concludes the poem is ironically deceptive. One proof that it is so is that one has so often to point out, even to bright readers, that the narrator initiates the repair, that the narrator is not one opposed to walls at all.

More often than we notice, Frost is playing a private game in his poetry, a poetry disguised as public through its particulars. In this respect, once more, one finds him akin to Poe and to that direct descendant of Poe, Wallace Stevens. The game in Frost is typically between fact and fancy, as in "Birches," where the reality of the ice storm is adorned metaphorically till fact is hardly extricable from fancy and is indeed of very minor interest. The more interesting game is in the dissolving of the point of view so that the remembering man becomes the boy and returns to being the man, a modulation of the awareness such as one finds less skillfully done in Whitman's "Out of the Cradle Endlessly Rocking." The game underway in "After Apple-Picking" lies in the dissolving of sense images into faint dream images veiled from the senses' actions in the world in order to please a weary body and yet not surrender the world. The body drifts toward sleep, but the "feelings" still reach toward the outer world. The mind won't surrender its images to oblivion, and so dream is the compromise it makes with the tired body. The "I" holds an impression of the world through the instep arch that "keeps the pressure of the ladder-round." And it keeps the body's larger feeling for the ambiguous outer world in the kinetic image of that line in which meter and sense (taken doubly) complement each other so effectively as to gently stir the body back to the world: "I feel the ladder sway as the boughs bend." The lover of that ambiguous outer world has had as much love as the body can take, but is reluctant to let go. The internal game that teases chaos is somewhat obscured to us by the very concreteness of Frost's images from the world adjacent to the senses. We too have seen stones like loaves, have filled cups up to the brim and over, have seen dirt on a spade. But what I suggest is that the surface virtues of Frost's poetry, for which he is generously praised, is in part a crafty disguise of that internal game. If Poe's rescue of his independence takes the form of rejecting the local, Frost's may be said to take the form of his hiding it deeply in the local.

Strategically, insofar as Frost's poems are deliberately dramatic, his celebration of the Self lies in his pitting heart against mind in their conjunction with consciousness. The dramatic game aims toward balance. One may take a poem which is not among his best, "On the Heart's Beginning to Cloud the Mind," as a paradigm—as a key to the bulk of Frost's poetry. The speaker sees a light in the darkness, through "wreaths of engine smoke," against which to play heart and mind. The light is seen first sentimentally with the heart, then realistically with the mind. The poem comes to rest in a balance, falling rather neatly into halves. This playful struggle between heart and mind carries the implicit message that the one is required for the pleasure of life and the other to prevent that pleasure from consuming one in illusion. The one is a "feminine" impulse, the other "masculine." If the "feminine" is victorious, it draws the consciousness off to "lady-land," a victim of chaos, however soothing the images of that chaos may be, as in woods filling up with snow. If the "masculine" overwhelms, it so isolates the consciousness from the threatening chaos that no game at all is possible. The game is most engaging on the precipice, so long as one has the option of taking one step backward.

When Frost's poems are most dramatically successful, the impulse of heart and the requirements of mind find embodiment in human figures, usually husband and wife. The drama is nicely balanced (in the old sense of *nicely*) in "Two Look at Two." The conflict is resolved in a softening of Warren in "The Death of the Hired Man," the turning point Warren's concession through his use of the familiar "Si." The conflict is left suspended in "Home Burial." It is played out but not resolved in "The Runaway," the feminine having the last word, the snow still falling. It is mischievously and playfully suspended in "Stopping by Woods on a Snowy Evening" by a reversal of roles through which the horse speaks horse sense, with the repetition of words in the final line leaving an afterglow of feminine irresolution. One might be tempted, reading these poems, to see as the dramatic center in Frost the battle of the sexes. But that would be a mistake. For he is fundamentally an allegorist of the alienated Self. One need only turn to those lyrics in which there is but the one character, the awareness of the poem, to correct the inclination. "Acquainted with the Night," "Desert Places," "Design," "For Once, Then, Something." The dramatic game between heart and head finds its dramatic form when played against the rolling clouds of nature, which when seen from the perspective of the consciousness behind the poems includes horses and woodchucks and woodland clearings and farmers and their wives and dead and dying children. It is a game which for itself alone might find few players, and that is one reason for its prudent disguise in the poems. For Frost, like Poe, seeing no meaning in existence beyond the individual present moment of the consciousness, is nevertheless and contradictorily hungry for audience. Like the drumlin woodchuck who knows the variety of his escapes, Frost through the game of verse can write, pretending to be the woodchuck:

> I can sit forth exposed to attack,
> As one who shrewdly pretends
> That he and the world are friends. (p. 282)

Such is the secret side of Frost's lover's quarrel with the world.

Notes to *Robert Frost: One Who Shrewdly Pretends* by MARION MONTGOMERY

1. "On Extravagance: A Talk," in *Robert Frost: Poetry and Prose*, ed. Edward C. Lathem and Lawrance Thompson (New York: Holt, Rinehart and Winston, 1972), p. 449.
2. *Memoirs and Opinions: 1926–1974* (Chicago: The Swallow Press, 1975), p. 104.
3. Quoted in Cleanth Brooks and Robert Penn Warren, eds. *Understanding Poetry* (New York: Holt, Rinehart and Winston, 1960), p. 370.
4. *Memoirs and Opinions*, p. 105.

Acceptance in Frost's Poetry:
Conflict as Play

MARJORIE COOK

T HE Dark Frost is by now familiar. For a decade scholars have
concentrated on Frost's portrayal of hopes shattered and lives dev-
astated by forces often presented as intentionally hostile. Scholars
who wish to praise Frost focus on his poems of fear rather than those
of acceptance—these latter somewhat embarrassing in the twentieth
century. Such positiveness seems glibly to avoid, rather than encompass, the problems that he faces more directly in his dark poems. If he
can keep his positiveness and playfulness when all about him are
losing theirs, perhaps he fails to understand the situation—or evades
the problem of his age.

Indeed, despite a generation of scholars documenting the dark
side of his vision, Frost is still attacked as a whimsical escapist. The
question is whether he confronts or avoids serious conflict. Does he
accept responsibility, or does he avoid commitment? My thesis is
that Frost finds balance through his ability to see conflict as play.

Basic to conflict viewed as a form of play is an acceptance of man's
limited capacities. Frost's view is that man lives in a world of flux
and paradox—in which opposing truths at various times obtain; and
man must judge which, how much, and when. Man's inability to
exist in the chaos of constant change makes conflict inevitable. He
needs purpose beyond drifting. Therefore he must struggle—decide
on worthy goals, take the risks, resist opposing forces; he must even
learn to live between opposing and destructive forces by trying to
keep them in balance. Frost sees that the limited human being must
be a courageous antagonist matching his skill against forces that
would destroy him. Part of his skill must be his ability to assess his
capacities.

Man must recognize his limitations, of which one of the most important is his inability to attain absolute truth. The principles of flux
and contrariety in the nature of the world eliminate the possibility of

223

absolute knowledge. Even systematizing knowledge violates the unpredictability of human experience. In "Boeotian" the speaker explicitly rejects systems, and in "The Bear" the speaker explains that any commitment to a position must be modified by a knowledge of the contrary. Balances are to be dynamic; visions are not to be interpreted as the completely expressed truth.

But Frost recognizes a danger in man's too easily accepting his limitations. In "The Times Table" and "On the Heart's Beginning to Cloud the Mind" the poet shows that focusing on limitations rather than on potential achievements can prevent man from accomplishing all he might. The defeat is a psychological one. In contrast, in "The Star-Splitter," the poet behind the poem clearly indicates that man is admirable in asking those unanswerable questions about man's place in the universe. Both Brad McLaughlin and the narrator know that Brad was right to burn down his house and spend the insurance money on a telescope because, as Brad says,

> The best thing that we're put here for's to see;
> The strongest thing that's given us to see with's
> A telescope. Someone in every town
> Seems to me owes it to the town to keep one.
> In Littleton it may as well be me. (p. 177)

The narrator is not quite sure what is the value of "splitting stars"; he observes, both at the beginning and at the end of his story, that man's light is "smoky." Even after their experience with splitting stars, the narrator concludes they still do not know much about man's place among the infinites or much about how it is between man and night. Still, man must construct his own working philosophy. The quest for knowledge and the determination of values are both inevitable and essential.

In "Too Anxious for Rivers" Frost emphasizes both the necessity of the quest and the frustration in the attempt. The opening image is effective: few people would insist on worrying about rivers failing to reach the ocean. Immediately, the reader grants the narrator the point: some things do not concern man, and he should accept his limitations, though he may not like to admit that he has "to cease somewhere" (p. 379). The danger in man's not recognizing the limits of his knowledge is that, as the speaker warns us, there is "No place to get lost like too far in the distance" (p. 379), which is what has happened to that "someone" who believes the distant mountain is the end of the world. Such is the danger of confusing speculation with truth, of categorizing absolutely in a world in which we must deliberately—and cautiously—*create* rough zones.

Insisting that reason alone will not produce final answers to ultimate questions, not even in great systems of epistemology, Frost seems at times to be attacking all rational thought. Although the principle of flux makes flexibility necessarily a value, Frost does not believe it makes meaninglessness the only alternative. Frost the synecdochist believes that the past can stand for and reveal the whole and that man's capability to discern pattern allows him to find meanings. He can achieve understanding though neither perfectly nor permanently. What man's accepting his limited capacity to know means to Frost is close to what Keats meant by "negative capability": "When man is capable of being in uncertainties, mysteries, doubts, without any irritable reaching after fact and reason . . . remaining Content with half knowledge." Frost the synecdochist values the part and is not too anxious about the whole. More conscious of change than of system, he prefers the dramatized experience. Nor does he wish disciples; it is enough to be able to live oneself. He is working at the edges of his own clearing in the wilderness; he has no desire to transform the whole area into a plantation.

But "remaining Content with half knowledge" does not mean for Frost that man should not ask those unanswerable questions. What is important is that he should realize that he is speculating. In "Too Anxious for Rivers" the poet himself ponders the First Cause: science portrayed as a mother putting her children to bed with a fairy tale implies that science's version of the beginning of things is also theory, metaphor:

> And how much longer a story has science
> Before she must put out the light on the children
> And tell them the rest of the story is dreaming?
> "You children may dream it and tell it tomorrow." (p. 379)

This fast, regular rhythm enchants like a fairy tale, and in this enchantment one probably does not at first realize that the final words do not rhyme, though they all have feminine endings—also enchanting. Speculating about First Cause is a kind of enchantment—a dangerous and necessary one. "Too Anxious . . ." suggests man accept the limitations of his capacity to know the First Cause and also encourages him to ponder "our place among the infinities (p. 177); the poem is itself such an exercise, and " 'You children may dream it and tell it tomorrow.' " Nonetheless, as the speaker reminds the reader, "It may be a mercy the dark closes round us/So broodingly soon in every direction." *Mercy* evokes conversational tones, and the casualness may keep the reader from seeing that *mercy* also implies the value of darkness. In "Dust in the Eyes" the poet asks for this unusual gift.

> If, as they say, some dust thrown in my eyes
> Will keep my talk from getting overwise,
> I'm not the one for putting off the proof.
> Let it be overwhelming, off a roof
> And round a corner, blizzard snow for dust,
> And blind me to a standstill if it must. (p. 265)

"Something," he concludes in "Good-by and Keep Cold," "has to be left to God" (p. 228). Frost concludes that man *can* have a great deal of the good life; only when man demands certainty, particularly on metaphysical questions, is he doomed to despair.

Inherent in this acceptance of human limitation is the necessity for struggle: man must realize he does know enough to act on and get ahead with, though he must make judgments carefully and then risk those judgments in actions. He has indeed succeeded only if the possibility of failure was real. Instead of being ashamed of having failed, man should protect his right to fail and respect his failures for what they contribute to his knowledge and his humanity. Simply, he must learn to live with his fallibility. With imperfect knowledge and errors in judgment along the way, he must learn to discern the "rough zones" of possibility. The speaker of "There Are Roughly Zones" sees a necessity for both struggle and acceptance in man's daring to transplant the peach tree to a northern climate. Nature, to be commanded, must be obeyed. However, which laws of nature must be obeyed and what they in fact mean are not at all clear. There are no absolute categories of good and bad, yet there are good and bad judgments. Man has many dreams but whether he succeeds or fails depends partly on chance. Knowing when to risk is of course the problem. In both "Sand Dunes" and "A Leaf-Treader" the speakers are admirable in not yielding to overwhelming opposition, but Brown in "Brown's Descent" must accept the impossibility of climbing back up that slippery slope and must take the long way to reach his destination. Frost accepts what he believes must be accepted; he respects prudence. Still, given good luck, skill, and courage, the speaker in "Willful Homing" can conclude, "Since [man] means to come to a door he will come to a door" (p. 341). Frost knows that man can accomplish much of what doesn't seem possible; for, after all, the limits of possibility are only roughly defined. Man's capacity for accomplishment, though remarkable, is ultimately limited, and man must not dream wildly. Even so, that "limitless trait in the hearts of men" (p. 305) makes them dare to do.

Donald Greiner finds some of Frost's acceptance to be ironic: the speaker pretends to accept the world, but the "acceptance" is defensive—a means for keeping the forces at bay as he prepares for battle. The irony allows Frost to recognize the terrors, but not be so overwhelmed that he throws up his hands in despair. Greiner concludes, "Frost is no pessimistic poet—a dark poet, perhaps; a poet who acknowledges life's chaos and confusion, but not a pessimistic one" (p. 56). Frost is not pessimistic because much of his acceptance is genuine, not just ironic.

Indeed, the speaker in Frost's poems seems to enjoy figuring out how to cope with the forces he must contend with. He is an antagonist par excellence, and he derives pleasure from even small successes he wins against the world. He sallies out to match wits with the worst the cosmos can muster against him, and he views the necessary conflict as a challenge. Frost shows both sides of conflict—the accomplishments man can achieve and the defeats he is sure to suffer. Frost clearly indicates that man's capacities, although finally limited, are remarkable. Understanding his limitations and knowing his resources, man can realistically set his goals and deal with opposing forces. This perception allows him to see conflict as a challenge. Man has to struggle; and if he performs well, he might win. That he might indeed succeed is what entices him to the conflict. If he disciplines himself to acquire skill, knowledge, and judgment, if he has courage, and if chance does not defeat him, he can accomplish near miracles. He delights in the prospect of outwitting the opposition, whatever it may be. Wit and play are essential; almost never can he simply match strength with the opposition. All the fun is in whatever success can be wrested from the surrounding hostile forces.

Conflict as challenge is serious play. If he can accept and even delight in the necessary struggle, he can find the play in even the most serious conflict. What is characteristic of Frost is his delight in the conflict itself. Accepting the struggle is the element of play in his philosophy. In conflict as play, the complexity in his acceptance is apparent.

This complexity has created the crucial issue in the interpretation of Frost's poetry: Does the play invalidate the serious? Frost often complicates the problem by blending playful and serious attitudes into a tone that seems merely whimsical. Given the circumstances, the cheerfulness of some protagonists, as in "One Step Backward Taken," seems downright unrealistic. Frost has warned his readers of the potential problems:

> It takes all sorts of in- and outdoor schooling
> To get adapted to my kind of fooling. (p. 470)

Such adapting is not easy, and the critical question remains: How playful can one be before he has indeed abandoned the serious responsibilities and become merely whimsical?

The charge of whimsical escapism is most often leveled against the poems about "strategic retreat" (p. 282). Can one retreat and keep his integrity? Does Frost show strategic retreat to be legitimate and respectable? Frost *has* shown that man's adaptibility is essential for survival. Given man's limitations, survival is often a matter of outwitting the opposition. Man learns to discern the rough zones of limitation and progresses toward his goals, but by a zigzag course, a "crooked straightness" (p. 421). Perhaps in accepting retreat as a legitimate strategy, Frost too easily loses sight of what has been lost. Perhaps he does overvalue the prudent and smaller victories; perhaps he dismisses failure too easily; perhaps he has a false sense of accomplishment. Can we adopt his attitudes and still respect ourselves?

If man sells his deepest commitments for mere survival, he has lost his integrity. Perhaps Frost seems vulnerable on this point because his protagonists, in "The Drumlin Woodchuck" and "The Bearer of Evil Tidings," for instance, seem to lack the noble commitments and capacity for real sacrifice that would validate such retreat. Still, there is no deception of self or others—except the opposition, which warrants it—in what they are doing and why, and one cannot accuse them of surviving simply to eat. In the late poems "Escapist—Never" and "[In Winter in the Woods . . .]" Frost's protagonists insist they are seekers and that any retreat is for survival to resume the serious pursuit.

Because Frost knows the difficulty of judging how best to risk and because, like Wordsworth, he knows that at times the world is in fact too much with us, he insists on retreat as a legitimate strategy. To Frost, such retreats are more about conflict than escape, or even acceptance; they are about surviving to resume the existential conflicts. In "One Step Backward Taken" the protagonist prudently accepts what he must and survives to take up the existential conflict. In the beginning the tone is light: Humorous images and sounds are evoked by "traveling" soils and "gulping muddy gallons." Yet this loss of balance is also very serious: boulders not easily shaken have shifted, even "Whole capes caked off in slices" (p. 377). In that line the assonance and the accents on the first four syllables call attention to the ground being lost. That emphasis and the figurative meaning of *standpoint* in the next line—"I felt my standpoint shaken" —indicate that the meaning of *ground* in this poem is figurative. The "universal crisis" can mean not only a crisis that is cosmic in scope, but also a crisis involving universally accepted concepts. In such a conflict man cannot win by insisting on his position when the ground itself has been shaken; he saves himself by being flexible and taking "one step backward." Pragmatically, such reaccommodation of principles to experience is constantly necessary and possible. Moreover, this metaphor of one's ground shaken is particularly appropriate for the predicament of modern man. Strategic retreat in these circumstances, the poet insists, is mandatory. Emphasis is increased by the pattern of accents, by the abruptness of a one-line sentence, and by the restraint of his matter-of-fact tone: "A world torn loose went by me." Indeed, in the last, climactic lines, the restraint is almost chilling: "Then the rain stopped and the blowing,/And the sun came out to dry me." The Power in the universe seems to approve of his backward step, supporting his instinct for survival. In these last two lines of the poem the speaker seems a new Adam in another pristine world. The unusual sentence structure of these lines evokes a sense of newness and significance. Although the situation at the end of the poem is still fanciful, the tone in the poem has changed from the lightly comic of traveling "sands and gravels" to the seriousness of a game played for mortal stakes.

The significance of the stakes creates the high seriousness here—and, in my reading, gives an overtone of the seriousness of existential conflicts to the thoroughly delightful poetic experiences of "The Drumlin Woodchuck" and even "The Bearer of Evil Tidings." Considering the human condition and the qualified successes, one could read these poems as ironic and pessimistic: man's chances of success remain slim, and who's kidding whom?

Despite interpretations of Frost as a tragic poet, his essentially comic vision of complex acceptance and balance keeps turning up; he finds it as important to write about realistic accomplishments as about realistic failures. The intricacies of Frost's amazing complexities and the complexities of his kinds of fooling are yet to be discerned and appreciated. Certainly Frost's poems reveal that he is aware of the seriousness of the conflicts; the potential for disaster, defeat, and tragedy is real. He does know the terrifying implications of the kind of world he sees: a universe of constant flux finally defeats all attempts to construct meanings and can lead to nihilism and despair. (A universe *without* change can lead to another kind of despair.) The poet has accepted the human condition which demands struggle—even for what may be unattainable. Heroism, even tragic heroism, is possible in Frost's world. In that Frost chooses to depict protagonists who are less than heroic, the poetry is less than tragic. This kind of protagonists is the principal of his poetry, and choosing this principal is a principle of his vision.

Serious play is the crux of Frost's poetics, and in no better way could he indicate the highest degree of seriousness than in his vision of play. Both playfulness and seriousness are required. How a man takes himself is his style, Frost says in his introduction to Robinson's

King Jasper. "If it is with outer humor, it must be with inner seriousness. Neither one alone without the other under it will do" (*SP*, p.
65). Given the essential ambiguity at the heart of the universe, man
must "keep his extrication" ("From Plane to Plane, p. 407), and that
detachment, made possible by the imagination's capacity to discern
and to create the discrepancies in irony and humor—that detachment keeps us sane. "The way of understanding is partly mirth"
(p. 306), he reminds us in "Not Quite Social." Without the perspective of detachment, effected by man's understanding of the ambiguity and his coping with it through irony and humor, he cannot
understand even "enough to go ahead with" (p. 483).

But despite the essential ambiguity, commitment is also essential.
And for Frost the archetypal commitment, accepting the challenge
of the conflict, is in poetry. Frost delights in the inevitable and often
overwhelmingly difficult and significant struggle to achieve essential
form: "What pleasanter than that this should be so?" he asks. "The
background in hugeness and confusion shading away from where we
stand into black and utter chaos; and against the background any
small man-made figure of order and concentration. What pleasanter
than that this should be so? Unless we are novelists or economists
we don't worry about this confusion; we look out on [it] with an
instrument or tackle it to reduce it. It is partly because we are afraid
it might prove too much for us and our blend of democratic-
republican-socialist-communist-anarchist party. But it is more because we like it, we were born to it, born used to it and have practical
reasons for wanting it there. To me any little form I assert upon it is
velvet, as the saying is, and to be considered for how much more it
is than nothing. If I were a Platonist I should have to consider it, I
suppose, for how much less it is than everything" (*SP*, p. 107).
But this activity is also perilous: "Life sways perilously at the confluence of opposing forces. Poetry in general plays perilously in the
same wild place. In particular it plays perilously between truth and
make-believe. It might be extravagant poetry to call it true make-
believe—or making believe what is so" (*SL*, p. 467).

The play of the imagination is essential to man's being able to
create and discover his meanings, his values, his self. Frost consistently emphasizes the importance of the imagination in its capacity

for metaphor and for ordering chaos—ultimately, two aspects of the same function. In such essays as "Education by Poetry" and "The Constant Symbol" Frost expresses his belief that most thinking is metaphorical, poetic: one learns the unfamiliar by imagining its relationship to the familiar. The imagination is the capacity to think in terms of "as if"; such a feat is, in effect, the means by which man can move outside himself and beyond the limits of the literal to "see" relationships even between strikingly unlike objects and concepts. Justified by this view of the imagination's function, Frost can delight in offering significantly complex and subtle poems under the guise of casual surfaces. Sometimes he is merely coy, as I think he is in "For Once, Then, Something"; sometimes he is profound, as I think he is in "Directive."

In the latter poem, the playful and the serious are indistinguishable: the make-believe turns out to be man's salvation. The speaker in "Directive" advises the reader to "Make . . . a cheering song" (p. 378) as they encounter situations which may overwhelm them. Even the successful attempt to reach the fountainhead is not enough for salvation; the poet brings further aid from the world of the imagination—from the children's playhouse a broken goblet, which is symbolic of the Grail. By indicating not only what man accepts but also how he *can* accept his condition, "Directive" shows how man achieves meaning. The creative, poetic act is the kind of achievement man must make to live "beyond confusion" (p. 379). In a world in which man can accept his limitations and know he must struggle to order chaos into meaning, poetry is possible—and necessary. Frost can accept and live in this world *because* it demands struggle, created order, poetry.

There is still more challenge and further delight in skillful expression of that created order. In "The Mountain" the poet can say, "all the fun's in how you say a thing" (p. 44). Frost delights in the challenge of performance, but not so exclusively as Richard Poirier suggests in *The Performing Self*. Frost knows that polemics is not the purpose of poetry—although he can be polemical about not being polemical, as in "The Lesson for Today" (p. 355). Frost knows that the material to be ordered into literary art form always has content, and he is not uninterested in what that material is. Poetry has finally to qualify as *"true* make-believe" (*SL*, 465).

In accepting the limitations of a world of flux and contrariety, of facticity and historicity, one is freed from admiring only idealized beauty. The world of the concrete particular can be appreciated for itself, because of itself. Frost celebrates the particular in "Hyla Brook." In this world the particular inevitably has its drawbacks. This specific brook runs dry, and what is left are weeds and dried, dull leaves. But the brook also has its moments of supreme beauty, and the contrast heightens the beauty. The lines describing the loveliness have a lilting music.

> (And taken with it all the Hyla breed
> That shouted in the mist a month ago,
> Like ghost of sleigh bells in a ghost of snow).... (p. 119)

Music and image contrast sharply with the matter-of-fact tone of the beginning and with the harsh sounds of the phrase "gone groping underground" immediately preceding the melodious lines. Those who have the capacity for loyalty, for remembering long, not only do not lose faith in the brook but, rather, love it exactly for what it is. Accepting his historicity allows man to live in the inconclusiveness of flux and even to rest in the mystery.

Acceptance is not an "easy out" in Frost's philosophy. Frost knows the difficulty of accepting the inevitable "end/Of a love or a season" (p. 30). He knows too that whether some acceptances are necessary is a matter of judgment and that the variables may effect tragedy. But Frost's vision is ultimately affirmative and therefore comic. The inevitable and terrifying conflicts are, essentially, absorbed in a vision which is comic because it acknowledges the goodness of the life in which tragedy is an inherent possibility but a life which also derives satisfactions from the conflict. The potential of tragedy is accepted—not glibly, I think—as necessary in the best of all possible worlds for man. With considerable balance Frost acknowledges both the difficulties and the satisfactions of the conflicts inherent in the human condition. Usually he avoids both Byronic melancholy and glib happiness. Even with all this emphasis on acceptance of struggle, the essentially comic nature of Frost's vision lies, finally, in his further response to conflict as challenge—a playfulness, a delight and satisfaction in the struggle. Life without the struggle would not really be any fun at all. Even Job does not want God to give us "Heaven at once," as Job's wife tells God in *A Masque of Reason.*

> Job says there's no such thing as Earth's becoming
> An easier place for man to save his soul in.
> Except as a hard place to save his soul in,
> A trial ground where he can try himself
> And find out whether he is any good,
> It would be meaningless. It might as well
> Be Heaven at once and have it over with. (p. 484)

Frost knows that ultimately man and his best dream may be defeated: "We all are doomed to broken-off careers,/And so's the nation, so's the total race" ("The Lesson for Today," p. 355). But despite—indeed, because of—the possibility of defeats and losses and tragedies, significant achievements are possible. The real reward for man remains the confrontation itself, the play. Man's failure to meet the challenge of that confrontation, as the Keeper in *A Masque of Mercy* observes, is often a failure of courage. But, as Paul says in that poem, even with man's greatest courage and effort,

> We have to stay afraid deep in our souls
> Our sacrifice—the best we have to offer,
> And not our worst nor second best, our best,
> Our very best, our lives laid down like Jonah's,
> Our lives laid down in war and peace—may not
> Be found acceptable in Heaven's sight.
> And that they may be is the only prayer
> Worth praying. May my sacrifice
> Be found acceptable in Heaven's sight. (p. 520)

Frost does see darkness, as scholars have shown, and he also sees reason to celebrate. What needs to be understood about Frost's acceptance, his comic vision, is that his affirmation includes the struggle. He does not choose between the dark and the bright. In a world in which the important successes are qualified, the question always is "what to make of a diminished thing" (p. 120). Like the oven bird, the poet *says* his song, aware of the diminished nature around him. Still, "the aim was song" (p. 224), courage is posited strong, and "happiness makes up in height for what it lacks in length" (p. 333). Thus, man can view conflict as a challenge to match wits against the opposition, and the more powerful the opposition, the more significant the success. With realistic hope of some success, he justly may take a positive, even playful, attitude—yet wary and not overly confident. Knowing the play is perilous, still he genuinely plays. His concern is with the dynamic balance of contrarieties. His concern is with the fundamental questions of his age—and all ages: What is the human capacity and how can the human being achieve the good life? The good life is accepting the necessary limitations and imperfections, playing perilously at the confluence of opposing forces, and creating true make-believe.

The Play of "Downward Comparisons":
Animal Anthropomorphism
in the Poems of Robert Frost

MARGARET EDWARDS

R OBERT FROST regarded the writing of poetry itself as a form of play. He says in "The Craft of Poetry," "I'd as soon write free verse as play tennis with the net down." He warned his readers: "It takes all sorts of in- and outdoor schooling/To get adapted to my kind of fooling" (p. 470). His kind of fooling was, first of all, poetry itself. His nonchalant attitude toward poetry and his recognition of writing as a playful enterprise may in part account for his being a popular as well as provocative literary figure. He did not strike a pose as a wizard; he presented himself merely as one who played a game well and strictly according to the rules.

Considering poetry as a sort of game disguised did not diminish Frost's serious literary purposes. He seems to have wished to avoid direct statement of strong feelings. Whimsy and wit become shields protecting the author and hiding both strong feelings and unpleasant convictions. This idea of poetry itself as play sets a context for discussion of Frost's playful use of animals.

The frequent appearance of animals in the work of a nature poet, especially a poet of the rural, is no surprise. Though his animals are always carefully and accurately portrayed, Frost presents many of them in the traditionally playful roles as human representatives. Animals behaving in inexplicably human ways seem remarkable, bizarre, and amusing. A circus, after all, is really a collection of people trying to do what animals can do best, and animals trying to do what people can do best. The anthropomorphic is innately comic.

In "Two Look at Two," a man and a woman walking in the woods see their own love reflected in the image of a buck and a doe. Both couples, human and animal, stop and stare a moment. The poem plays with perspective and concludes: "Two had seen two,

236

whichever side you spoke from" (p. 230). Nature, which is the "earth" mentioned in this poem, seems to be blessing the human union by granting the man and the woman a vision of animal love. "Departmental," a more comic poem, offers a view of animal efficiency. It compares the social structure of an ant colony to bureaucracy, and Frost's outline is too clear to need discussion.

"Stopping by Woods on a Snowy Evening" presents comic anthropomorphism with a twist. The poet says:

> My little horse must think it queer
> To stop without a farmhouse near
> Between the woods and frozen lake
> The darkest evening of the year.
>
> He gives his harness bells a shake
> To ask if there is some mistake. (p. 224)

Strictly speaking, the horse *thinks* and *asks*. The playful conceit extends the visual content and emotional context of the poem. A standing horse shaking its head hard enough to make harness bells ring seems, indeed, to show forceful disagreement. The horse appears to offer an opinion. In "Stopping by Woods..." this particular bit of anthropomorphism not only provides a clever, playful aside but also deepens the poem's psychological portrait. The sleigh's driver is alone, cut off from his fellow men by the dark, the snow, the countryside; therefore, he must feel strongly the temptation to ascribe a personality to his horse for the sake of companionship. Anthropomorphism, in this case, reinforces the narrator's isolation. We assume that the narrator needs to believe, at least for the moment, that the horse is a conscious friend and adviser. We accept this jest about a thinking horse and do not demand that the poet assure us it is only a bit of self-indulgent fun. We understand suddenly that such playfulness has a grimly serious side, for this man's impulse to perceive feelings in his horse could be saving him from freezing.

In other poems concerning animals, Frost does not indulge in anthropomorphism at all. He depicts animal behavior as if only to point out the gulf between human and animal consciousness. The refusal to anthropomorphize is as interesting as the technique itself.

"The Runaway" might easily have been a poem centered in an anthropomorphic jest, yet it is not. The poet and the poet's companion, who stop by a pasture wall to watch a colt, perceive that he is terrified by the falling snow. The colt bolts and runs, then races back to the wall, rolling his eyes, lifting his tail, and "shudders his coat as if to throw off flies" (p. 223) as the snowflakes alight on him. The poet's companion remarks sympathetically: " 'He isn't winter-broken. It isn't play/With the little fellow at all.' " There is no way the human beings can communicate to the young horse that snow is "only weather." The colt's fear, starkly depicted and unmistakeable, drains all humor from the situation. Thus a poem about the colt's misapprehension of the world and failure to comprehend the superior knowledge of human beings is a poem that "isn't play" as well.

Frost usually anthropomorphizes animals with a careful consideration of the reader's need to realize the joke behind it. His most successful poems of this sort elaborate in exquisite detail the actual, visually obvious behavior of the animal. The ascription of human motive or feeling is rarely seriously presented and never allowed to be the "point" of any poem. "The White-Tailed Hornet" is essentially a creed of the *whys* and *why nots* of such anthropomorphic playfulness. First of all, Frost suggests that human similes cannot accurately suggest the wonderful complexity of animal nature. The hornet exits "like a bullet" from his nest; but by "having the power to change his aim in flight,/He comes out more unerring than a bullet" (p. 277). Yet, to believe that animals are so remarkable as to be beyond human failings as well as human metaphor is to forget that animals, too, will make mistakes. The hornet in the poem hunts flies by the kitchen door, misses one fly, then attacks a nailhead, and then a huckleberry. At this point, Frost delivers a very cunning anthropomorphic association:

> But for the fly he might have made me think
> He had been at his poetry, comparing
> Nailhead with fly and fly with huckleberry:
> How like a fly, how very like a fly. (pp. 278–9)

"But for the fly" is crucial. Frost decides to reject the comparison of hornet with poet because, as he says in the next lines, "the real fly he missed would never do;/The missed fly made me dangerously skeptic." He continues the poem by elaborating a skepticism about the faith put in animal instinct. We might miss here Frost's latent skepticism about the faith we put in human art. "But for the fly" the hornet could be a poet comparing one image with another. Frost might have tolerated the anthropomorphic association and let it stand had not the "missed fly" made of the hornet's erring comparisons a series of life-threatening mistakes. A poet's faulty comparisons or ridiculous metaphors will result in bad poetry; the hornet's mistakes, on the other hand, will result in starvation. Again, Frost is considering poetry itself a game, a form of play. The concept of a game implies that the stakes are not too high; victory is gratifying, yet loss is only symbolic, never actual. (If the losing team, for example, must die, then the game is no longer really a game.) So Frost seems to be saying that the hunting of words is not the same as the hunting for food. Bad poems, and poems that fail to live up to the poet's ambition, are not the same as starvation.

Yet the game of art does have consequences. Frost asserts in "The White-Tailed Hornet" that bad poetry is a form of erroneous thinking and feeling which can and has harmed us. He laments that

> Our worship, humor, conscientiousness
> Went long since to the dogs under the table.
> And served us right for having instituted
> Downward comparisons. . . . (p. 279)

He seems to be saying that anthropomorphism, applied without skill, is harmful play. It is an institutionalized "downward comparison" that degrades both man and animal. It confuses, it obscures. Frost, then, would have us take what is playful in life seriously and what is serious in life playfully. Bad poets have left us a legacy of inaccurate observation, and thus "We were lost piecemeal to the animals,/Like people thrown out to delay the wolves" (p. 279).

If "downward comparisons" are potentially so harmful, can any comparison of man with animal or animal with man be justified? Frost seems to believe anthropomorphism is safe, provided the comparison is not an end in itself, not seriously presented or crucial to the poem's deepest meaning. "A Drumlin Woodchuck" depicts animal personality outrageously, creating a woodchuck that speaks for itself. Exaggeration insures the comedy. The woodchuck's voice is an obvious disguise for the poet, who discourses on the value of a safe home in a hostile world. The formality of the woodchuck's speech—his use of the royal "we," his direct address of a reader as "my dear"—subverts any superficially serious or sentimental interpretation. No doubt Frost is mocking such anthropomorphism even while employing the technique. To make certain readers won't misunderstand the playfulness of the conceit, the woodchuck as poet's spokesman points out: "We allow some time for guile" (p. 282). It's the poet's guile to hide behind a woodchuck's voice, even as it's the woodchuck's guile to construct a "two-door burrow" and make use of it.

The woodchuck dives into his burrow and reemerges only "after the hunt goes past/And the double-barrelled blast/(Like war and pestilence/And the loss of common sense)" (p. 282) has missed him. If the hunt and the hunter's gun were equated only with "war and pestilence," this poem would be a simple tribute to the practical, rugged individual whose forethought and hard work save him from holocaust. But the "blast" is also "the loss of common sense." Thus the woodchuck speaks for the intelligent man in a world of fools. What the thinking man must do to survive "still for another day/Or even another year" is behave as the woodchuck "who shrewdly pretends/That he and the world are friends," yet is "instinctively thorough" (p. 282) in the construction of a safe hiding place. The poet, faced with dangerous foolishness and a world of enemies, will follow the woodchuck's example and very adroitly "dive down under the farm." Thus the poet's rural life and his nature poems become the "two-door burrow" of a man who perceives himself as threatened but clever.

Frost occasionally uses another sort of anthropomorphism far less outrageous and arch. It dares to reach beyond playfulness. In the last lines of "The Rabbit-Hunter," the poet's voice describes the "shadowy hare" that is running toward the hunter, toward death. It is a death, says the poet, "That he nor it/(Nor I) have wit/To comprehend" (p. 360). Confusion about the meaning of life and death is common to man and animal. This discovery of the ultimate fate we share with beasts is the most serious revelation Frost's use of anthropomorphism provides. "To a Moth Seen in Winter" deftly probes the mortality of both moth and poet. Frost begins with a characteristic close and accurate observation, describing in detail the physical appearance and behavior of his subject:

> Bright-black-eyed silvery creature, brushed with brown,
> The wings not folded in repose, but spread. (p. 356)

He then constructs the poem around a series of inquiries, interpretations, and blessings. He addresses the moth, yet the form of his address is strictly rhetorical, for he never seems to expect a response. His injunction, "But stay and hear me out," and his later command, "But go. You are right" (p. 356) are tailored to the moth's activity as it rests, then flies. Frost interprets the moth's flight as its search for a mate, for "the love of kind," which is a doomed search in wintertime. The moth, like the white-tailed hornet, is being betrayed by instinct. It is making a fatal error. It will suffer and die, a victim of "the old incurable untimeliness" that afflicts all mortal endeavors. The poet warns it:

> You make a labor of flight for one so airy,
> Spending yourself too much in self-support.
> Nor will you find love either, nor love you.
> And what I pity in you is something human. . . . (p. 356)

What makes this poem an exception in the "animal" genre is that Frost does not use the "playfulness" of anthropomorphic comparison to elude an exploration of powerful feelings. The moth finally flies from the poet's hand, but is not dismissed with a wave or a witty double meaning. The tone stays genuine; the despair is unremitting. The poet says goodbye to the moth by acknowledging "pity cannot help" and in the last lines of the poem confesses his pity is really not so much for the moth but for himself.

> I cannot touch your life, much less can save,
> Who am tasked to save my own a little while. (p. 357)

However, this sort of effect is rare in Frost's use of anthropomorphism. Some readers might say "To a Moth Seen in Winter" does not merely skirt the sentimental but also falls headlong into it. Frost does, as a rule, seem to prefer humorous play over sorrowful conceits.

Another poem more sentimental than playful in its portrayal of an animal is "On a Bird Singing in Its Sleep." The technique of anthropomorphism is muted. Frost suggests that the bird "sang ventriloquist/And had the inspiration to desist" (p. 302) singing because of an inborn wariness, an instinctive reticence, that has saved it from giving away the secret of its position to its enemies. This observation of the bird's behavior leads the poet toward reassurance that the natural design of things will save us all and allow us to pass "through the interstices of things ajar" (p. 303) from generation to generation. The half wakened bird is not as endangered as he seems. And perhaps half wakened persons are not so endangered as they fear. The assumption is understated, but nonetheless present.

"A Considerable Speck" is an interesting example of an anthropomorphic jest which implies much but seems at the same time to be rejecting any broader meaning. The poet sees a moving speck on his sheet of writing paper and, just before mashing it with his pen, stops himself and observes the speck closely. The fact that the speck moves of its own will and is not being blown about convinces the poet that it is no speck of dust but a living creature. The two beings, man and bug, are thus poised in a confrontation. Each is portrayed as initially feeling contempt for the other. Says the poet of the speck: it "would have been beneath my sight/On any but a paper sheet so white." And when the speck crawls far enough to reach the recent, still-wet lines of the poet's manuscript, it "Then paused again and either drank or smelt—/With loathing, for again it turned to fly" (p. 357). Whereas we were sobered by the consideration of the moth's "false hope" which *was* so human, here we are amused by the speck's "loathing" because it *seems* so human. The fact that the speck cannot read, while the author implies it can, makes us laugh.

What adds a grim, exciting touch to the poem is the fact of the poet's pen lifted to annihilate, yet pausing. We are gripped by the absurd drama: will the poet spare the speck or not? Yes, he will. The poem elaborates the reason for this stay of execution. The poet does not want us to believe that common pity moved him. (He gave pity to the moth, but this is a different sort of poem.) He avows,

"I have none of the tenderer-than-thou/Collectivistic regimenting love/With which the modern world is being swept." So this is no liberal's mawkish queasiness. The poet says he refrains from killing the speck for two better reasons: first, the speck is not yet known to be "evil," and second, it manifests at least a rudimentary sort of thinking process. Ascribing his mercy to a respect for a fellow creature, the poet says:

> I have a mind myself and recognize
> Mind when I meet with it in any guise.
> No one can know how glad I am to find
> On any sheet the least display of mind. (p. 358)

And we gather that such a respect is not readily accorded fellow writers whose pages may often show not even so much as a "considerable speck" of intellectual worth. This is a clever criticism of modern poetry or the state of modern letters in general that allows Frost at the same time to be "just joking" about a bug that ran across his page. The poem masks the sentimental with the hyperbolic and hides strong criticism beneath what could be a mere trivial conceit.

"The Bear" is another study of a "display of mind" which compares man and bear, suggesting that the advanced human intellect imprisons the spirit, whereas the bear's relative stupidity liberates it.

> The world has room to make a bear feel free;
> The universe seems cramped to you and me.

The assertion is made while the poet shows the bear behaving almost humanly, embracing a fruit tree as if it were a lover. This is the condition of the wild, free bear. Man, on the other hand, is behaving like a caged bear:

> He paces back and forth and never rests
> The toenail click and shuffle of his feet,
> The telescope at one end of his beat,
> And at the other end the microscope.... (p. 269)

This reversal of classic anthropomorphism, the assigning of animal characteristics to a human being, is Frost's playful way of presenting a serious point. His rather disturbing distrust of the intellect as an agent of happiness is cheerfully accepted as we enjoy the comic similarity between a thoughtful philosopher and a zoo's captive bear, both frustrated, disheveled, "baggy," and "equally pathetic." The description of the antics of a caged bear is acute; the bear "sits back on his . . . butt/With lifted snout and eyes . . . shut/. . . And back and forth he sways from cheek to cheek" (p. 269). The most searing critique is presented parenthetically: "(He almost looks religious but he's not)." The bear represents a "scientific" mind torn by extreme points of view. Such a mind cannot explain the world or integrate its meaning philosophically. The activity of such a mind "may be thought, but only so to speak." This stinging rebuke to the scientific community is couched in a delightful portrait of bears.

Another poem which uses anthropomorphism in much the same way, pointing out a desperate human circumstance while at the same time entertaining with a clever "downward comparison," is "Range-Finding." A bullet aimed by one human being at another passes through the lives of a bird, a butterfly, and a spider before reaching its destination. The bird returns to its nest and the butterfly to its perch after a momentary disturbance. The bullet's passage through a spiderweb likewise causes a reaction:

> The indwelling spider ran to greet the fly,
> But finding nothing, sullenly withdrew. (p. 126)

This conceit of the disappointed "sullen" spider emphasizes the gulf that exists between the lives of men and beasts. As the spider misinterprets human activity as being relevant to his life, so we may in turn be misinterpreting the spider. More crucially, the murder of one human by another is certainly not a "natural" act when seen in this context of Nature and Nature's creatures. What is of great moment in human life hardly touches the animals here; therefore, it may not be of such importance after all.

In almost all of Frost's poems that depict animals, anthropomorphism is a playful conceit used to lighten a dark tone, distract from strong feeling, and vivify realistic animal behavior. Frost was never so naïve as to insist that we respect animals as more noble, sensitive or "human" than ourselves. He never sought to obfuscate evolution's separation of man and beast. Yet one feels that Frost may have been drawn to animals as subjects for poetry precisely because they seemed with all of their exuberance, persistence, instinctual motivation, their urge to survive and their sense of leisure and fun, to mimic the wisest and best aspects of the personality of an artist.

Technique and the Sense of Play
in the Poetry of Robert Frost

WALTON BEACHAM

ECAUSE poetry is an encounter between the poet and reader, in the broadest sense all poetry is play. That is, poetry is the interaction and coordination of two people toward one end within a given set of rules and traditions. The poet "plays" with the reader insofar as the poet must withhold insights until the exact moment when the reader has been prepared for the revelation. All good poetry possesses this quality, but poets play with their craft, and their readers, in other, more specific ways. Robert Herrick plays with equivocation, Ogden Nash plays with humor, e.e. cummings plays with syntax.

Robert Frost plays with irony, almost as a cat plays with a cornered bug, and it is this quality of his poetry which has led critics to praise Frost's cosmic vision and sense of the absurd. But if we are to equate "play" with "irony," then we must be careful to recognize that Frost is also "playful" in a manner and attitude quite distinct from his play. "Playing" involves the whole spirit, while "playfulness" can be the result of detached observation without real commitment to the game. Frost is full of horseplay in almost every poem, in a spirit closely akin to the American tradition of folk humor, but it is play—his dexterity with irony—that has established his critical reputation, while "playfulness" has contributed greatly to his popular success.

In dealing with Frost's play, or irony, the difficulty is that while all irony is personal and subjective, it is particularly troublesome with Frost because he intentionally eludes and deceives all but the cleverest readers. As critics, we have aptly recognized the importance of analyzing Frost's work on as many levels as possible in order to discover the irony which, in many cases, reverses more traditional readings of the poems, but we have only begun to explicate the depth of irony in Frost's poems.

In attempts to come to grips with Frost's evasive play, I've found it useful to establish some patterns of poetic tools which operate whenever Frost seems to be most ironic, and it's clear to me that Frost lays many clues which reveal his themes through his particular use of six technical devices: dramatic situation, rhyme, stanzaic structure and tradition, overall structure, meter, and personification.

Dramatic situation in Frost's poetry is one of his most nearly unique and important achievements, and it, alone, accounts for his unparalleled popularity among general readers. If we define dramatic situation as the setting, action, or situation in which the personae must function, or if we reduce the definition even further to what one might see or infer from a photograph depicting the poem's setting, then what we are really talking about is the visual appeal of poetry. Everyone enjoys looking at picturebooks, and Frost's canon is a catalogue of pictures created by dramatic situation, not through images as most other poets create their pictures in the reader's mind. It is this firm sense of setting—giving the reader a seat from which he can view the stage—that accounts for Frost's ability to make the reader identify with his narrator, and creates his frame for raising questions and establishing ironies: inexperienced readers can enjoy the theater even if they don't quite understand the play, while experienced readers can appreciate the irony as well as the setting.

Take, for example, "Stopping by Woods on a Snowy Evening," in which the dramatic situation could be reduced to something like: "A man in a horse-drawn vehicle has stopped by woods to watch snow fall. There is no one around, and there is no farmhouse between the woods and lake where he has paused. It has been cold enough for the lake to freeze, but it is now snowing. The only noises are the sounds of harness bells, the wind blowing easily, and the snow falling." Although some very important aspects of dramatic situation are deliberately left unanswered—such as: where did the narrator come from and where is he going; why did he stop; what time of day is it; why is he in a horse-drawn vehicle; why should there be a farmhouse near—we have a very clear description whose strength stems from the freedom which Frost permits the reader in forming his own images. For trained readers, the opening lines of "Stopping by Woods on a Snowy Evening" are philosophical, while for untrained readers the image projected might be that of some villainous landlord who posts "No Trespassing" signs and doesn't like people snooping around his property. Likewise, each succeeding stanza allows maximum flexibility to the reader's imagination so that each reader essentially draws his own picture of the dramatic situation.

By allowing the reader to absorb himself into the poem through free imagery, Frost reduces the objectivity which one might otherwise bring to the dramatic situation, and it becomes more difficult for the reader to understand the irony being worked on him. In "Stopping by Woods," for example, one reader might imagine a rather cozy communion with nature, while another might feel fear and apprehension because he is trespassing on forbidden ground at dusk. "After Apple-Picking" might give some readers the satisfaction of a job well done while others would identify with the futility of touching ten thousand thousand fruit. Unlike many other poems contemporary with Frost's, such as "The Love Song of J. Alfred Prufrock" or "Sunday Morning," the dramatic situation is not presented as it will later be interpretted by astute readers and, unlike "Prufrock" and "Sunday Morning," harmless, everyday objects turn into unique and sometimes terrifying symbols. It is one thing to suspect the connotative possibilities of yellow fog and ragged claws and quite another to be duped by a woodchuck. With Frost, what is excluded from the dramatic situation is as important as what is included; and until we verify the missing elements, we will certainly have trouble with irony.

One of the most important discoveries I've made about Frost's use of dramatic situation is that he will not tamper with it in those poems which are merely playful, and the narrator's own relationship to his dramatic situation is entirely different in the poems where irony is most prevalent. That is to say, when Frost is hardest at play, he is most involved, and the stronger the presence of a narrative persona, the more likely the opportunity for irony. In an important way, Frost is most ironic toward himself; and although, in his playfulness with readers, he may pull a dirty trick by presenting a cliché surface which contains depths unsophisticated readers can't see, he becomes most poignant and bitter when he sees that he is his own victim. In this respect, Frost seems closer to Thomas Hardy than to any other modern poet.

Two fairly comparable poems, "At Woodward's Gardens" and "Birches," illustrate the importance of involvement of the narrative persona in the dramatic situation. Although "Birches" is longer, both poems deal with boys and things out of nature common to New England boyhood; both poems are blatantly metaphorical; both poems draw strikingly similar closing statements; both are unrhymed narratives. Yet, in spite of all the similarities, the poems are remarkably different: "Birches" is considered and remembered by most readers as profound, while "At Woodward's Gardens" commands almost no attention, and the reason is quite obvious. In "At Woodward's Gardens" Frost is playful, amused by a much too clever comparison between people and monkeys, while in "Birches" he is searching for connections which he doesn't fully understand. He is involved in the whole organic process in "Birches," while being quite detached from the zoo in the garden. When Frost is aloof and haughty, the irony is weakened, and the strength of the narrative persona in "Birches" clearly defines the distinction between the poems.

If dramatic situation is the most important single element for establishing irony in the longer poems, and particularly in the long, unrhymed poems, then rhyme is the most important element in the shorter poems. Frost must have translated emotions directly into rhyme, for there is an amazing consistency between rhyme and tone. In selecting rhyme scheme, Frost sticks pretty evenly with the traditional uses of form, a method which, in turn, influences the irony. With few exceptions, the poems written in couplets are playful because the composition of couplets, in a century marked by cynicism, makes the form difficult to sustain the solemnity which irony demands. One might argue that in the eighteenth century couplet tradition Frost might have achieved marvelous satire, but he apparently had no desire or talent for transforming ridicule and satire into irony. Thus, the couplet poems reflect a kind of longing or sadness vitiated by the form's playful tradition. And though Frost's couplet poems are generally more sincere than ironic, Frost is often at his ironic best when he uses double, triple, and quadruple rhymes in other poems, such as "Stopping by Woods on a Snowy Evening" and "After Apple-Picking."

Progressing from the least ironic rhyme scheme to the most, the *abcb* poems tend to ask personal, philosophical questions of such magnitude that no answer is possible and, therefore, no real irony. Poems such as "A Serious Step Lightly Taken," and "In Hardwood Groves" consider questions which can only, by the nature of their content, be directed to a fairly disengaged narrator. There is some intellectual playfulness about these poems, but little irony. The most curious poem among this rhyme group is "Come In," which could easily have turned more ironic than it does. In many ways, it is a companion poem to "Stopping by Woods," but the last two lines refuse to push the narrator into the depth of observation of "Stopping by Woods." Frost turns potential irony into playfulness, and I'm convinced that if his emotion had been locked into alternating rhymes or framed segments, the poem would have been entirely different. An incantation appears in both poems: the woods beckon the narrator in "Stopping by Woods," while the thrush seduces the narrator in "Come In," but the modified Rubaiyat stanza in the first poem, combined with more regular meter, offers the narrator much less chance of escaping, while the feeling of entrapment in the second poem is much more like: "come into my parlor, said the spider to the fly."

Somewhat more adaptable to irony, but still more removed than one might expect, are the alternating quatrains, octaves, and sonnets. These poems are more openly philosophical than any of the other forms Frost uses, and they convey a sense that the poet has stumbled onto a pleasant discovery after so many years of not being able to see past himself. But the poet does finally see, and isn't resentful that he's been deprived of insight. It's as though the subject matter just occurred to him, unlike the more ironic poems in which the narrator has lived with some enigmatic emotion which nagged and evaded him for a long time. The quatrains, octaves, and sonnets are playful because the narrator feels good about his discovery, and even the somewhat exceptional poems, "Two Tramps in Mud Time" and "Design," contain only elements of irony without making a final ironic statement. Frost seldom plays with alternating rhyme, and the one element which makes "Mowing" ironic is personification.

By far, the surest sign that Frost is developing irony in the rhymed poems is through his use of framed segments (e.g., *abba, abca, abbba, aaba*). In rhymed stichic poems, like "The Grindstone" and "After Apple-Picking," and in the four-line strophic poems, like "Tree at My Window," "Stopping by Woods on a Snowy Evening," and "Choose Something Like a Star," the ironic tone is strong, and when Frost begins shortening lines, or using catelexis or anacrusis, then the probability of irony is even higher. The opening of "After Apple-Picking" (and the entire poem) illustrates Frost's use of framed segments to achieve irony; and with the combination of enjambment, a shortened second line, and the couplet between lines five and six, there can be little doubt that Frost is presenting a poem which we cannot accept at face value. Frost's uniquely rhymed poem, "In a Disused Graveyard" is a good illustration of the difference rhyme can make on play.

> The living come with grassy tread
> To read the gravestones on the hill;
> The graveyard draws the living still,
> But never anymore the dead.
>
> The verses in it say and say:
> "The ones who living come today
> To read the stones and go away
> Tomorrow dead will come to stay."
>
> So sure of death the marbles rhyme,
> Yet can't help marking all the time
> How no one dead will seem to come.
> What is it men are shrinking from?
>
> It would be easy to be clever
> And tell the stones: Men hate to die
> And have stopped dying now forever.
> I think they would believe the lie. (p. 221)

The first stanza, rhyming *abba*, conveys solemn irony as Frost plays with the union which the graveyard demands between the living and dead. Not only does the graveyard continue to attract the living, but it also "draws the living still," meaning that the living are sketched in a kind of animation. The dead, who are already drawn still, require the services of the graveyard in a different manner from the living. The second stanza, however, rhyming *cccc*, conveys a lighthearted spookiness which, like a haunted mansion, makes us only ostensibly afraid, while the third stanza begins in the same spirit as stanza two but is changed to playful sarcasm when we feel the force of couplets rather than quadruple rhymes. The fourth stanza possesses good potential for irony but, like most of Frost's alternating quatrains, tends to present itself with more earnestness than play. "In a Disused Graveyard" there is certain playfulness, and its meter and personification make it somewhat ironic, but not to the extent it might have been had the middle stanzas not weakened it.

Frost's use of stanzas and verse paragraphs is a secondary but important means by which he can build to, and reinforce, the irony established by dramatic situation and rhyme. Using "Tree at My Window" as one example of a typical strophic poem, we can see that the stanzas represent divisions in ideas and emotions which fuse in the final stanza and give meaning to the poem. That the poem is divided into four equal parts indicates that each stanza will bear equal weight and importance in developing the impact. Structurally, the poem sets up a pattern for development. Stanza one suggests the idea of a boundary between man and nature and, in doing so, anticipates that the poem will consider this boundary. Stanza two, however, seems to break from this idea, suggesting that man's imagination as he looks at nature might lead to profundity. While stanza one suggests the importance of separation, stanza two implies that profundity lies in the union of man and nature. Stanza three again sets up the notion of a boundary between the tree and the man, but this time shows how they are alike in their separate domains. Stanza four, like stanza two, returns to whatever element it is that bridges man and nature. The basic stanza-by-stanza structure of the poem, then, is:

1. A desire to bridge the *separation* between man and nature.
2. The notion that a *union* between the two will lead imaginative man to profundity.
3. A realization that in *separation* the crux of unity is similarity.
4. The recognition that the tenuous unity of similarity is the profundity about man and nature desired in stanza two.

The structure certainly sustains the poet's notions of a dichotomy and parallelism between man and nature and may suggest the notion that separation makes unity possible.

The importance of structure as it relates to irony lies in the duality which Frost presents in so many of his poems. When he pits two things against each other, whether it is man and tree, two men on each side of a stone wall, lovers looking at a pair of deer, or a boy climbing upward away from earth, he is creating a situation for irony because he can illustrate the differences between the opposites. What ought to be is contrasted by an opposing force, which becomes a theme of overbearing importance in Frost's poetry. The gap is never quite breeched, as Frost believes it shouldn't be, and no one can build a bridge across West-Running Brook or ever be married to it. Frost does not lament having taken the road that he did; he doesn't wish for another vocation or avocation, or regret having picked his apples, but he does insist that we become aware of how far we have come on the road, and what that means to us; and the pattern of development, particularly in the strophic poems, reinforces that theme.

Frost's short poems composed of strophic divisions usually give equal weight to the idea presented in each stanza and develop in one of two ways: a presentation of separate ideas whose union forms a larger, more complete observation than any of the individual parts, as in "Tree at My Window" or, in a step-by-step progression of ideas or events, as in "Desert Places." Stanza one of "Desert Places" describes a general scene: snow falling into a field. In stanza two the woods are described as belonging to the field, and the animals to the woods, which gives a more specific situation. In lines seven and eight the poet compares himself with the animals, and because the poem is structured so that we are moving from the general to the specific, we can expect that the poet will move to himself. The movement is from:

very general to less general to more specific to very specific
    lines 1–4   line 5   lines 6–8   lines 9–12

In addition to movement created through stanzaic divisions in many of Frost's poems, there is movement and tradition within the stanza form. In "Tree at My Window," the stanza is basically iambic tetrameter, rhyming *abba*, with the last line containing only two feet and some lines containing an extra syllable. Although the form is somewhat irregular, the form might be considered a modified "In Memoriam" stanza, which is traditionally used for meditative or introspective subjects. Because of the central couplet which is interlocked by rhyming lines, great emphasis is placed on line three, giving the form a natural focal point. In "Tree at My Window," Frost maintains the full rhyme of the "In Memoriam" stanza but makes variations on the form by adding and reducing syllables. There are, indeed, so many long lines that Frost's stanza might be considered a Brace (pentameter *abba*) were it not for the short last line which reduces the tension created by the traditional Brace stanza.

The syllable count for each stanza of "Tree at My Window" is:

I–8	II–9	III–10	IV–9
8	8	9	11
9	9	11	9
5	4	4	6

As with the "In Memoriam" form, the third line of each stanza in "Tree at My Window" does command focus, particularly in stanza three, but line four brings it quickly to a resolution, unlike the traditional "In Memoriam" which uses the fourth line to reflect on the first three. However, in Frost's poem, the shorter third line in stanza four and the longer fourth line delay the resolution and cause the reader to slow down and reflect.

"Stopping by Woods on a Snowy Evening" is another example of Frost's modification of a traditional stanza form, the Rubaiyat stanza, to set up a forum for irony. As with the Rubaiyat, whose five feet give it a heavy solemnity, the tetrameter *aaba* achieves a focus on line three which causes line four to become anticlimactic and hyperbolically profound. After the initial couplet, the third line's deviation in rhyme causes the stanza to build to a climax, while the fourth line, in returning to the original rhyme, creates a sense that it is reflecting on the climax reached in the first three lines. Because the fourth line possesses this reflective characteristic, it must be profound or poignant, and this is frequently impossible except through irony.

Thus, in "Stopping by Woods on a Snowy Evening," Frost has chosen a form which has as its principal characteristic an emphasis on line three with commentary following in line four. When, in "Stopping by Woods," he repeats the fourth line, we are forced into a situation in which the climax and reflection appear to be the same, but both intuitively and analytically, it seems certain that Frost intends lines three and four in stanza four to communicate entirely different meanings. Line four, in Rubaiyat tradition, attenuates the seriousness of line three, which Frost has presented in enormous overstatement.

Although Frost opts for using strophic verse more times than not, he attempts to achieve similar balance through verse paragraphs when he writes stichic poems. Take, for example, a short stichic poem, "Fire and Ice," which Housman might have written in strophic verse (as he did "Epitaph on an Army of Mercenaries").

> Some say the world will end in fire,
> Some say in ice.
> From what I've tasted of desire
> I hold with those who favor fire.
> But if it had to perish twice,
> I think I know enough of hate
> To say that for destruction ice
> Is also great
> And would suffice. (p. 220)

The title, "Fire and Ice," suggests that some comparison or balance between the concepts (and allusions) of fire and ice will be made, and presents a tempting subject to set up in eight lines. That Frost chose nine stichic lines suggests that if balance is to be achieved, the first and the last four lines will center on line five. This is not to say that most nine-line poems will take on a four-one-four structure, but that in "Fire and Ice" there is an antithesis which is important; and were the poem divided into a five-four structure, one of the two dichotomies would receive greater emphasis. So it's not surprising to find that Frost does, indeed, set lines one through four in fire, and lines six through nine in ice. Our surprise comes not from the overall structure, but from a rhyme scheme which, at first glance, doesn't seem to have the potential for delicate balance that say, ababcdede or ababbcbcb, might attain. We are struck by the absence of symmetry in the *abaabcbcb* pattern, and not until we correlate rhyme with line length and meaning can we appreciate the skill with which balance has been achieved.

After considering the context of the poem, we'll probably conclude with Frost the necessity of ending the fire section with authority so that we can move cleanly into fire's antithesis, but this final authority can't be established with only a full stop after line four; a period might accomplish a syntactical close but would not give this section the finality necessary if fire is to be abandoned. Realizing this, Frost forms lines three and four into a couplet, uses exact rhyme in line four, and indicates a full stop, all of which close this section with a tight lid.

Because line five begins a new section, but also contains a rhyme common to both halves, the line becomes a strong binding force between fire and ice. Not only is the *b* rhyme common, line five is the first time the *b* rhyme is repeated, which gives line five a strong associative power with line two. This force which binds lines two and five is counterbalanced by the fact that line five comes after the strong closing of the fire section and is, therefore, more closely connected with the section about ice. The imbalance which might have occurred because the couplet makes line five cling to the second part rather than the first is again balanced by the first repetition of the *b* rhyme.

As Frost presents the material, fire and ice deserve the same amount of emphasis; so we might ask why the last four lines rhyme *cbcb* rather than with a couplet if Frost should, by analogy, establish the same finality for ice as he does fire. One answer is that were Frost to conclude the ice section with a couplet, only the last half would be closed. What Frost is attempting, it seems, is a fusion of both ideas and a finality to the entire poem rather than to the last part and, having used the couplet once for that purpose, can't offer us that technique again for the same effect. So, in order to achieve the finality he wants, Frost shortens the tetrameter lines to dimeter with the effect that short lines coming after the longer ones make the poem end very quickly, with an abruptness that shakes us to a sudden halt. Had Frost not anticipated the dimeter ending with line two, we might have been shocked or annoyed by the dimeter device, but the fact that the first dimeter line comes early in the poem and isn't repeated until the end gives the dimeter lines power to close the poem.

In summary, we might diagram the structure of "Fire and Ice" as follows:

	line	length	rhyme	function
	1	tetrameter	a	
	2	dimeter	b	anticipates later dimeter lines; the short b rhymed line helps to balance the three *a* rhymes in section 1.
fire				
quatrain	3	tetrameter	a	couplet gives finality to section 1.
	4	tetrameter	a	
	5	tetrameter	b	central line unifies the parts because of the binding *b* rhyme.
	6	tetrameter	c	
ice	7	tetrameter	b	
quatrain	8	dimeter	c	
	9	dimeter	b	dimeter lines give finality to both sections and establish the balance between parts, emphasizing the middle line.

Obviously Frost has very carefully worked out the structure so the sections would take equal emphasis, and when analyzing meaning, we might argue that on the basis of structure the center line serves as a hypothesis around which the poem's philosophy is based. Certainly, the careful structure established by rhyme scheme and line length would suggest that the middle line is ironic.

Similar to his use of stanzaic structure and tradition, Frost's precise sensitivity to meter creates a forum which makes irony much easier to achieve, and while meter is not ironic in itself, it is an important contributor to both play and playfulness. Frost is an amazingly adept metricist whose craft delights anyone who recognizes how his lines operate, and one of the important contributions which Frost has made to prosody is his brilliant demonstrations of the strong Anglo-Germanic impulse which readers have for base meter.

Though Eliot is the master of variable verse (maintaining a sense of the accentual-syllabic base meter while deviating from it at will, including interspersing Anglo-Saxon four-stress lines), Frost is equally good. Usually calling on a tetrameter (e.g., "Tree at My Window") or pentameter (e.g., "Mending Wall") line for his base, Frost achieves variation not only through unparalleled use of substitution but also through the substitution of entirely different lines into his base. "After Apple-Picking" is a reasonable example of this variable verse technique. Opening with two lines which are metrically confusing:

> My long two-pointed ladder's sticking through a tree
> Toward heaven still,
> And there's a barrel that I didn't fill
> Beside it, and there may be two or three
> Apples I didn't pick upon some bough.
> But I am done with apple-picking now (p. 68)

Frost begins establishing his pentameter base in line three, but because of the "still/fill" association between lines two and three, the reader can't be comfortable with the base for at least several more lines which finally do establish a metrical contact. Through the first twelve lines (with the exception of one and two), Frost maintains a rhymed, fairly regular, iambic pentameter base while permitting the reader to establish dramatic situation through free imagery in his usual manner. For this first section, Frost allows the reader to interpret, or misinterpret, the religious significance of apples as symbols, panes of glass as allusions, and the end of apple-picking season as a metaphor for man's life, before varying the length of his lines.

The first section, then, establishes an iambic pentameter base, but once the poem embarks from the physical with line thirteen, moving into dreams, and finally to the metaphysical with the closing six lines, the measure varies from one to five feet. It's not enough to notice that Frost intersperses short lines, enjambment, and rhyme in order to challenge the reader's comfort with a regular pentameter base, thereby creating tension through technique which reinforces an obvious theme (a simple interpretation of man's fears at the end of life). With an almost pauseless end to line fourteen moving into line fifteen ("But I was well/Upon my way to sleep before it fell"), the reader doesn't reach a caesura until after "sleep" in line fifteen.

Visually, there are two lines, supported by masculine end-rhyme, but metrically the reader feels the presence of five feet between "but" in line fourteen and "sleep" in line fifteen. In other words, "But I/was well/upon/my way/to sleep" seems to function as a pentameter line. However, in contrast to our sense of that pentameter base, there is a faint notion of a heptameter line reminiscent of the long, essential six-footer which opens the poem, and this adds to the tension generated by the variations on the metrical contract. Throughout the entire dream sequence, Frost keeps pushing at our sense of balance, appropriately ending with a final trimeter line which emphasizes the importance of each syllable.

Similar to the tension which Frost creates through his base meter and rhyme is his use of the foot within the line. Where he wants the most emphasis, he will almost always establish a rising or falling line, then counterpoint with the succeeding line or deny the natural rise and fall within that given line. Taking the first line of "After Apple-Picking" as an example, it is quite clear how Frost denies the reader's longing for balance. Scanning the line and reading it as an iambic base, we get:

My lŏng/twŏo-point/ĕd lăd/der's stick/ĭng through/ă tree

  1   2   3   4   5   6

Except for the spondaic substitution in foot two, the line is regular; but because Frost has split the four middle feet, the natural rising rhythm which iambs should create becomes a means for recreating the imbalance of the ladder swaying in the tree. The words "point/ed," "lad/der," and "stick/ing," which have a strong natural falling rhythm, are forced into an iambic base. Because the stress is so strong on the first syllable, whenever we encounter these words we insist on reading them as they would be pronounced in isolation, but splitting them by imposing the iambic base forces us into a disparity between rising and falling rhythm.

"Mending Wall," shows Frost using the same technique with a twist. In the line:

Ănd sends/ the froz/ĕn-ground-/swell ŭn/der it

   1   2   3   4   5

tension is created because of our determination to read "frozen" and "ground-swell" as complete, unsplit words and Frost's insistency that "frozen-ground-swell" constitutes a complete phrase. Unlike the first line from "After Apple-Picking," Frost isn't playing against our sense of rising and falling rhythms, but on our desire to read "frozen" as one complete unit and "ground-swell" as another. Instead of permitting us this luxury, Frost forces us through the strong pentameter base meter (which is firmly established throughout the poem as well as being ingrained into our normal speech patterns and traditional verse) to associate the "en" in "frozen" with "ground" (rather than with "froz"), and to separate "swell" from its natural partner. Not only do we feel the ground swelling, but there is a psychological swelling in the reader, and the tension which passes from neighbor to neighbor is sustained by the superficial balance of the boulders (line eighteen) and the saying, "Good fences make good neighbors."

Splitting feet, substitution, depressed feet, feminine endings, and truncation are some of the techniques Frost uses to make us feel tension within the line; that Frost judges his reader with consistent accuracy is a tribute to the poet's genius. The larger tensions which he creates when ladders are swaying, boulders are balancing, or boys are climbing birch trees are matched through subtle, less flamboyant channels to the reader's emotions in other poems. In "Tree at My Window," for example, Frost splits the third foot of the first line after an initial trochaic substitution, so that the effect is almost a statement for the first three and a half feet, "Tree at my window," and a reflection stated by the last foot and a half: "window tree." The tension established by the split third foot causes the narrator to think after the caesura, "I've said that the tree at my window is a window tree, but now that I consider it, what is a window tree?" The reader's response is that if the narrator wonders about the identity of the tree, then we must too. It's not a heavy touch, nor is it such an important part of the poem that we are tempted to make some scholarly point with it, but the narrator's bewildered voice established by a falling rhythm within an iambic base does fit the decorum of the poem perfectly, and suggests a tone which allows good flexibility for irony.

Considering all the technical devices which contribute to play, it seems obvious and consistent with the theory of irony that Frost establishes dichotomy whenever he can. Meter is used to contrast and render imbalanced emotions which we would like to feel and which are superficially suggested by the subject matter, thereby creating a difference between comfort and insecurity. Stanzaic structure forces the reader in one direction, but in doing so demands that he consider the nature of direction and the contrast possible between where he is and where he could be. Personification provides Frost a voice and a point of view when he specifically wants to focus on observations which the narrator dare not say. The effect is to establish a distance between things human and things of nature, and personification is a sure sign of irony. Rhyme, through its associative power, and especially when combined with line length variation, enjambment, and catalexis, establishes reflective powers, as well as greatly influencing the sound (and consequently the tone) of the poem. Finally, dramatic situation provides the means by which a persona is given the impetus and inspiration to confront his environment so that he can establish, and hopefully reconcile, the distances between himself and nature. The degree of irony is usually proportionate to the number of these techniques which a poem contains; and while no mechanical yardstick will inevitably measure irony, it is certainly a helpful and consistent indication of the poet's intentions, if not the poem's effect.

The Control of Play and the Play of Control in Robert Frost's Poetry

STEPHEN D. WARNER

Wᴴᴇɴ I was a child my uncle was still a farmer in upstate New York. He was mechanized as all farmers had to be to earn a decent living, but he also kept a team of oxen with which he tended his garden plot beside the house. It was an extravagance, as my aunt often reminded him, but his answer was that it gave him a direct sense of what he did that tractors didn't allow. Whenever strangers visited and watched him work the oxen, often only verbally with both hands on the plow, they would remark at how easy it seemed to be to direct such well-trained beasts. My uncle would "allow as how" it was pretty easy, and offer the guest a try the next time he took out the team. (They were always "ready for the barn" at that particular time). Of course, the guests always failed to get the team to move. I was convinced of my uncle's magic until my father told me, when he thought I was old enough to keep a secret, that my uncle always reversed the oxen in the yoke—put them on the side they weren't used to—to be worked by the strangers. The beasts, confused to be where they rarely were, either stood stock still or worked against each other. I was amazed to learn what a simple trick made my uncle's control so impressive.

Perhaps because of my uncle and his simple magic I have grown suspicious of magic in others and look for its cause. I think I have discovered Robert Frost switching oxen in a significant number of cases. Frost's switch is in the persona and the traditional assumptions we make about his wisdom as interpreter of the substance he relates. The effect is to give the impression of control. This control of form is often confused by the reader as the control of substance. It seems, as developed by Frost, a pragmatic poetic game.

Through game metaphors and play, Frost establishes conditions in his early poetry which develop a false impression of mastery on the part of the persona. In control of the game, the persona seems in control of all aspects of the game. Play in Frost's poetry often disguises what metaphors in poetry usually seek to clarify.

The clearest early example is "Mending Wall," a poem whose surface presents a reasonable persona dealing with an unreasonable neighbor, an "old-stone savage armed" with his father's saying. The speaker seems to be seeking the reasons behind his neighbor's urge to mend the fence. But there is no "reasoned" motivation, only the belief in the father's saying that "Good fences make good neighbors." Superficially considered, the poem seems to confront a man of reason with a man of tradition, with the man of reason reflecting the mischievous condescension we all feel toward that "old-stone savage." The poem, we conclude, is a comment on fences and on the men who build them. After all, "Something there is that doesn't love a wall."

The problem in this surface reading comes when we go behind the game metaphor in the poem. The persona compares the process to tennis: "Oh, just another kind of outdoor game,/One on a side. It comes to little more." The mending brings neighbors together to construct and to compete. The man of reason serves with speculations on the logic of what they do; the neighbor volleys with convictions that don't require logic.

We easily can be persuaded of the mastery of the persona in this situation. He baits the neighbor: "Spring is the mischief in me, and I wonder/If I could put a notion in his head:/'Why do they make good neighbors?'" But careful scrutiny of the poem reveals the mischief to be more than play. It is the persona who initiates the yearly rite ("I let my neighbor know beyond the hill"); and it is the persona who, as a man of reason, demonstrates through his questions that his yearly mending is even less logical than the neighbor's.

Thus the magic of control in "Mending Wall" is the distortion, through the game image, of the persona's own situation in the poem. When we question why the persona builds and rebuilds, the evidence undermines the tone we traditionally assume the poem to have: the mastery of the situation, both its substance and its form.

While Frost later more directly engaged substance through the control of form, his early public career reveals a number of instances like "Mending Wall" where that control is deviously arrived at through games within the poem or games between the poem's speakers. For instance, the play of persona and situation has a slightly different turn in "The Mountain." In this poem, the play is between visitor and native and focuses on the caprice of nature in making a lake which seems warm in the winter and cold in the summer. This is the play, or by-play, in the poem, and it is one of several Frost poems which place the poetic persona outside local lore and metaphor. For instance, when the local resident waxes metaphoric about the sprinkling of houses about the mountain's foot, the persona returns mischievously to the curious local legend of the lake: "Warm in December, cold in June, you say?" The question seems to demand a confession of belief from the local, but instead draws the logical reply:

> "I don't suppose the water's changed at all.
> You and I know enough to know it's warm
> Compared with cold, and cold compared with warm.
> But all the fun's in how you say a thing."

Here the persona of the poem is outpoetized and has explained to him the reasons he assumed didn't reside in local perceptions. The persona is ignorant of the real nature of the native, whereas the native was not ignorant of the real mystery of the lake. The native controls the situation (not the persona; see also the town-bred farmer in "The Code") and responds to the question "You've lived here all your life?" with more proof of control: he ends the conversation with the same cool decisiveness with which he controls his oxen:

> He drew the oxen toward him with light touches
> of his slim goad on nose and offside flank,
> Gave them their marching orders and was moving. (p. 44)

Increasingly for Frost the play *in* poetry became the play *of* poetry: the business of control is essential to the process of poetry. Frost explains in "The White-Tailed Hornet." The hornet has struck at a number of inanimate fly-like objects. Then he strikes at and misses a real fly. The persona theorizes:

> But for the fly he might have made me think
> He had been at his poetry, comparing

Nailhead with fly and fly with huckleberry:
How like a fly, how very like a fly.
But the real fly he missed would never do;
The missed fly made me dangerously skeptic. (pp. 278–79)

He continues to bring the whole matter of animal instinct under consideration. He raises, playfully, the questions of fallibility and control, blaming man's low self-esteem on downward comparisons. But both the play in the poem and the play of thought seem to indicate a further evidence in Frost of the importance of control in play. The poet, by the sureness of his comparisons, makes his control over poetry the control of poetry's substance; the hornet, missing the fly, shows that control is perhaps the *human* instinct and that the poet, always busy about his comparisons, never really risks missing the real fly.

Poetry, particularly Frost's poetry, acknowledges that life's real flies are elusive and goes about comparisons with particular control. Two examples which show how Frost uses games and play as the heart of the comparison are "The Bonfire" and "Directive." In "The Bonfire," the play represents the ritual comparison as catharsis. How shall we learn about fear? "The best way is to come uphill with me/ And have our fire and laugh and be afraid" (p. 133). It is through games and play we learn, for games are the analogues of reality. In "Directive" the persona bids us advance until "you're lost enough to find yourself" in a "children's house of make-believe." That house stands next a house "in earnest," a real house which is the reality mirrored by the play house. I believe it important in that important poem that the "drinking goblet like the Grail" comes from the *play* house: "Here are your waters and your watering place./Drink and be whole again beyond confusion" (p. 379).

The importance of the sense of play is to provide respite from and insight into reality. Play represents a rehearsal in miniature of those roles and agonies we meet in life. Psychologists have discussed the importance of play to children; surely imagination, and its play, provides the adult the same ability to accustom oneself to a situation which will eventually be real, or which is real.

Play then, for Frost, is control of the metaphor for reality. In poems like "Mending Wall" this metaphor is a disguise for the persona who gives the appearance of control. In later poetry the control will be directly in the voice of the poems, and the play will be between voice and form.

For example, toward the end of Frost's career the control of play became less explicitly the play of games and more the play of poetry. No single poem of *In the Clearing* is without the confidence earlier disguised as the play of the game. At least the control is explicitly declared in the confidence of a master poet's voice. In the collection's penultimate poem Frost warns "It takes all sorts of in- and outdoor schooling/To get adapted to my kind of fooling." Even the title "How Hard It Is to Keep from Being King When It's in You and in the Situation" clarifies the role of poet laureate which Frost assigned himself in "Kitty Hawk," the central poem of the collection:

> Nature's never quite
> Sure she hasn't erred
> In her vague design
> Till on some fine night
> We two come in flight
> Like a king and queen
> And by right divine,
> Waving scepter-baton,
> Undertake to tell her
> What in being stellar
> She's supposed to mean. (p. 442)

These two, the pilot and the poet, give meaning to nature because "We may get control,/If not of the whole,/Of at least some part . . ." (p. 441). This sense of spokesman, hinted earlier in "Directive," gives a lunatic quality to the verse, a confidence and control that make the play of poetry.

Frost's house of poetry had become, in the terms set out in "Directive," both a house in earnest and a house of play. Frequently the part through which Frost established control was the play within the poem. Like my uncle's manipulation of his oxen, the apparent ease with which Frost moved toward his objective was achieved by the arrangement of elements and their playful inversion. It is mastery of such parts which convinces us of mastery of the whole.

Revelation as Child's Play
in Frost's "Directive"

DAVID ALAN SANDERS

We understand then do we not?
What I promis'd without mentioning it, have you not accepted?
What the study could not teach—what the preaching could not
accomplish is accomplish'd, is it not?

Whitman, "Crossing Brooklyn Ferry"

I have heard "Directive" described as a grim poem, a Frostian version of Eliot's "Waste Land," offering the "clear and disenchanted perception" that in nature everything, physical or cultural, "simply goes."[1] But though the poem strips away illusions, it does not do away with fictions. It insists that all we can marshal against nature is rooted in the simplest make-believe—that the acts of imitation and identification in the play of children are models for the processes of poetry and ritual alike. As the world of the poem implies—a world minutely factual yet highly metaphorical—the poem is about transformations, about conversion. Touching childhood and death at once, "Directive" implies that to see as the poet sees will save us as nothing else can: it will show us what life comes to in nature, and what else we can make of it. "Poetry," Frost said, "begins in trivial metaphors, 'grace metaphors,' and goes on to the profoundest thinking that we have."[2] "Directive" says as much for play.

Actually, "Directive" illustrates two kinds of play, two inventive efforts requiring different degrees of belief. From the start we see nearly all the kinds of playfulness we are used to in Frost: games with syllables, verbal tricks, dramatic ploys and ironies to keep us off balance. But there is also the play that, even with irony, works in earnest, turning make-believe ritual into a ritual make-believe

267

that carries the poem to its denouement. Venturing beyond the decorum of the literal, Frost implies that the Jesus of St. Mark's account is a poet addressing an elite,[3] further hinting that his own parable—like that of the seed on rich and barren soils—also concerns figuration and election. Yet, by claiming to have "stolen" the communal goblet from the children's playhouse and to have kept it "under a spell," he characteristically denies these mysteries their accustomed solemnity.

The truth at the poem's center is sobering enough. The point of this poetic journey is first to face our mortal vulnerability by feeling the dignity and value of other lives already spent. To feel this isolation and loss, we must know these lives intimately; we must leave our world and enter theirs. Yet, if we would not take refuge in our accidental differences from them, they must be anonymous as well. Each reader must become that "someone" whose "road . . . from work this once was," making himself "at home" in a world where even evidence of eating, drinking, working barely survives—where "the only field/Now left's no bigger than a harness gall."

Yet, even amidst these ruins, emphasis falls on the play which once made something special, as it does again here, of these ordinary acts—made them worthy of imitation:

> First there's the children's house of make-believe,
> Some shattered dishes underneath a pine,
> The playthings in the playhouse of the children.

To "Weep for what little things could make them glad" is not only to lament the littleness of what life clings to but also to sense how much its value is conferred by imagination, and to be moved by both. The next four lines only seem to leave the children's house behind:

> Then for the house that is no more a house,
> But only a belilaced cellar hole,
> Now slowly closing like a dent in dough.
> This was no playhouse but a house in earnest.

The playhouse is not so much put aside as merged with what it leads us to; an impermanent house whose "earnestness" it still bears witness to; for the "shattered dishes" tell us all we know and need to know of the actual kitchen—of its life and its death, each evoked again by the "dent in dough" which vivifies the earth's effacement of it. The children's house is "first" now because it is last, outliving the "real" house in almost the way that poetry survives experience.

We could easily underestimate the thematic importance of this make-believe, which is hardly less earnest than what it imitates. Like most ritual, it reenacts in simpler, more vivid form the life which it once looked forward to and again, in the poem, invokes. The repetition and slowing cadence in "The playthings in the playhouse of the children" even confer a hint of formal dignity which asks us merely to linger a moment and to ponder. By beginning the climactic episode with the children's house, Frost asks us to confront the life lost here, and life itself, as the children face it—without familiarity, without a personal past. To see life as children, whether Christian[4] or Wordsworthian, is the final step in seeing through "all this now too much for us."

How the poet portrays the children's play makes all the difference, for if we are to "Weep for what . . . could make them glad," what matters to them must matter to us. And it does. Unlike Wordsworth's satiric "Darling of a pygmy size,"[5] these are not children to be seduced into conning shallow roles in rapid sequence. Their few remains have a simplicity which lets us concur in their concern for form, for how things are done, which clarifies the lives we undertake, and which finally makes their play a model for the poet's own, supplying even the "broken drinking goblet" in which he extends to us his vision of wholeness. The handing down of the vessel to the children, to the poet, and finally to us, suggests how life renews itself imaginatively *as* it does so physically; for, as children, we first confirm that human life is art as well as nature—that we, as well as nature, have something to say about the form our lives shall take. This confirmation is the task of such play, as it is the task—the work—of art.

Even more important than the ritual implement, then, is the model the children's play provides for projecting one's *self* into another *body*. Asked to weep for their joys, we must even drink from the same source they drank from:

> Here are your waters and your watering place.
> Drink and be whole again beyond confusion.

Taking "the water of the house," we exchange our tears for the essence of other lives broken off, dissolved again into earth, as ours will be. We encompass the stream of time that might merely have carried us away and, by making it a part of ourselves, change it into a stream of lives that might otherwise never have touched. Though we die our individual deaths, the poem thus preserves our humanity. If I am the poet, it can even sing my song.

To drink as the speaker commands, then, is also to save him, for he lives on in a world made possible by his language and made actual by each reader who enters it fully.[6] If we lose ourselves to his make-believe, the present tense of his voice, already reaching to past lives, extends through us to the future. And if we give ourselves to what he sees, we step—for the duration of the poem at least—from our lives doubly into community.

The speaker's own references ("if you'll let a guide direct you"; "if you're lost enough")[7] make quite clear the conditional aspect of this communion. Like many initiatory rites, including the Grail quest alluded to, the poem is a test of the worthy; setting out guarantees no illumination, nor will going through the motions suffice. As Jesus says in the passage to which Frost refers, some "may indeed see but not perceive, and may indeed hear but not understand" (RSV, Mark 4: 12). And like Jesus, who uses parables to hide the truth from those outside the kingdom, Frost hides his revelation "Under a spell so the wrong ones can't find it,/So can't get saved, as St. Mark says they mustn't." This single declaration of motives intensifies the challenge already contained in his second-person address to the reader. For, where the normal, first-person lyric voice lets us eavesdrop upon a poetic world, such direct invitations and instructions expose us, confronting us with the alternatives—to enter or feel left out—that most poems leave implicit. The pose is less startling in a poet who often toys with readers' expectations, who has admitted to shaking loose the unwary by "snapping the whip,"[8] and has even boasted of being too clever for some, "saying things that suggest formulae . . . but don't quite formulate. I should like," Frost has confessed, "to be so subtle at this game as to seem . . .

altogether obvious. The casual person would assume that I meant nothing or else I came near enough meaning something he was familiar with to mean it for all practical purposes. Well well well."[9] But despite precedents and warnings, the direct challenge surprises us in "Directive," especially so late in the poem. We might feel, as one critic has put it, that "Frost . . . has his nerve."[10]

But Frost does not discriminate between the sheep and the goats quite arbitrarily. Unlike Jesus—at least as he saw him in Mark's fourth chapter—Frost does not designate a faithful for whom he spells things out. Nor does his parable test us all at once, but provides instruction in its method, exercising us step by step in the mysteries we must master. Almost from the start, it is true, the speaker makes his reader something of an adversary, proposing a kind of Follow-the-Leader as he turns his gentle concern ("if you'll let a guide direct you") into a threat of adandonment ("Who only has at heart your getting lost"). Nor is his reassurance wholly honest as he raises the very specters he pretends to banish: "You must not mind a certain coolness . . ./Still said to haunt his side of Panther Mountain"; "Nor need you mind the serial ordeal/Of being watched from forty cellar holes"; "Make yourself up a *cheering* song" (italics added). Yet, if the speaker seems to enjoy our uneasiness with him, and in this wilderness, we are scared only enough to make it an adventure, as he says. More important, our mythic lostness has begun unawares, and in our confusion we give ourselves, like children, to one who seems in control. Fittingly, even the promise of a clarity beyond our initial (and partly syntactical) confusion, even the assurance of something "Back out of all this now too much for us"—namely, of the house "no more a house," or the farm a farm, or the town a town—has a "once-upon-a-time" quality in the recitation.

That we are powerless and lost, if not yet aware of it, is the first of "Directive's" object lessons, and the poet, to dramatize our passage from old to new ways of seeing, devises verbal mysteries through which he can guide us to revelation. But we are not simply at *his* mercy. Our confusion, especially in the poem's first half, stems also from what, in "Carpe Diem," Frosts says life always is in the present, "Too crowding, too confusing—/Too present to imagine." Here the poet plays on this natural uncertainty not only to sharpen our need for poetic resolution but also to remind us how baffling and uncertain the familiar world really is. As a natural creature, he too feels vulnerable in a nature whose "monolithic knees" expose the "pretense" of culture, whose glacial "coolness" toward us never passes, whose glacial lines, "ruled" and "chiseled," mock the "grave-yard marble sculpture" and all other lines of human definition "dis-solved and broken off"—the road, the two villages, the houses, the names. The speaker, then, shares his own disquiet in the familiar Frostian jokes that half-neutralize fear by half-admitting it. To pro-ject anxiety as "the woods' excitement.../That sends light rustle rushes to their leaves" recalls the "little horse" who "gives his harness bells a shake" because the poet "think[s] it queer" to be stopping by woods on "the darkest evening of the year" (p. 224)—or the "little bird" in "The Wood-Pile" "who takes/Everything said as personal to himself" and "let his little fear/Carry him off the way I might have gone" (p. 101). The question aimed here at the "upstart" woods—"Where were they all not twenty years ago?"—seeks a similar re-assurance in condescension, but the short time it takes undergrowth to shade out orchard has obvious implications. "People," says Frost in "Education by Poetry," "say 'Why don't you say what you mean?' We never do that, do we, being all of us too much poets? We *like* to talk in parables and in hints and in indirections—whether from diffidence or some other instinct."[11]

Because without imagination we would be irretrievably lost to nature, we must, like the poet, learn to "sing"—to make a world that compensates our loss of this one. Whether our song puts a traveler ahead of us "on foot" or "creaking with a buggy load of grain" makes no difference; what counts is the power of invention we marshal against nature's reduction of artifacts back to elements. Nor does it matter that our initiation begins without our active participation, for the first paradoxes need only prepare us to find meaning within negation by equating effacement of human mark-ings with clear sight. If this implicit directive for imagination re-mains general, none is more central, for it points to a continual con-version of nature back into art—to the necessary salvation of things broken and lost that the poem is about.

As we are not ready at the outset to be fully lost, the speaker keeps us in touch with the physical terrain without betraying us to a literal nature. Thus, while the anthropomorphized glacier, with its lingering "coolness," departs from any geological "story in a book about it," such transparent fictions do not match nature's power. Turning the road back into "monolithic knees" covers its hardness no better than earlier cultural "pretenses." Imagining a giant artisan who "chisels" his lines into stone really dwarfs man more than it humanizes nature, just as condescending to the "upstart" woods only exposes the impermanence of human cultivation. The "cheering song" which admits to fear by countering it captures the doubleness of all these images, which sustain us just long enough on the wrong sort of road.

They fail in the poem as they are meant to fail, for, to save us, imagination must surpass merely fanciful alternatives to nature. We thus reach a major transition in the metaphoric journey when that part of us which has been clinging to a familiar reality through such comforting fictions is baffled.

> The height of the adventure is the height
> Of country where two village cultures faded
> Into each other. Both of them are lost.
> And if you're lost enough to find yourself
> By now, pull in your ladder road behind you
> And put a sign up CLOSED to all but me.
> Then make yourself at home.

Though we do not get the village cultures we are led to expect, the words "Both of them are lost" augur something important. We are asked to cast loose into a metaphoric world, and the transition from one "lostness" to another refines our notion of the journey by redefining the "height of adventure." To get "beyond confusion" into wholeness, we must cross this uncertain ground, give up the specificity, the naming that suggests a map of actual terrain, and accept a "height of country" we can find only in the poem. In directing us to "put a sign up CLOSED to all but me" the speaker assumes that we follow and are ready to be illuminated, and his tone aids our advance toward the final communion. As his tutelary distance yields to fuller reciprocation of our trust, his solicitousness turns to direct intimacy; and we, having "let a guide direct" us, having "made [ourselves] up a . . . cheering song," now make [ourselves] at home" and hear no more conditional instructions. We are simply told to "weep," as we will be to "drink."

For the speaker, as we have seen, the figurative communion retains a more personal dimension, for the poetic action that engages us in his vision becomes a living embodiment of his presence. The poem *is* his survival beyond the natural body—though only under certain conditions. As the metaphor of the Eucharist implies, both we and the speaker are necessary to give this body life. Only if we see does his imagination live; if we cannot identify with him, he is dead. As our salvation depends on him, so his survival depends on us. If the poem is necessary for him to save us, we are necessary if the poem shall save him.

This relation of poet to reader is admittedly the condition for all lyric poetry. If the poem works, then for its duration we become the poet and he is each of us. As Auden said of Yeats in his elegy, "he became his admirers." Wallace Stevens has said the poet's "function is to make his imagination theirs." [12] We need poets to survive imaginatively, and to survive imaginatively all poets need us—though the terms mean something slightly different in each case. But "Directive" is unique in Frost's poetry, and among all poems I know, in dramatizing intentionally the process by which it becomes the figurative body incorporating poet and reader. Of course, being guided and lost, challenged, reassured, and finally perhaps saved is normally so unstated that we hardly realize it goes on in every poem we read.

Only "The Pasture" invites the reader as explicitly, and as the frontispiece to almost every volume of Frost's collected poems since 1914, it became the overture to his verse as a whole: "—You come too." Yet, this gentle urging, closing each of two stanzas, remains an afterthought in a larger sense, conveying a wish to share, but no compelling need. The reason is the poem itself. Images of emergence and birth, verbs in the future tense, make it rich in expectation, befitting spring. Death is hardly evident: a detritus of dead leaves needs only be skimmed away. And because nature seems enough, we are extra: "—You come too." In "Directive," a nature that has all but submerged culture has clarified the poet's need for a reader who can know the worst and not turn from it. He prepares a thorny path and a prickly invitation because he tests us for struggle.

Understanding the poem as a process rather than an artifact, and realizing how it saves the poet, helps to explain the mood of acceptance, almost transcendence, implied by a brook described in terms—"lofty and original"—that merge poetic and religious "sources." Only some assurance of a body beyond the literal could relieve the anxiety attached to the flow of waters in so many other lyrics of Frost;[13] and only from some figurative elevation such as our identification with the poet could we look upon nature without the defenses of humor and irony which reassure both poet and reader through more than half this poetic journey. Contradictory though it may seem, the poet's personal salvation helps also to explain the defensive irony that flashes once more as he takes obvious delight in having hidden the priceless truth beyond reach of the "wrong ones." Though we might find other examples of such crustiness in the later Frost, we can do more than forgive the poet a familiar vice, especially when we know how such assertiveness typically betrays a mortal anxiety. The speaker condescends to us here as he does earlier to glacier and "upstart" woods—to reassert the upper hand. As he wished to deny his vulnerability to nature, he would now deny all dependence on his reader, who has him at his mercy in a different way. He may also feel the helplessness of not knowing whether he has done enough, for any salvation resting on human powers must remain uncertain. The poet's real adversary, then, is the death which makes him need us at all. His pretense of control over us is thus, even more, a primitive outburst against that final helplessness. The direct emergence of the "I" in these lines emphasizes his need to register an indelibly personal voice over his efforts toward community with us.

Another lyric from *Steeple Bush* alludes to such distinctly personal survival. In "To an Ancient" the speaker addresses a stone-age forerunner whose meager evidences—an eolith and bone ("The second more peculiarly your own")—seem "as expressive of the human race/As meeting someone living, face to face." The speaker nonetheless ends with a question:

> You make me ask if I would go to time
> Would I gain anything by using rhyme?
> Or aren't the bones enough I live to lime? (p. 382)

Clearly, such mute endurance, however human, is not enough. The dead man's anonymity haunts the poet: "Sorry to have no name for you but You." His particular need for language is more poignantly expressed in "To a Moth Seen in Winter," where the speaker pities "something human" in this fellow creature (and traditional emblem of the soul) who, "lured . . . with false hope/To . . . the venture of eternity," makes such a "labor of flight." "But go," he concludes; "My pity cannot help":

> the hand I stretch impulsively
> Across the gulf of well-nigh everything
> May reach to you, but cannot touch your fate.
> I cannot touch your life, much less can save,
> Who am tasked to save my own a little while. (pp. 356–7)

So cut off in its dying, the moth quickens the poet's fear that his words will fail. Like that last anxious assertion in "Directive," this terror measures the pull of the tragic in Frost—the sense that in nature we are finally, simply left.

His commitment, then, must be to his poem, and, however reluctantly he accepts our part in saving him, however he may vaguely threaten to exclude us, the poem needs us. Nor is his reference to St. Mark a wholly exclusive gesture. Like Jesus, who explains his parabolic method to the faithful, Frost, while threatening exclusion to the wrong ones, reassures himself by confirming the right ones, telling us where to find the truth by showing *how* it is hidden. His simple analogies between goblet and Grail, between his directives and the gospel, hint at the figurative process—at meaning within meaning, the Word within words. "Your waters and your watering place," are, he tells us, "here": at the brook so near its source, at the old cedar where the goblet is hidden, at the children's playhouse from which it was "stolen." But as all these places at once, "here" is a locale existing only in the poem, which unfixes all these things from nature and time, giving them new life and new relations to one another. In this sense the poetic action is the vessel in which the waters of natural dissolution are made the outward sign of continuity for all who can drink as directed. The poem itself is thus like the goblet which it saves, for without imagination, both would be broken and wasted by time. The real poem is the goblet "hidden"—

not merely the artifact, "broken" by nature, but the figurative play of the poet's imagination, which ours must help to save. It is play which changes us through acts of sharing, sustaining human form through time, keeping our word for other men.

Notes for *Revelation as Child's Play in Frost's "Directive"* by DAVID ALAN SANDERS

1. The attitude, and the words quoted as I recall them, belong (as of November 1973) to Jonathan Bishop of Cornell University. About that time, William Hedges of Goucher College suggested the comparison to Eliot.
2. "Education by Poetry," *Robert Frost: Poetry and Prose*, ed. Edward C. Lathem and Lawrance Thompson (New York: Holt, Rinehart and Winston, 1972), p. 332.
3. This he has done both within the poem (ll. 55–62) and, less obliquely, without. Robert Francis—in *Frost: A Time to Talk* (Amherst: University of Massachusetts Press, 1972), p. 5—reports: "We discussed again Mark 4: 1–12, to which he refers in his poem, 'Directive.' . . . He maintained that Jesus had said it and meant it, and that he (Frost) agreed. Namely, not merely the fact that some people were for one reason or another excluded, but that they needed to be and ought to be excluded." In reference to the same passage, Frost has also been quoted as saying, "It seems that people weren't meant to be saved if they didn't understand figures of speech." See S. P. C. Duvall, "Robert Frost's 'Directive' Out of *Walden*," *American Literature*, 31 (1960), 87.
4. See Matthew 18:3: "unless you turn and become like children, you will never enter the kingdom of heaven." (I quote the Revised Standard Version in this and other Biblical references.) Marie Borroff, in "Robert Frost's New Testament: Language and the Poem," *Modern Philology*, 69 (August 1971), 53, offers (in addition to some relevant bibliography) a concise summary of the main New Testament passages which "Directive" echoes and alludes to.
5. See Stanza seven of the Intimations Ode.
6. The emphasis on reciprocity between poet and reader, especially as evidenced by tears in the reader, suggests Horace's advice to poets in the *Ars Poetica* (ll. 102–3), "Si vis me flere, dolendum est/Primum ipsi tibi," which I read: "If you would have me weep, there must first be suffering on your part." As I am reminded of it, though certainly no Latinist, Frost, quite a good one, may well have had it in mind. As he says in "The Figure a Poem Makes," "No tears in the writer, no tears in the reader" (*Poetry and Prose*, p. 394).
7. Especially important here is Matthew 10: 39: "He who finds his life will lose it, and he who loses his life for my sake will find it" (or Luke 17: 33).
8. "On Extravagance," Frost's last public talk, given at Dartmouth College, 27 November 1962, rpt. in *Poetry and Prose*, p. 452.
9. From a letter to Louis Untermeyer (1 January 1917), quoted by Lawrance Thompson, *Robert Frost: The Years of Triumph, 1915–1938* (New York: Holt, Rinehart and Winston, 1970), p. 300.
10. Borroff, p. 53.
11. *Poetry and Prose*, p. 332.
12. "The Noble Rider and the Sound of Words," in *The Necessary Angel* (New York: Vintage, 1951), p. 29.
13. See, for example, "West-Running Brook," "A Hillside Thaw," "Hyla Brook," "The Onset," "Spring Pools," "In Time of Cloudburst."

BACKGROUND
AND BIOGRAPHY

Thomas Daniel Young's essay is in effect a narrative with a surprise ending, though the reader should allow the author to tell the story and not anticipate him by peeking at the last page. Professor Young talks of the association between Frost and Ransom and, gradually moving to a discussion of Ransom's point of view, reveals an appraisal of Frost's work. By chance Peter Stanlis adds a note of interest (in a letter to the editor): "Frost's remark of Ransom that he 'had the art and . . . the tune' is consistent with the high praise I have heard Frost give to Ransom as a poet. When I was at Bread Loaf as a student I had three courses with Ransom, and I recall talking with Frost about Ransom. Frost regretted that Ransom spent so much of his time and energy on criticism, and wished he would turn exclusively to writing poetry. He said that in the long run Ransom would be remembered much more as a poet than as a critic. This was at the height of Ransom's reputation as a critic. I have always remembered these remarks by Frost, since they were intended as high praise for Ransom. They also are another instance of many in which Frost showed himself to be completely devoted to poetry, as against other literary activities." Professor Young says he agrees with Frost's opinion that Ransom should have spent more time with poetry.

Perry Westbrook's excellent essay provides the kind of background material that really illuminates biography as well as the poetic process. Readers will be surprised to find "Directive" included in the several poems that may have their origins in Frost's knowledge of a New England by no means pastoral. (Professor Westbrook is careful to allow that this poem, and others, may retain its wholeness for those who find it a meaningful statement of Frost's

279

ideas.) The essay leads to further speculation about Frost's kinds of fooling, and studies of this kind reintroduce the question of Frost's pastoral world, specifically, to borrow again from Professor French, the nature of Frost country. To what extent was Frost deliberately creating a poetic world and for what reasons? Did his poetic mind require creation of a country of his own? And when one looks into or through Frost's kinds of fooling, what in fact are the human values?—to borrow from Professor Nitchie's book title.

Dorothy Tyler's beautiful essay must simply be *read*. Would the poet have appreciated the irony? The last essay in *Frost II* is an epitaph that says Robert Frost lives.

J. T.

Our Two Worthies:
Robert Frost and John Crowe Ransom

THOMAS DANIEL YOUNG

WHEN John Crowe Ransom went overseas in the fall of 1917, he carried with him early drafts of many of the poems that were published two years later in *Poems About God*. His military duties demanded so much of his time and attention during the first few months of his assignment in France that he was able to do little writing. In the spring of 1918, however, after serving nearly four months at the front as an officer in the field artillery, he was reassigned to the base at Saumur. In his first tour of duty at this post he had received instruction in the operation of the 155 Howitzer; in this second tour he was to pass along the information he had received to the officers who were just beginning their tour of overseas service. During his two years in France, while his friend Christopher Morley was attempting to find a publisher for *Poems About God*, Ransom had given as much time and thought as he could to revising this early verse. Although Morley was trying to place individual poems with magazines at the same time he was searching for a publisher willing to bring out the first volume of an unknown poet, he was having little success. He placed one poem with the *Independent*, but at least a dozen other journals returned everything he sent them.

Partly because of the discouraging news he received from New York and partly because of his dissatisfaction with these early poems, Ransom decided that if a publisher was not found soon, he would withdraw the manuscript, completely revise it, and send it out again when he returned to the States. He wrote Morley on 13 May, 1918, that the volume was "clean done," that he had "outgrown" it, and that it had become "a bit artificial" with him.[1] Ransom requested that if Henry Holt, whom Morley planned to ask to reconsider the volume, turned it down, it be held for him to pick up when he came through New York after the war.

In the letter with these instructions Ransom sent four new poems, many suggested changes in the old ones, and a most unusual introduction, one in which he indicated his dissatisfaction with the volume and hinted that it might soon be suppressed. As soon as Morley received this revised manuscript, he sent it to Henry Holt with his strong endorsement. What neither he nor Ransom could know was the identity of the reader to whom Holt would send the manuscript for an official reaction, a reader who would share Morley's genuine enthusiasm for the volume. At this time Holt was paying Robert Frost a small retainer, and he was expected to read and evaluate any poetry manuscripts the company was considering for publication. One of the two or three requests Frost received for this service was for a report on *Poems About God*. His reaction strongly supported the endorsement of Morley, for, as he recalled many years later, the young Tennessee poet "had the art and . . . the tune" (Brooks and Warren, p. 12). Frost's recommendation, added to that of Morley, apparently persuaded the publisher to bring out, in those war years when the demand for poetry was very slow indeed, a volume of verse by an unknown poet.

Although some of the reviewers of *Poems About God* saw a strong influence of the New England poet in these poems about growing up in middle Tennessee around the turn of the century, Ransom said he had not read much of Frost until after the volume was published. In the years just before he began writing verse, Ransom read with great interest and enthusiasm the poetry of Robert Browning, A. E. Housman, and Thomas Hardy. These were the poets who influenced him most before he became acquainted with the work of the French Symbolists immediately after World War I. When he returned to Nashville in 1919 and renewed his associations with the Fugitives, however, he began to read as much contemporary verse as he could. Among the poets he read then was Robert Frost, and he was somewhat envious, he said years later, of the New Englander's ability to write quality verse in a manner to appeal to the modern reader whose taste was shaped by popular fiction. He was one of the few American poets of his generation—the only one of consequence except E. A. Robinson and, perhaps, Edna St. Vincent Millay—in whose hands "poetry as a living art" had not "lost its public support."[2] Although evidently influenced by modernism, Frost had avoided the extremes found in the work of such "pure" poets as Wallace Stevens and such "obscure" poets as Allen Tate. He later did a complete about face in his attitude toward T. S. Eliot, but in the mid-1920s he speculated that Eliot's poetry would not last. "The genius of language," he wrote in *The Literary Review* for July 14, 1923, "is notoriously given to feats of hospitality; but it seems to me it will be hard pressed to find accommodations at the same time for two such incompatibles as Mr. Wordsworth and the present Mr. Eliot; and any realist must admit that what happens to be the prior tenure of the mansion in this case is likely to be stubbornly defended."

About two years later Ransom wrote a short piece for the *Fugitive* in which he argued that irony is "the ultimate mode of the great minds" because "it is most inclusive" and because the "whole mind has been active in arriving at it, both creation and criticism, both poetry and science."[3] Although the "trim and easy" poetry of Robert Frost is "anything but pretentious," it marks its author as modern because it "contains plenty of this irony." Its spirit goes back beyond the Romantic poets of the nineteenth century to Donne and his contemporaries in the seventeenth. Frost's attitude toward nature is "immensely metaphysical": "When this poet sees the bent birches in the wood, he 'likes to think a boy's been swinging them,' a hypothesis which would immediately put man and nature into sodality of merry play. But he is too skeptical to believe that; he is forced to consider that ice storms have bent the birches, and thereupon his romantic impulse, baffled but not yet defeated, takes a new tack and begins to personalize the trees, imagined under their ice-coating. . . . Whenever he dwells on Nature, he is the same; as when he finds the rotting timbers attempting to warm the forest with the 'slow smokeless burning of decay.' It would indeed seem that Nature never otherwise puts in an appearance in human art— whether poetry or painting. Always the natural processes are personalized, and art consoles us with its implication of far-flung analogies between our order and the natural order. Mr. Frost is more than ordinarily delicate in making this implication."

Despite his admiration for Frost's verse, Ransom's speculation

on the nature of poetry, as well as his attempts to justify the existence of art to the members of a society whose compelling interests
were almost entirely in material values, led him to defend a kind of
poetry Frost seldom produced. Although he came to believe the
term too restrictive, he called this kind of verse "metaphysical,"
and declared it "the most original and exciting, and intellectually
perhaps the most seasoned that we know in our literature." The
staple of such poetry is the conceit, a "meant metaphor," one which
is "developed so literally" and "predicated so baldly that nothing
else can be meant." In this kind of poetry a "miraculism arises when
the poet discovers by analogy an identity between objects which
is partial, though it should be considerable, and proceeds to an
identification which is complete."[4] This kind of poetry can be
justified in a world dominated by science because it provides man
with a kind of knowledge he can receive from no other source. His
efforts to point up the differences between poetry and prose brought
him to his well known structure-texture formulation. In addition to
a loose logical structure, "which is not so tight and precise on its
logical side as a scientific or technical prose structure generally is,"
poetry, unlike prose, has an "irrelevant local texture." The structure
includes the poem's logical content, with its beginning middle and
end, its appropriately interspersed transitions, and its rhyme (if any)
and meter. Although the poem's "determinate meaning" may be
expressed by its paraphrasable content, its "indeterminate or final
meaning" may be represented only by taking into consideration the
"residue of meaning" which does not go into the logical paraphrase. This "residue of meaning" resides in the "irrelevant local
texture"; that is, in diction, imagery, sound, and figurative language.[5] In his theory as in his practice, then, Ransom was drawn
toward what Donald Davidson has called the "packed line" with its
"closely woven inferential and referential scheme."[6] Although Ransom often insisted that the real value of a Frost poem was seldom
enclosed within the apparently innocent simplicity of its paraphrasable content, he desired poetry with a textural richness that he seldom found in the poems of Frost. Obviously Ransom would agree
with Eliot's explanation of why contemporary poetry must be difficult. "Our civilization comprehends great variety and complexity,"

Eliot wrote in "The Metaphysical Poets," and this variety and complexity, playing upon a refined sensibility, must produce various and complex results. The poet must become more and more comprehensive, more allusive, more indirect, in order to force, to dislocate if necessary, language into meaning."[7]

Although Ransom concurred with Allen Tate in the conviction that Frost "wrote some of the finest poems of our time," he also agreed with that critic's statement that Frost was not "my kind of poet."[8] He simply did not believe that much of Frost's verse was of the sort designed to "realize the world," to enable the reader to see it better. But if Ransom's personal preferences did not make Frost's poetry appealing to him, he often said that his New England contemporary was making a valuable contribution to the cultural life of his time because Frost's public readings of his verse were the most successful example he knew of the serious artist attempting to bring his work to the people. Consequently, in the middle thirties, when a committee of the Centennial Club of Nashville asked Ransom to recommend a poet to appear before that group, he presented, as his first choice among the several poets he suggested, the name of Robert Frost. After Frost accepted, Ransom agreed to host a small dinner party in his honor and to introduce him before his reading to the club members and their guests. Although many well known writers—including Witter Bynner, Louis Untermeyer, and John Gould Fletcher—were giving readings in Nashville during this period, no one attracted a crowd as large as that gathered to hear Frost. Every seat in the auditorium was taken and a few late comers were seated in the aisles or standing against the wall in the back. After Ransom's introduction Frost read and commented on his poems (Donald Davidson said he chanted them, seldom referring to a manuscript) for almost two hours. No poet in their memory, Ransom and Davidson agreed, had ever been received so well by a Nashville audience. In addition to prolonged applause and a standing ovation at the end of the reading, Frost obviously had the complete attention of his audience for the entire time. His work was so well known that his announcement of the poem he was to read was often lost in a spontaneous burst of applause. Frost was understandably pleased by the reception he received and he told Ransom and

Davidson, who drove him to a party given for him following the reading, that the Fugitives had created in Nashville a "climate for poetry."

Everyone was in a good mood and the party went long beyond the time originally set for it. Frost's chair in the corner where he stationed himself shortly after his arrival was completely surrounded all night and conversation never waned. Davidson reported that the talk that evening was about as good as he had ever participated in, and Ransom thought Frost appeared "absolutely exhilarated." It was almost three o'clock, therefore, when Ransom set out to take their visitor back to his hotel. When they arrived there, both men were deeply involved in a discussion which they wished to continue; consequently Ransom parked his car and walked with Frost to the hotel. There before the front entrance—both still in tuxedos—and in the lobby, the two poets talked until daylight. Milkmen were on the street, Ransom recalled many years afterwards, before they went inside, and "there we stood in our dress clothes, in the morning sun, still talking. People passing by must have thought it funny."[9] Just before he was due at school for an eight o'clock class, Ransom rushed home to change clothes. His wife, whom he had dropped off on his way downtown, was awakened and heard him complain as he searched for appropriate clothing, "I must go to class, but Robert Frost can sleep."

What Ransom was not aware of at this time, of course, was that this association with Robert Frost very likely changed his entire future and placed him in such a position that he would have a significant effect on the course of American literature for two decades or more. Less than two years after he and Frost reluctantly broke off their conversation in the lobby of the Maxwell House, Ransom had moved from Nashville to Gambier, Ohio, and was deeply involved in planning the first issue of the *Kenyon Review*, which quickly became one of the most distinguished and influential journals of its time. He had left Vanderbilt after more than twenty years to join the faculty of Kenyon College because of a series of negotiations which had been set in motion by Robert Frost. In the spring of 1937 when Gordon Keith Chalmers was appointed president of Kenyon College, almost his first official act was to invite his old friend Robert Frost to join him as poet-in-residence. Chalmers and his wife, Roberta Teale Schwartz, the author of two books of poetry, wanted to establish at Kenyon a journal of the kind and quality of the *Yale Review* or the *Virginia Quarterly Review*, and they knew that having Frost's name associated with such a venture would go a long way toward assuring its success. But Frost did not wish to leave New England, nor did he want any kind of position that would impede his freedom of movement. His reputation was so firmly established that he was receiving more invitations to lecture or to read his poems than he could comfortably fill; therefore he refused Chalmers's offer. In declining, however, he suggested that the "man for the job might be available down there in Tennessee." [10] One cannot help wondering how much the pleasant memories of his visit to Nashville contributed to the warmth with which Frost recommended Ransom. Roberta Chalmers, who had published some of her first poems in the *Fugitive* and who was an admirer of Ransom's poetry, supported Frost's recommendation, and Chalmers came to Nashville to persuade Ransom to accept the position. This meeting occurred in the spring of 1937. Barely six months later Chalmers and Ransom had begun to formulate plans for the *Review* and a few years later they organized the Kenyon School of English. The impact of these two developments on the literary world was such that a small liberal arts college with little more than a local reputation for excellence soon became the focus of some of the most important literary activity that occurred in England and America for twenty years or more.

Once Ransom was settled in Gambier the association between him and Frost continued without interruption. Frost came to Kenyon almost every spring to visit the Chalmers and often stayed for a week or longer. During these visits he not only gave public readings, but he was also available for informal sessions with students and faculty. Since he and Frost were "in the same business," as Ransom said, they saw a good deal of each other. Often they appeared together on formal programs, and Ransom arranged as many occasions as he could to allow his students to meet their famous visitor. There were formal dinners at the Chalmers and elsewhere and many of a more private character, usually at the Ransoms or in the home of

Phillip Blair Rice, the associate editor of the *Review*. During the early forties Ransom spent many of his summers in Middlebury, Vermont, as a member of the faculty of the Bread Loaf School of English. Among his most enjoyable experiences of these summers were the frequent visits of Robert Frost, who had a home just down the road from where Ransom and his family lived with other members of the summer school faculty. Once after dinner at the Ransoms, Robb Reavill Ransom recalled many years later, the two poets sat on the porch and talked until almost midnight. When Frost started home, Ransom offered to walk a part of the way with him. At Frost's gate, they paused and talked for a while. When Ransom started home, Frost accompanied him, and the two poets spent the remainder of the night walking from one gate to another, so engrossed in conversation they did not realize they had talked the night away until Mrs. Ransom called them in to breakfast.[11] Frost was to be away for the summer of 1942, and he invited the Ransoms to live in his house, an arrangement which pleased Ransom very much because at meals in the living quarters supplied by the school he was expected to preside "over little tables of old maid students in the dining room."

The close personal relationship between the two poets continued through the years, although few letters were exchanged, and Frost's opinion of Ransom's poetry did not change. In 1956, during one of his visits to Kenyon, he told a student audience, "you have right here on this campus the greatest living American poet." As one might expect, the undergraduate writer who reported Frost's statement took exception to it, insisting that the person deserving that honor was the speaker.

But Ransom was never able, apparently, to make up his mind completely about Frost the poet. During the 1950s and after, he taught on several college campuses a course he called "Poetry of Our Own Age," and though he usually included a few poems by Frost, he concentrated on the poetry of T. S. Eliot and Wallace Stevens, in later years devoting more attention to W. H. Auden than he did to Frost. The rich evocative texture of the poetry of Eliot and Stevens, he told his classes, could fully engage the faculties of readers "fully aged in the academic disciplines" and assist them in realizing a world "made of whole and indefeasible objects." In 1961, when he was invited to offer a seminar in the poetry of Stevens and Eliot at the Ohio State University, he was delighted to accept because the preparation for this assignment would require him to do some work he had intended to do for many years. Since completing *The New Criticism* twenty years before, he had wanted to write another extensive essay on Eliot, who he was convinced was the most important poet of his generation. On two previous occasions he had been less than generous in his comments on this poet, he said, and he wanted "to write him up" again so he could indicate formally his conviction of Eliot's greatness. He had also changed his mind about Stevens, whom once he had classified as "just below the rank of greatness," but whom he now regarded as a "major poet whose magnitude had only gradually dawned" upon him.[12] Among the last of Ransom's essays were reappraisals of Eliot and Stevens, but he never wrote extensively about Frost, a poet whose achievement he considered of lasting importance and a man whose companionship he cherished beyond almost all others. One explanation for this long silence may be included in a letter he wrote Allen Tate shortly after Frost's death: "I felt very sad about Frost, though I didn't go to the funeral. I generally had the curious feeling about him of being indebted to his achievement, in this sense: he was at his best a fine poet, but he chose not to be at his best generally, and therefore discharged the debt to the less literate society which we can't find in us to take seriously. That's a sort of missionary feeling, with relief that somebody else is doing the job."[13] That Ransom was never able to see the whole of Frost's greatness was, in part at least, the result of a consistent application of aesthetic principles developed by one of the most significant theoretical critics of this century. Except in a few poems, Frost did not produce the miraculism that Ransom sought in poetry.

Notes to *Our Two Worthies: Robert Frost and John Crowe Ransom* by THOMAS DANIEL YOUNG

1. Ransom's letters to Christopher Morley are in the Haverford College Library.
2. "Poets Without Laurels," *The World's Body* (New York: Charles Scribner's Sons, 1938), p. 55.

3. "Thoughts on the Poetic Discontent," *Fugitive* 4 (June 1925), 63–4.

4. *The World's Body*, pp. 135, 139.

5. *The New Criticism* (Norfolk, Conn.: New Directions, 1941), pp. 281–82.

6. "Poetry as Tradition," *Still Rebels, Still Yankees and Other Essays* (Baton Rouge, La.: Louisiana State University Press, 1957), p. 7.

7. *Selected Essays* (New York: Harcourt, Brace and Company, 1932), p. 248.

8. *Memoirs and Opinions* (Chicago: The Swallow Press, 1975), p. 96.

9. Quoted by Louise Davis in the Nashville *Tennessean Magazine*, June 7, 1964.

10. For a full discussion of the circumstances surrounding Ransom's leaving Vanderbilt see Thomas Daniel Young, "His Own Country," *Southern Review*, 8, n.s., no. 3 (Summer 1972), pp. 572–93.

11. Interview, Robb Reavill Ransom, February 12, 1971.

12. "The Planetary Poet," *Kenyon Review* 26 (Winter 1964), pp. 233.

13. Ransom's letters to Allen Tate are in the Firestone Library of Princeton University.

Abandonment and Desertion
in the Poetry of Robert Frost

PERRY WESTBROOK

I

IN much of Robert Frost's poetry is an element of sentimentalism, though not, in most cases, in damaging amounts. Indeed, often sentimentalism emphasizes more important aspects of a poem by allowing effective use of irony. Instances easily come to mind: the children's playthings in "Directive," the minister's comments on the old woman in "The Black Cottage," or the details of Silas's plight in "The Death of the Hired Man." Most frequently, moreover, the presence of sentimentality (one hesitates to say intrusion of it, since the poet apparently includes it intentionally) characterizes those of Frost's poems which depict the scenes of desertion and abandonment so common on the New England countryside during his lifetime. In addition to "Directive" and "The Black Cottage," notable poems in this category are "Ghost House," "The Generations of Men," "The Birthplace," "The Need for Being Versed in Country Things," "The Census-Taker," and "In a Disused Graveyard." Only rarely, as in "The Wood-Pile" and perhaps "The Hill Wife," does Frost treat the themes of abandonment and desertion without at least a trace of sentimentality and a liberal infusion of irony as a counter-irritant.

The fact is that deserted houses, overgrown cellar holes, disused graveyards, abandoned roads, and miles of stone walls threading forests that once were meadows and pastures inevitably give rise to emotions and thoughts that border on, or slip over into, sentimentality. Comparable scenes of desertion and decay have, of course, long been stock subjects of literature, as the churchyard musings and the meditations among ruins recorded by authors like Thomas Gray, Constantin Volney, and Lord Byron amply testify. To a poet or philosopher, or to any person of sensitivity, relics of the past suggest mortality and the transitoriness of human affairs. Nowhere in America were such reminders more evident than in the New England to which Robert Frost, at the age of eleven, came from the West Coast, and they were extremely evident in the northern areas in which he lived and worked for much of his life.

But the time for a frankly romantic, much less a sentimental, treatment of such materials—in the manner of a Byron or a Longfellow— had long since passed; and doubtless Frost, except perhaps in several very early poems, never contemplated following a frankly emotional approach—an approach to which his turn of mind and character were alien anyway. The problem, then, was how to treat these subjects without excess of sentiment. But before examining Frost's solution of this problem, one should take a closer look at the New England scene itself and give some attention to the potential for artistic treatment this scene possessed.

II

The past has long been a frequent preoccupation of New Englanders and of persons, like Frost, descended from New Englanders. In fact, within thirty years of the settlement of Plymouth Colony, William Bradford, one of its founders, was praising the past of the community, which he already considered fallen on evil days. Along with such laments for a past that was better than the present, developed a veneration for ancestors which amounted almost to a religion and which has by no means disappeared. Genealogy became, and remains, a widespread concern, and not solely among "leading" families. But New England genealogy was not simply a regional concern; it commanded nationwide interest. The reasons are obvious but can bear a brief summary.

The original New England settlements were, of course, on the coast. But almost immediately—beginning with the migrations to the Connecticut River Valley in the 1630s—expansion inland commenced. As population pressures increased and new land to the northward became more accessible, expansion assumed the proportions of an explosion. Large areas in Maine, Vermont and northern New Hampshire, not to mention parts of New York and Pennsylvania, were overrun with land-hungry Yankee farmers. Mountainsides and hilltops, terrain where farming should never have been attempted, were cleared of trees; the innumerable glacial stones were built into walls sometimes ten feet wide; houses and barns were erected; and churches and schools were established. Almost all available land of the slightest agricultural potential was occupied well before the mid-nineteenth century.

The abandonment of much of this area was as rapid as was its settlement. For many reasons the population drained away, leaving houses and barns to tumble down and fields to revert to forest. In numerous burial plots, the stones were toppled by encroaching trees, and the inscriptions were erased by weather and lichen. In Frost's day and in ours, travelers among New England's hills may observe these remnants of former flourishing human habitation and experience the melancholy engendered by the knowledge of something that has been lost, never to be retrieved—a melancholy scarcely to be dispersed by a realization that the people who once lived on these rocky farms were probably much happier and much more prosperous in their new homes.

The reasons for the exodus, which continued for several generations, are multitudinous, but the major ones were obviously the harshness of the climate and the sterility of the soil. Many of the farms yielded barely a subsistence. Short growing seasons, lengthy and vicious winters during which the farmers' wives would frequently become insane, and inaccessibility to markets—all combined to make life in the hilly back-country unrewarding and unpromising. In the meanwhile other parts of the nation offered better things—or so many of the hill people thought. Steady wages in down-country factory towns lured some; others in large numbers poured westward to take up land that was as fertile as New England's was barren.

The Erie Canal and later the railroads made travel to the west easy. Sometimes whole neighborhoods, the larger parts of townships, would emigrate en masse, establishing beyond the mountains replicas of the communities they had abandoned. The Civil War, during which many New England men saw at first hand regions and ways of life that seemed to offer greater rewards than were possible in their own hills, added one more stimulus to emigration. Inertia was the only incentive for remaining.[1]

III

Such extensive emigration, of course, had disastrous economic effects on all but the more fertile regions of rural New England. For decades, restoring any earlier prosperity seemed impossible. Efforts to encourage tourism and summer vacationing were reasonably successful in localities that could offer scenic or recreational attractions. But the large areas not so endowed benefited little from what later became known as "the summer industry." Other attractions were needed to lure people and money.

Prompted by a realization of this need, a state senator later to become governor of New Hampshire, Frank W. Rollins, suggested the idea of an annual Old Home Week, during which emigrants and the descendants of emigrants from New Hampshire would be requested, by the towns of their origin and, perhaps, a general call by the governor to return home, renew their contact with their ancestral soil, and reestablish their New England identities. While these benefits would accrue to the returning sons and daughters of New Hampshire, the impoverished towns would pick up a bit of cash, would be roused out of their normal lethargy for at least one week in the year, and would, perhaps, occasionally receive a handsome donation of a church, a school, or a monument from some wealthy homecomer with a particularly lively sense of the value of his New England background. Also, some of the participants in these in-gatherings might contribute to local prosperity by purchasing abandoned farms to serve as vacation houses. The eloquence summoned by Rollins in support of his idea deserves a sampling; the following effusion is from an article in the *New England Magazine* of July 1897: "Sons and daughters of New Hampshire, wherever you are listen to the call of the old Granite State! Come back, come back! Do you not hear the call? What has become of the old home where you were born? Is it still in your family? If not, why not? Why do you not go and buy it this summer? Is there any spot more sacred to you than the place where you were born? No matter how far you have wandered, no matter how prosperous you have been, no matter what luxurious surroundings you now have, there is no place quite like the place of your nativity. The memories of childhood, the friendships of youth, the love of father and mother cling about it and make it sacred. Do you not remember it—the old farm back among the hills, with its rambling buildings, its well-sweep casting its long shadows, the row of stiff poplar trees, the lilacs and the willows? I wish that in the ear of every son and daughter of New Hampshire, in the summer days, might be heard whispered the persuasive words: Come back, come back!"[2]

Whether Frost read the article containing this outburst is a matter of conjecture, though he did, of course, later publish several poems in the *New England Magazine*. He also may have read other articles on related matters by Rollins appearing in *The Independent* or in *Country Life in America*; or, even more likely, he may have run across an essay " 'Old-Home Week' in New England," by a Thomas Anderson, in the *New England Magazine* for August 1906, the year before Frost's "A Line-storm Song" was printed in the same periodical.[3]

In all events the idea of Old Home Week caught on quickly in New England and soon hundreds of towns celebrated it. Entertainments, contests, and rousing, tear-jerking speeches marked the occasions; a gala atmosphere not unlike that of a county fair obtained, and no one could say that the fun was not clean, and even—in good Puritan fashion—edifying. Despite the commercial impulse behind the custom—which continued in full force for thirty or more years—Old Home Week seemed to meet some need in the American psyche, though in a crude, at times perhaps vulgar, way. One is reminded of Robert Lowell's poem describing "ten thousand Fords" converging on Concord "in search of a tradition."[4]

IV

Quite literally Robert Frost's "The Generations of Men" is a poem about Old Home Week. Less literally "Directive" reflects the Old Home Week impulse. No one, probably, will take issue with this comment on "The Generations of Men," which seems to have been sedulously ignored by the critics (perhaps because they are unaware of its context and hence do not enjoy its many ironies). But the suggestion that "Directive"—that poem so loved by the explicators because, as Frost suggests,[5] it presents problems of interpretation comparable to those of some of T. S. Eliot's major poems—is in any way associated with so banal, so Babbitty an institution as Old Home Week will not meet with a uniformly favorable reception. Yet the two poems, though different in the level of their literary sophistication, have much in common, as to both theme and intention, and these likenesses deserve notice.

Doubtless Frost looked upon Old Home Week (many a celebration of which he must have witnessed) with a great deal of amusement. Yet there are many types of amusement; it may be derisive, it may be sympathetic, it may be warily ironic. I suggest that in writing "The Generations of Men" Frost's amusement was a composite of the latter two—irony and sympathy. After all, Frost did not take his own New Hampshire ancestry lightly, and he too was a returnee to New England, not for a week but for a lifetime. No one could hold greater pride in a New England background or admire its cultural traditions more. At the risk of being trite, one might say that Frost found his identity in New England. He had returned *indeed* to the source, had bucked the western migration, much as his own West-Running Brook and the eddy within it moved counter to customary directions. Symptomatic of his feelings was his addiction to buying farms, none of them very fertile, in New Hampshire and Vermont. The impulse behind at least some of these purchases is half-humorously described in "A Serious Step Lightly Taken," the persona of which asserts that on his newly acquired land he will complete another three-hundred-year cycle of his family's cultivation of New England soil.

We are told that Old Home Week generated innumerable sappy, doggerel poems on subjects connected with the event. Frost's "The Generations of Men" and other poems on related themes obviously do not belong in this large group of trash. Fortunately Frost took steps to neutralize the sentimentality inherent in the subject by including an irony, a humor, that he must have realized was directed against a tendency within himself. He was later irked that Amy Lowell failed to see and appreciate this humor (Thompson, II, 59, 534).

"The Generations of Men" begins:

> A governor it was proclaimed this time,
> When all who would come seeking in New Hampshire
> Ancestral memories might come together.
> And those of the name Stark gathered in Bow,
> A rock-strewn town where farming has fallen off.... (p. 73)

As the poet tells it, the cellar hole of the original Stark homestead[6] has been discovered up a back road in the township. Each returning Stark has been provided with a card indicating his or her exact position on the many-branched tree of this famous New Hampshire family, and a day has been set for the whole relationship to meet at the cellar hole (incidentally Frost's first title for the poem was "The Cellar Hole"). The arrangement is quintessentially in the spirit of Old Home Week and is marked by a pointless sentimentality exploited for the economic interests of town and state, harmless but surely laughable. Yet to many, including Frost, beneath the fanfare and folderol lay a significance having to do with the perpetuation of traditional values.

The Stark descendants, however, do not take the matter very seriously—and here is one of the ironies of the poem—for a light rain on the appointed day keeps all but two of them from the meeting that had been so elaborately prepared as the culmination of their return to Bow. The two who did keep the appointment are a young man and a young woman, who "idled down" to the spot from opposite directions. The man has a card proving his Stark ancestry; and the woman has three such cards, for she is descended from three branches of "the old stock." (Note that "stock" and Stark, as pronounced in New England, constitute a pun—another of Frost's desentimentalizing touches and a way of universalizing the poem's subject.) The humor of the situation is not lost on these two, whose intellectual sophistication is revealed by their highly literate speech, the wit of their repartee, and their literary and mythological allusions. Yet it is just such persons who would discern whatever of value or substance lay beneath the surface effusions of Old Home Week. These two might seriously

> try to fathom
> The past and get some strangeness out of it.

Frost is on very thin ice in this poem and at any moment could break through into schmaltzy depths of sentiment. As the poet makes very clear the couple who meet here at the ancestral cellar hole are about to embark on a courtship which will eventuate in marriage, after which they will build a summer home on the old foundation, including in their new house, perhaps as doorsill, a piece of charred timber from the original structure. Thus the dearest wish of the governor—that of enticing persons of New Hampshire origins to buy an abandoned farm as a summer residence—is to be realized, with sentimental overtones that would delight the governor beyond his wildest dreams. And what better subject for Old Home Week doggerel! Yet as Frost wrote it, poking gentle fun at the whole concept of Old Home Week, "The Generations of Men" is obviously not doggeral and it is sentimental only to a degree. The realistic depiction of the site and the low-keyed, restrained dialogue keep sentimentality within bounds, as does, of course, the ironical treatment of the whole charade of the reunion. But more than anything else the sense of proportion exhibited by the two young Starks—their New England suppression of whatever pride they may have covertly taken in their ancestry, their playful evocation of their progenitors' comments—makes the poem a meaningful statement on the perennial human need of having roots, identity, and, above all, a code to live by. The most serious remark in the poem— perhaps the only serious one—is:

> What counts is the ideals,
> And those will bear some keeping still about.

We are told that Frost constantly quoted or paraphrased these lines (Thompson, II, 561). Yet even in this statement, he has slyly left us with an ambiguity based on two meanings of the word "still." Does he mean that one should not speak about the "ideals" or that they should be retained? To a New Englander, Frost's words might imply that the two interpretations are reconcilable. New Englanders tend "to keep still"—say nothing—about really important matters—about "ideals," for instance—that they still believe worth preserving. Of course, another possible interpretation, for which a somewhat plausible case could be made, is that the "ideals" were rather unimpressive, if they ever existed at all, and one had better not talk about them.

V

"The Generations of Men" is an early poem, but in subject and theme it anticipates "Directive," published thirty-three years later. We have seen that Frost himself was somewhat sarcastic about the favorable critical reception of "Directive." The fact is, his sarcasm was not without cause. "Directive" advances an idea, or an attitude, that had its first statement in 1913 in "Ghost House" and had been restated many times in the ensuing decades in poems dealing with the desertion of New England farmlands—the idea that "what counts is the ideals" (p. 80). Furthermore, over the years much the same set of images kept reappearing in these poems: uninhabited houses or the cellar holes of houses already vanished; lilac or raspberry bushes, or appletrees, near the housesite; roads that no longer lead anywhere but usually ascend a hill or a mountain; a well, or spring, or brook; meadows and pastures reverting to forest; and disused graveyards. What each of these objects may symbolize, if anything, in the various poems in which they appear, can not be definitely determined, as the myriad differing interpretations of "Directive" make evident. Each reader may, and should, assign his own meanings and values to these recurring objects.

Of one thing, however, we may be certain: a major purpose of Frost in these poems was to evoke the atmosphere of a region, of a culture, that had been abandoned and left to return to a state of nature. Obviously the spectacle is a disturbing and saddening one to the poet, who sees in it implications involving more than New England. "The land was ours before we were the land's," (p. 348) Frost wrote in "The Gift Outright." The hill country of New England was the settlers' for a few decades, but the ruinous evidences of their brief sojourn proclaim all too clearly that the land did not possess them. Did these fugitives from New England become possessed later by the lands they fled to in the West, or did they withhold themselves there also? The answer need not be given here, but Frost seems to say that America is still not spiritually possessed by its people. At any rate the experience of the emigrant farmers during their New England stay had been fragmentary and incomplete, and thus they left the New England hills as fragmented, incomplete persons.

Though it is too late to begin over again, a return, in spirit at least, to the deserted villages and abandoned farms and even a sacramental drink from the ancestral wells might be needed if our culture, marked with incompleteness, is ever to "be whole again" (p. 379), the wholeness being derived from a realization of the continuing presence of the past—in this case, the hill-country phase of the past. The "tireless folk, but slow and sad" (p. 6) of "Ghost House," Frost's first poem on the desertion of the New England countryside, live in the American present, and the recognition of this existence is essential to the wholeness of American society. Obviously, not only New England is involved here, but the whole of American pioneering and the transitory relations with the soil that it fostered.

VI

The success of Old Home Week, which was by no means confined to New England, derived from the human need for a contact with the past, the need for a sense that one's life exists not in temporal isolation but in continuity with former generations. A return, after a long absence to one's childhood home or the home of one's ancestors is an emotion-arousing experience that has been celebrated in song and poetry as long as those arts have existed. Frequently, of course, such song and verse are of a rather shallow, platitudinous quality, and this seems to have been especially true of the Old Home Week doggerel already alluded to. Thus the dilemma is great for a poet who recognizes, as did Frost, the validity of the spiritual or emotional impulse behind the desire to return home but realizes he must repudiate the materialism that exploits the impulse and the mawkishness that tends to degrade it. Frost, as we have seen, resorted to irony and humor as decontaminants. So far as was within his powers, which were very considerable, he appeals to the impulse, honors it, but spares it from the usual Old Home Week dishonesties. He could also present rural New England as it actually was, a deserted and abandoned region of crumbling houses and weed-choked cellar holes, and not pretend that nothing had changed since the exodus fifty or more years before. The returnees would find something very different from what they or their forbears had left. They would find ruin and decay instead of an energetic, thriving, if perhaps misdirected, society, and the spectacle, to the sensitive at least, would not so much sate their nostalgia as generate in them feelings of regret, even misgivings concerning the past of which they were a continuation.

"The Generations of Men," and "Directive" are, of course only two of a sizable number of poems dealing with New England's past. "The Black Cottage" ranks high among such poems and provides a remarkable example of Frost's use of irony—in this case the minister's irony directed against himself—to keep sentiment within bounds. Another poem in this category is "The Birthplace," which has received less than its share of critical attention. In it the poet describes an abandoned homestead—with its accompanying spring and surrounding network of stone walls—where a large family of boys and girls has grown up and later scattered far and wide. Here again the danger of lapsing into bathos is severe, but Frost surmounts the danger by a clever personification of the mountain, which, he writes, "seemed to like the stir" for a while but then "pushed [the family] off her knees" (p. 265). A similarly high potential for excessive emotion is present in the subject of Frost's "In a Disused Graveyard." But he short circuits this potential by a simple half-humorous, half-serious remark—which, moreover, is based on fact—that now even the dead avoid this cemetery, for no one is buried there any more. He ends with a quatrain in which he again resorts to personification:

> It would be easy to be clever
> And tell the stones: Men hate to die
> And have stopped dying now forever.
> I think they would believe the lie. (p. 221)

The mood of gentle irony reminds one of Emily Dickinson's treatment of a graveyard as an ever-growing community in the poem beginning "Who occupies this house."[7]

Frost's irony borders on the comic in "Of the Stones of the Place," in which the persona offers to send to a New Englander in the West a stone from the emigré's ancestral farm to "keep the old tradition safe" (p. 365). The recipient can say of it that it serves as

> The portrait of the soul of my Gransir Ira.
> It came from where he came from anyway.

The appropriateness of the stone as a reminder of New England and its past deserves some comment. Where New Englanders tried to farm they had first to remove innumerable stones from the soil, and to dispose of them they built them into walls. The toil, the hopes, the disappointments these walls represent go beyond the power of words to tell, and Frost, sensibly, never made the attempt —directly at least. But in one of his most famous—and most variously interpreted—poems, "Mending Wall," he calls attention to these monuments of the epical struggle of former generations of yeomen. The wall in Frost's poem does not really need rebuilding, since it serves no present purpose, and perhaps never did, aside from being a means of getting rid of unwanted rocks. But the persona himself has initiated the mending because he feels the wall deserves preservation for other than practical reasons—though certainly not for the fatuous reason given by his neighbor. The "something . . . that doesn't love a wall" (p. 33) is the same something—nature—that the original builders of the wall struggled against and overcame, at least temporarily. To preserve the results of their labor is to pay respect to the tradition, perhaps the "ideals," they represent; but very wisely Frost does not lecture us to this effect. A lecture would be far less impressive than a simple description of the act.

The "something . . . that doesn't love a wall" in New England does not love a meadow either, as Frost makes clear in "The Last Mowing," which may be taken as a companion piece to "Mending Wall." The building of a wall is only a part of the process of creating a meadow from a rock-strewn forest, and the meadow is the place where the farmer's labors reach fulfilment—a place even of joyous labor, as Frost intimates in "Mowing" and "The Tuft of Flowers." Thus the decision to let a meadow revert to woodland is a momentous one which would touch the most insensitive feelings. Even nature, as she takes over, proceeds gently, filling the meadow for a few seasons with flowers, like offerings on the coffin of a dead hope, before the final obliterating onslaught of the forest.

Yet, as Frost states in "The Need of Being Versed in Country Things," the witness of these natural processes must hold his emotions in check or he will fail to undertsand the human significance of what is happening. The pervasive thought in the background of the aggregate of Frost's poems of desertion and abandonment is that human beings are responsible for what they do or do not do—for the desertion, for example, of a farm or a countryside—but that nature acts with signal indifference to human failures and successes. When a family or a group of families leaves land they or their forbears have prepared with great industry and hope for human uses, an act of rejection has taken place, and a sense of that rejection, with all the disappointment and disillusionment it implies, remains as a sort of aura on the land which the settlers briefly possessed but which failed to possess them. The question which haunts Frost's poems on such subjects is whether something less tangible but more important—such as the original settlers' confidence in themselves and their land or the sense of rightness and goodness that sparked their pioneering efforts—may not have been rejected along with the acres that in a sense had, of course, failed them.

Have the "ideals" of the first settlers vanished from New England's hills along with the settlers themselves? Have the "ideals" perhaps vanished from all America and not from New England alone? Was Emerson right when he wrote:

> The God who made New Hampshire
> Taunted the lofty land
> With little men?[8]

In his poem "New Hampshire" Frost skirts these questions, either not choosing or not being able to answer them. Instead, having quoted Emerson, he quotes another Massachusetts poet, Amy Lowell, who disparaged the people of New Hampshire. Frost continues:

> And when I asked to know what ailed the people,
> She said, "Go read your own books and find out." (p. 166)

The reader is left to surmise whether Frost accepted this comment about his poems. The fact that he does not bother to reject it is perhaps his way of answering the questions posed above, though more likely it indicates that he had thus far no definite answers, or that no final answers are possible.

Notes to *Abandonment and Desertion in the Poetry of Robert Frost* by PERRY WESTBROOK

1. Accounts of the expansion and decline of rural populations in northern New England may be found in Lois Kimball Mathews, *The Expansion of New England* (Boston: Houghton, Mifflin, 1909); Harold Fisher Wilson, *The Hill Country of Northern New England: Its Social and Economic History, 1790–1930* (New York: Columbia University Press, 1936); and Stewart H. Holbrook, *The Yankee Exodus: An Account of Migration from New England* (New York: Macmillan, 1950).

2. Frank W. Rollins, "New Hampshire's Opportunity," *New England Magazine*, 16 (July 1897), 542. *The Hill Country of Northern New England* (pp. 270–76) deals interestingly with the subject of Old Home Week.

3. The Anderson article, which contains several specimens of Old Home Week doggerel, appears on pp. 673–85 of the *New England Magazine*. The two other articles by Rollins are "The Renaissance of New England," *The Independent*, 53 (January 10, 1901), 69–70; and "The Abandoned Farm in New Hampshire," *Country Life in America*, 18 (September 1910), 531–34.

4. Robert Lowell, *Lord Weary's Castle* (New York: Harcourt, Brace, 1944), p. 27.

5. See Elizabeth Shepley Sergeant, *Robert Frost: The Trial by Existence* (New York: Holt, Rinehart and Winston, 1960), p. 394. "This is the poem," Frost said of "Directive," "that converted the other group. The boys [followers of T. S. Eliot] call it great. They have re-estimated me. This is great and most of the rest trivia."

6. Perhaps Frost had in mind the very first Stark home in America, which was at Derry near Frost's farm. This house burned (note charred wood in the poem) in 1736. Starks later settled in Dunbarton a few miles from Bow, but the seven-generation removal of the couple in the poem from their common ancestors suggests that Frost was thinking of the Derry site.

7. *The Poems of Emily Dickinson*, ed. Thomas H. Johnson (Cambridge, Mass.: The Belknap Press of Harvard University Press, 1958), p. 657.

8. *Poems* (Boston: Houghton, Mifflin, 1884), p. 72, quoted in Frost's "New Hampshire," p. 166.

The Strong Are Saying Nothing

DOROTHY TYLER

Living as I now do in Robert Frost country, with the Green Mountains and the Berkshires at the rise of the roads to the east, I am sometimes intensely aware of the last resting place of Frost. It is in the hallowed burial ground of the First Church, Congregational, in beautiful Old Bennington, which was made Vermont's Colonial Shrine in 1937. Frost was himself present for that service of dedication, as he said in a letter to Louis Untermeyer. Properly called the Bennington Center Cemetery, it is older than the church itself, older than the graves of Revolutionary War soldiers and the Hessian soldiers buried in a mass grave. Frost was one who would appreciate the pathos of the fate of Bridget Harwood, buried there in 1762, who died just seventeen months after arriving with the first party of settlers.

From every direction of approach, the Bennington Monument looms over the scene, though it is common knowledge that the Battle of Bennington was fought over the border in New York State, in Walloomsac, at a well-maintained battleground reaching its peak of fame during the bicentennial years. One cannot visit it in the present day without feeling some grief for the soldiers, on both sides, who were too occupied with their bloody encounter to enjoy the great beauty of the scene. All this was in Frost country, and that "Fourth of July American," as he called himself, knew it well.

There is still a link between the two states, New York and Vermont, in this border country, for directly across from the church stands the old and unrestored Walloomsac Inn, which has its share of history. At the Inn in 1842 the distinguished Ellery Channing, founder of the Unitarian Church, died in 1842, and there is a cenotaph honoring him in the cemetery. No doubt Frost knew about its presence there, for Emerson was one of the authors he most honored, and the Channing family were his associates.

But to return for a moment to the road that leads to Frost's grave:

From Troy, New York, known as the home of Uncle Sam, whose original was Samuel Wilson, the traveler takes Route 7 eastward. It is a route that even now has its trace of eeriness—and Frost must have traveled this way on his barding trip to Russell Sage College. On this road, in the early days, the French and Indian hordes swept through on their way to attack New England, not once but many times. And before Bennington or the state line is reached, one passes between dense woods, the Tibbits State Forest, with a stream in the ravine—a perfect setting for "Stopping by Woods on a Snowy Evening." Snow there is in quantity in winter, and there is no farmhouse near. It is hill and river country here, and soon one crosses a big bridge and passes the village of Hoosick and is at the high border and into the Green Mountain State.

What is the difference one feels at once? There *is* a difference, though New Yorkers from Downstate have contributed much, especially in wealth, to Vermont; and even some of their famous maple syrup comes from this sister to the west. But, as Carl Carmer has noted, "Every State is a country," and Vermont has cultivated its differences.

And now, unless you make the left turn immediately, past the ruinous but still used Walloomsac Inn, you may go straight ahead into the cemetery, to the side of the church, until you are stopped by chains stretched between posts. The poet could have made a metaphor, or at least a simile, from all that. He knew this cemetery well, for in 1937 he had attended the ceremonies that made the Bennington Center Cemetery, with the Old First Church, Vermont's Colonial Shrine. His rather deprecatory manner toward all that, as expressed in a letter to Louis Untermeyer, was to change, as his opinions often changed. For in March of 1938 his beloved wife Elinor died in Gainesville, Florida. Cremation followed, and a memorial service in the chapel of Amherst College. Elinor Frost had wished her ashes to be scattered on the grounds of their farm in Derry, New Hampshire, and Frost had traveled there to sound out the feelings of the owner. He was not met with cordiality; and sensitive spirit as he was from first to last, he gave up the plan. As Carol's wife Lillian noted, he had not taken the urn with him. It

remained on the shelf of a closet in Stone Cottage, South Shaftsbury, and Lillian once found a flower decorating it. It had become a
kind of shrine.

But a few years later, in 1941, Frost purchased a lot in the cemetery in Old Bennington, and in the crypt prepared to receive them,
placed the urns of Elinor, his wife, and Carol, their son, who had
died, a suicide, in October 1940. Only his grandson, William Prescott Frost, son of Carol and Lillian, and Lillian herself, were with
him for the private ceremony.

Many years passed, "Years of Glory," as Lawrance Thompson
would call them, when Frost would achieve world fame as man and
poet and would become as well one of the best loved great men
of our time. But "Great and Troubled," as Edmund Fuller of *The
Wall Street Journal* would call him, for he was still "a man of
sorrows and acquainted with grief." It was not for nothing that
he carried a Bible in his pocket and that its words crept into his
mind, among them "sorrows" and "acquainted." The Book of Job
led all the rest, but he knew the others as well. He sometimes
thought of his poems as an offering that he hoped would be "acceptable in Thy sight."

For Frost was a religious man, though some might think otherwise, even if not a churchgoer. He called himself "an Old Testament Christian," and his beliefs tended toward the Judeo part of the
Judeo-Christian tradition. Or was it the Swedenborgian beliefs of
his mother, or the Universalist Church he had attended with his
Frost grandparents, or his own private mixture of beliefs that governed his outlook? As John Milton is said to have followed "The
Religion of John Milton," it may be that biographers in the future
will identify "The Religion of Robert Frost." It is known, certainly,
that he read *Paradise Lost*, and it is possible to read "Two Look at
Two" and remember the last lines of Book XII of the great Miltonic
poem:

> The world was all before them, where to choose
> Their place of rest, and Providence their guide!
> They, hand in hand, with wandering steps and slow,
> Through Eden took their solitary way.

Had not the Frosts, Robert and Elinor, often been left to "the way they had taken," with the world all before them, where to choose?

If Frost feared death, his own especially, he was a lover of life, and believed it was the main task of the living to return to the tasks of daily life, even after the death of those near and dear. His wife Elinor could not follow him in that philosophy, as the early poem "Home Burial" makes clear. Where else will you find lines that transfix the reader as effectively as those on death?

> The nearest friends can go
> With anyone to death, comes so far short
> They might as well not try to go at all.
> No, from the time when one is sick to death,
> One is alone, and he dies more alone. (p. 54)

Whatever may be true in other parts of the country, there were many "home burials" in New England and eastern New York State, and a wanderer through the countryside will find not only the "be-lilaced cellar holes" of which Frost wrote, but many a forlorn and forsaken family burial plot. Though the name of Elliott Frost and his dates are on the stone in Old Bennington, it is probable that he, the firstborn son who died before age four, was the subject of "Home Burial." That was one of the first "sorrows."

Others came in its train, but none so severe as the death of Frost's wife in 1938. If he had been able to bear the other deaths—except possibly that of Marjorie, the lovely and greatly loved daughter of the Frosts, in May 1934—which may have hastened Elinor Frost's death,[1] the death of his wife was a sorrow too great for him. He was for years "beside himself," an accurate expression in this instance. Hervey Allen and other friends came to his rescue, and then Kathleen and Theodore Morrison, who knew what must be done for him. Like the "Tree at My Window," they had seen him "when I was taken and swept/And all but lost."

Kathleen Morrison, who had known Frost first when she was a student at Bryn Mawr College, and who has written of him faithfully and truly in *Robert Frost: A Pictorial Chronicle*,[2]—dedicated to the memory of Lawrance Thompson, Frost's biographer—became his secretary-manager for the last twenty-five years of his life. He could not have managed his life or career without her, and how much he valued her his letters attest. Indeed, he had the care and affection of the entire Morrison family. It was their daughter, Anne Morrison Gentry,[3] who not only took his dictation of letters and poems at Peter Bent Brigham Hospital in Boston, as relief for her mother, but was also to inform her parents by messenger of Frost's death during their very brief respite—for Frost died on January 29, 1963, while they were staying at the Whale Inn in Goshen, a village near Amherst, during what must have been the coldest days of that winter. They had left Cambridge on the twenty-sixth, only to be called back to Boston early on the twenty-ninth.

Now the outpouring of news reports on Frost's illness and possible recovery was over, and long obituaries and memorial reports began. Frost had been sensitive to death all his life, as readers of his poems know. He had written in an early poem, "Out, Out—" (published in *Mountain Interval* in 1916):

> They listened at his heart.
> Little—less—nothing!—and that ended it.
> No more to build on there. And they, since they
> Were not the dead, turned to their affairs. (p. 137)

But it was in the volume *A Further Range* twenty years later, in 1936, that he had written, in a poem comparing the body in the grave to the seed that is sown:

> There may be little or much beyond the grave,
> But the strong are saying nothing until they see. (p. 300)

That poem provided both title and text of a perceptive review in the *Times Literary Supplement* (London, January 26, 1973) of the *Family Letters of Robert and Elinor Frost*. Anonymous as always in the *TLS*, the writing proved both knowledge and insight in the author. "For all the large family and the many friends and devotees," so the reviewer would end, "his was a lonely life, self-contained, self-besieged, and self-scarred by his own 'desert places.' "

Those lines would not do for an epitaph, but Frost made provision for that in his long poem, "The Lesson for Today," published in *A Witness Tree* in 1942.

> I hold your doctrine of *Memento Mori*.
> And were an epitaph to be my story
> I'd have a short one ready for my own.
> I would have written of me on my stone:
> I had a lover's quarrel with the world. (p. 355)

"Earth's a hard place in which to save the soul," he had written, but he might have said, with Whitman, "At the last, tenderly"; though "Strong is your hold, O mortal flesh!" he had glided noiselessly forth. Surely he knew the poem, enviously as he sometimes viewed the great poet who had preceded him.

I remember the grief with which I, among many who had known Frost, heard of his death. After all, he had been in Detroit, where I then lived, as recently as November 1962, vibrantly and unmistakably himself. I was reminded of a poem that surely Frost, with his acquaintance with the classical tongues, knew as well—the poem "Heraclitus," in the beautiful translation from Callimachus by William (Johnson) Cory:

> They told me, Heraclitus, they told me you were dead,
> They brought me bitter news to hear and bitter tears to shed.
> I wept as I remember'd how often you and I
> Had tired the sun with talking and sent him down the sky.
>
> And now that thou art lying, my dear old Carian guest,
> A handful of grey ashes, long, long ago at rest,
> Still are thy pleasant voices, thy nightingales, awake;
> For Death, he taketh all away, but them he cannot take.

It was Frost's dearest wish to "lodge a few poems where they would be hard to get rid of," and that wish he was granted. His nightingales are still awake, and Death will not take them.

Memorial Services, Amherst

Many were the memorials of Frost after his death, not least the editorial in *Life* (Feb. 8, 1963) and their pages on "Passing of the Poet," in which they said that Frost's death was felt "in a deeply personal way, by millions of his countrymen." It was *Life* that provided some of the best pictures of the poet whose "craggy face and rumpled figure, whether in an English field or behind a college lectern, became a symbol of poetic simplicity," though they were aware that Frost was a complex man who "lived for ideas."

But chief among the memorials, certainly, was the service held in the chapel at Amherst College on February 17, 1963.[4] There the Right Reverend Henry Wise Hobson of Ohio spoke of the strong and deep religious faith of Frost, of his constant and unwavering search for truth. It was Mark Van Doren who read the Frost poems printed in the memorial program—and who would himself die in December of 1972. And President Calvin H. Plimpton, in his "Reflections," made a true and remarkable comment about Frost:

> His poetry is with us, but what I will miss is the man. . . . It was here that many of us met and knew Robert Frost, the man.
>
> I am sorry for those of you who did not see him or know him even as little as I did. But it is a funny thing. There is almost no one who ever met him, however briefly, who does not claim him for his own. You never felt you knew a little of Robert Frost, and no one ever knew him all. The part you know was given to you with such intensity—the part you saw was so vivid—that while his poetry belongs to the ages, Frost the man, the teacher belongs to us.

Those who came to the Amherst Memorial Service were given a handsome edition of the tribute by Louis M. Lyons, Curator of the Nieman Foundation for Journalism at Harvard University, and news analyst for Boston's educational television and radio stations. It had been broadcast on the very evening of Frost's death in the early hours of January 29. His opening words were greatly inspired:

> Robert Frost died this morning, leaving a void of greatness in the land. Great poet of our land. More than poet. Taken as sage and seer by Presidents and people. Great in all dimensions. Wise with an olden wisdom. Rugged as that craggy face. Thorny as any Yankee farmer. Rock sturdy in his individualism. Universal in his themes as all humanity. Out of the land. Out of our land, "North of Boston," "West-Running Brook," "Mending Wall," "The Wood-Pile," "Dust of Snow," "Mountain Interval," "Birches," "The Sound of the Trees," "Stopping by Woods on a Snowy Evening," "The Need of Being Versed in Country Things."

The Robert Frost Library at Amherst

There are several schools named for Frost, including one in the Detroit area, but the biggest and best memorial is the Robert Frost Library at Amherst College. He knew it would be named for him, and it was well in the works when he died. "He was pleased by the honor of having a library named for him. He *was* tickled!" said President Plimpton at the Memorial Service. Frost had attended a dinner in the autumn of 1962 when the Frost Library gift was announced, and had made some characteristic remarks. The college man, he said, "knows there's a book-side to everything."

Before the year of his death was over, on October 26, 1963, Amherst celebrated the "Ground Breaking for the Robert Frost Library," with a "Convocation to Honor the President of the United States," John F. Kennedy, who on that occasion made one of his best addresses, fully reported in *The New York Times*[5] of the following day. Frost would have liked the Quotation of the Day, selected from the President's speech:

> When power leads man toward arrogance, poetry reminds him of his limitations. When power narrows the areas of man's concern, poetry reminds him of the richness and diversity of his existence. When power corrupts, poetry cleanses.

His words and his appearance that day would have gone far to heal the breach between poet and President which had existed since Frost's interpretation of Khrushchev's words to newsmen as meaning "We are too liberal to fight," on his return from Russia the year before. Not even during his last illness had Frost received a word of sympathy from the President who had been the first to invite a great poet to appear at his Inauguration. If Frost was well known before, he became familiar to millions all over the world through his appearance on television that day.

Yet he had said in his last letter to daughter Lesley, "Life has been a long trial, yet I mean to see more of it." He was at least spared the great shock of President Kennedy's assassination in Dallas, on November 22, less than a month after his address at the ground breaking in Amherst.

Frost's Own Library Given to New York University

A year after Frost's death, and only a few months after the ground breaking for the Library at Amherst College, there was another shock in store for the friends of Frost, and especially for Amherst, when it became known that the poet's own fine library of some 3,000 volumes would go, not to the Robert Frost Library, but to New York University. The decision was made by the daughter of the poet, Lesley, whose husband, Joseph W. Ballantine, was then a member of the faculty of New York University.

Among the reasons given for her decision, Lesley noted[6] that the Jones Library of Amherst had one of the greatest collections of Frost of any place in the country. So it has, and the late Charles R. Green, Librarian and then Curator, and friend of the poet for many years, was the person responsible for the collection and the establishment of the Robert Frost Room in that handsome stone library building on the well-named Amity Street.

The Grave of Robert Frost

Many of the family duties now fell to daughter Lesley, the only surviving child except for Irma, who had succumbed to mental illness. So it was that Lesley, in June 1963, with private ceremony, committed the urn containing the ashes of her father to the grave in Old Bennington.[7]

But, as the *Bennington Banner*, chief newspaper of the area, was to report,[8] it was not until April 9, 1964 that an inscribed tombstone marked the grave of Robert Frost, more than fourteen months after his death. As the *Banner* noted, there were reasons for the delay. The original stone, a block of handsome granite from Westerly, Rhode Island, certainly the whitest granite to be found, for it resembles marble, did not provide room for Frost's name and dates, and one of the life dates of Elinor Frost was given incorrectly.

Under a contract with Lesley Frost Ballantine, the *Banner* reported, the firm of Bai Rossi Art Memorials, Inc. of Brattleboro, Vermont, represented in Bennington by David E. Carver, had worked most of the winter "on the delicate job of shaving down the old inscription three-eighths of an inch, and sandblasting the new ones." The firm deserves credit for its work, for seldom if ever has a tombstone been inscribed as handsomely. There is a border of laurel leaves to honor the great poet, who might have said, with Housman:

> We'll to the woods no more,
> The laurels all are cut.

Though pilgrims come to see the grave of Robert Frost, the stone is a memorial to the family of Robert and Elinor. However, only the two have epitaphs.[9] The inscriptions follow:

ROBERT LEE FROST
Mar. 26, 1874 – Jan. 29, 1963
"I had a lover's quarrel with the world"

His Wife
ELINOR MIRIAM WHITE
Oct. 25, 1873 – Mar. 20, 1938
"Together Wing to Wing and Oar to Oar"

MARJORIE FROST FRASER
Mar. 29, 1905 – May 2, 1934

CAROL FROST
May 27, 1902 – Oct. 9, 1940

ELLIOTT FROST
Sept. 28, 1896 – July 28, 1900

ELINOR BETTINA FROST
June 20, 1907 – June 21, 1907

Several changes have taken place in the gravesite since 1964. Within a year or two there was a substantial marker at the head of the path, with an arrow: ROBERT FROST GRAVE. The persons in charge at Old First Church were no doubt weary of directing the many who came to the church door. Some years later, when it became clear that the grass leading to the grave would always be trampled to the roots, a Vermont marble step and walkway were placed there. Then an identical granite stone was placed beside the first. Its purpose was not apparent until some years later; then the name of Lesley's husband, Joseph W. Ballantine, with birth and death dates, was inscribed. He had died in January 1973, ten years to the day after Robert Frost. Beneath his name was that of Lesley Frost Ballantine, with her birth date. The rest was so far blank, awaiting mortality.

A Place of Pilgrimage

Visit the grave of Robert Frost in Old Bennington Cemetery almost any time of the year, but especially after spring returns to the earth, and you will find others there before you, or walking down the path on their way to the place. In summer whole New England tour buses full of travelers will have stopped on the roadway above. Sometimes one will encounter familiar friends of Frost. Usually they are strangers. They have been coming before the stone was placed there, as the *Bennington Banner* reported, and were disappointed not to find his name there. I know a former editorial writer for the Troy *Times Record* who told me he visited the grave often when the world was too much with him, as the world often is in our times.

Explain it who can, but there was in Robert Frost some greatness Americans sought for, both in his life and in the memory of the man and the poet. Perhaps, as he would say, he offered something "to stay our minds on and be staid." For Frost it was "something like a star" that provided that power. For others, it was Frost himself and his poetry, in which the careful reader can find depths beyond depths.

As for the man himself, who appeared on so many public platforms, at great cost to himself, playful as he was at times, he had in extraordinary measure an *aura*—a concept of personality that meant much to architect Eliel Saarinen. The granite head of Frost, the craggy face that showed the suffering and sorrows he had undergone—these were part of the aura he carried about, and their meaning was evident to many.

There is a Robert Frost Mountain near Ripton, Vermont. It is well named.

Notes to *The Strong Are Saying Nothing* by DOROTHY TYLER

1. On a visit to Frost in South Shaftsbury, Vermont, with two friends (RF had ridden the runningboard, directing the driver), I was aware that then, in the summer of 1934, after the death of Marjorie in May, all was not well with the family. "You have heard about Marjorie?" Frost asked me. I nodded that I had. But Mrs. Frost, who was never really well after Marjorie's death, did not leave the house to greet us, and Carol, who looked around the corner of the house, was not invited to join us, to "come in." The meaning of these events did not reach me for some years.

2. Kathleen Morrison, *Robert Frost: A Pictorial Chronicle* (New York: Holt, Rinehart & Winston, 1974).

3. The name is so given in *Selected Letters*, ed. Lawrance Thompson (New York: Holt, Rinehart & Winston, 1964), p. 596. However, in Morrison, p. vii, it is given as Anne Morrison Smyth.

4. Copies of the memorial publications from Amherst and Cambridge were sent to me by Sue Bonner Walcutt, to whom my thanks are due.

5. *New York Times*, Sunday, Oct. 27, 1963, 1, pp. 2–3; text, p. 87. Article by Warren Weaver, Jr. "Kennedy, Honoring Frost, Bids U. S. Heed Its Artists." Archibald MacLeish, poet and friend of Frost, was quoted as saying the only other library named for a poet was the Pushkin Library in the Soviet Union. (He referred, no doubt, to important libraries, for certainly there are many branch libraries named for poets, including the Countee Cullen Library in Harlem.) A quotation from MacLeish's address is given as the motto for Section V, "On the Highest Plane," in Morrison's book.

6. Reported in the *New York Times*, January 11, 1964. Lesley Frost Ballantine was reached at the Tilton (New Hampshire) School, where she had been lecturing on poetry.

7. *Selected Letters*, p. 445, headnote to Letter 341.

8. *Bennington Banner*, Saturday, April 11, 1964. The report is illustrated by a photograph of the stone, with the Old First Church shown at the top of the hill. Many changes have occurred in the newer side of the cemetery since that time. Down the hill where the cemetery is located the Bennington Museum may be seen, its roof and higher windows visible from Frost's grave. On the Museum grounds is the Grandma Moses schoolhouse from Eagle Bridge, New York.

9. Frost's epitaph, "I had a lover's quarrel with the world," is from "The Lesson for Today," in *A Witness Tree*, 1942. The epitaph for Elinor White Frost is from the sonnet "The Master Speed," in *A Further Range*, 1936. The volume is dedicated "To E. F."

Bibliography

PRIMARY SOURCES

Abbreviations in the Text:

SL—Selected Letters of Robert Frost. Ed. Lawrance Thompson. New York: Holt, Rinehart and Winston, 1964.

SP—Selected Prose of Robert Frost. Ed. Hyde Cox and Edward Connery Lathem. New York: Holt, Rinehart and Winston, 1956; rpt. in paperback by Macmillan, Collier Books, 1968. References are to the Collier edition.

Thompson, I—Thompson, Lawrance. *Robert Frost: The Early Years 1874–1915.* New York: Holt, Rinehart and Winston, 1966.

Thompson II—Thompson, Lawrance. *Robert Frost: The Years of Triumph 1915–1938.* New York: Holt, Rinehart and Winston, 1970.

Untermeyer—*The Letters of Robert Frost to Louis Untermeyer.* Ed. Louis Untermeyer. New York: Holt, Rinehart and Winston, 1963.

SECONDARY SOURCES

While some of the following items are cited in notes, they are elsewhere abbreviated in essays that otherwise would have had but one or two notes. The items are listed again here both to give proper credit and to avoid confusion with other works by the same authors.

NOTE the separate listing of "Conversations on the Craft of Poetry," cited as Brooks and Warren in the essay by Thomas Daniel Young.

Barry, Elaine. *Robert Frost.* New York: Frederick Ungar Publishing Co., 1973.

———. *Robert Frost on Writing.* New Brunswick: Rutgers University Press, 1973.

Brooks, Cleanth and Warren, Robert Penn. *Understanding Poetry*, 3rd edition. New York: Holt, Rinehart and Winston, 1960.

Brower, Reuben. *The Poetry of Robert Frost: Constellations of Intention.* New York: Oxford University Press, 1963.

"Conversations on the Craft of Poetry." A transcript of the tape recording made to accompany *Understanding Poetry*, 3rd edition, separate paging.

Cox, Sidney. *A Swinger of Birches*. New York: New York University Press, 1958.

Greiner, Donald J. "The Use of Irony in Robert Frost," *South Atlantic Bulletin*, 38 (May 1973), 52–60.

Jarrell, Randall. *Poetry and the Age*. New York: Knopf, 1953.

Lynen, John F. *The Pastoral Art of Robert Frost*. New Haven: Yale University Press, 1960.

Montgomery, Marion. "Robert Frost and His Use of Barriers: Man *vs* Nature Toward God." *The South Atlantic Quarterly*, 57 (Summer 1958), 339–353.

Winters, Yvor. *The Function of Criticism: Problems and Exercises*. Denver: Alan Swallow, 1957. The essay on Frost is reprinted in James M. Cox, ed. *Robert Frost: A Collection of Critical Essays*. Englewood Cliffs: Prentice-Hall, 1962.

In addition to the bibliography noted in the Preface is Peter Van Egmond, *The Critical Reception of Robert Frost*. Boston: G. K. Hall & Co., 1974.

Contributors

Walton Beacham is director of creative writing, Virginia Commonwealth University, Richmond, Virginia.

Marie Borroff is professor of English at Yale University, New Haven, Connecticut.

Marjorie Cook is assistant professor of English at Miami University, Oxford, Ohio.

Margaret Edwards is assistant professor of English at the University of Vermont, Burlington, Vermont.

Warren French is professor of English at Indiana Universtiy-Purdue University, Indianapolis, Indiana.

Joseph Kau is associate professor of English at the University of Hawaii at Manoa, Honolulu, Hawaii.

Thomas McClanahan is writer in residence at the South Carolina Arts Commission, Columbia, South Carolina.

David L. Miller is teaching associate at the University of California at Irvine—California.

Marion Montgomery is professor of English at the University of Georgia, Athens, Georgia.

Stearns Morse is emeritus professor of English at Dartmouth College, Dartmouth, New Hampshire.

George Nitchie is professor of English and chairman of the department of English at Simmons College, Boston, Massachusetts.

Laurence Perrine is Frensley Professor of English at Southern Methodist University, Dallas, Texas.

Richard Reed is associate professor of literature at the University of North Carolina at Asheville—North Carolina.

Karen Lane Rood is a doctoral candidate and a teaching assistant at the University of South Carolina, Columbia, South Carolina.

David Alan Sanders is at Germantown Friends School, Philadelphia, Pennsylvania.

Peter J. Stanlis is professor of English and distinguished professor of humanities, Rockford College, Rockford, Illinois.

Dorothy Tyler is a writer and editor residing in Troy, New York, who was a student of Frost at the University of Michigan.

Patricia Wallace is assistant professor of English at Vassar College, Poughkeepsie, New York.

Stephen D. Warner is assistant professor of English at State University College, Fredonia, New York.

Perry Westbrook is professor of English at the State University of New York at Albany.

David M. Wyatt is assistant professor of English, University of Virginia, Charlottesville, Virginia.

Thomas Daniel Young is Gertrude Vanderbilt Professor and chairman of the department of English at Vanderbilt University, Nashville, Tennessee.

Index

321

05